Crossing the
49th Parallel

ALSO BY BRUNO RAMIREZ

La formazione dell'operaio massa negli USA, 1898–1922 (Milan, 1976), with Gisela Boch and Paolo Carpignano

When Workers Fight: The Politics of Industrial Relations in the Progressive Era, 1898–1916 (Westport, Conn., 1978)

Les premiers Italiens de Montréal: l'origine de la Petite Italie du Québec (Montréal, 1984)

La vida social en angloamerica (Caracas, 1988)

The Italians in Canada (Ottawa, 1990)

On The Move: French-Canadian and Italian Migrants in the North Atlantic Economy, 1860–1914 (Toronto, 1991)

If One Were to Write a History . . . : Selected Writings of Robert F. Harney (Toronto, 1991), co-edited with Pierre Anctil

The Italian Diaspora: Migration across the Globe (Toronto, 1992), co-edited with George Pozzetta

Sarrasine: A Screenplay (Toronto, 1995), with Paul Tana

Crossing the 49th Parallel

Migration from Canada to the United States, 1900–1930

◆

BRUNO RAMIREZ

with the assistance of Yves Otis

Cornell University Press

ITHACA AND LONDON

First published 2001 by Cornell University Press

Printed in the United States of America

Library of Congress Cataloging-in-Publication Data

Ramirez, Bruno.
   Crossing the 49th parallel : migration from Canada to the United States, 1900-1930 / Bruno Ramirez, with Yves Otis.
      p. cm.
   Includes bibliographical references and index.
   ISBN 0-8014-3288-X (alk. paper)
   1. Canadian Americans—History—20th century.   2. Immigrants—United States—History—20th century.   3. Canada—Emigration and immigration—History—20th century.   4. United States—Emigration and immigration—History—20th century.   5. United States—Relations—Canada. 6. Canada—Relations—United States.   7. Northern boundary of the United States—History—20th century.   I. Otis, Yves.   II. Title.
   E183.8.C2 R32 2001
   973'.0411–dc21

                                                                    00-011450

Cornell University Press strives to use environmentally responsible suppliers and materials to the fullest extent possible in the publishing of its books. Such materials include vegetable-based, low-VOC inks and acid-free papers that are recycled, totally chlorine-free, or partly composed of nonwood fibers. Books that bear the logo of the FSC (Forest Stewardship Council) use paper taken from forests that have been inspected and certified as meeting the highest standards for environmental and social responsibility. For further information, visit our website at www.cornellpress.cornell.edu.

Cloth printing   10 9 8 7 6 5 4 3 2 1

FSC FSC Trademark © 1996 Forest Stewardship Council A.C.
         SW-COC-098

For Christiane,
witness and accomplice

Contents

Preface

The 49th parallel is both a metaphor and a geographic reality. As a metaphor it has been commonly used to evoke the point of territorial contact or separation between Canada and the United States, two nation-states with distinctive histories and cultures. As a geographic reality, the expression is often synonymous with the physical and legal border that separates the two national territories. But only a portion of that border, roughly one-third, actually follows the 49th parallel. Much of the nearly 5,500–mile boundary follows a sinuous course across the North American continent. From Minnesota, the boundary line turns gradually southward through Lake Superior, and then almost vertically down through Lake Huron as far south as the 42d parallel, not far from the Ohio shoreline. From there it keeps climbing, cutting through Lake Erie and Lake Ontario, and reaching its northernmost point at the tip of Maine before plunging down again to the Bay of Fundy.

But it is the border as a physical and legal entity, not as metaphor, that takes center stage in this book; for it was the crossing of that line that turned Canadians on the move into international migrants who sought in their neighboring country the opportunity to improve their life conditions.

Estimates covering the years 1840 to 1940 place the number of Canadians who moved and settled in the United States at 2.8 million, two-thirds of them from Anglo-Canada, the other third from French Canada, which makes the northern confederation one of the leading contributors of population and labor in U.S. history. Yet, considering its magnitude, this population shift has left only a small—and at best partial—trace in the national narratives of the two countries. In the United States, despite the growing interest in immigration and ethnic history, researchers have been attracted only to that portion of the movement originating from Quebec. Likewise, when Canadian historians finally began to acknowledge the significance of this phenomenon, they also focused on French-Canadian emigration, and their research was most often circumscribed within the field of French-Canadian history. Only recently have a handful of Canadian and U.S. scholars turned their attention to the Anglo-Canadian component of the movement, producing important regional studies that unfortunately have not generated among researchers the degree of attention their efforts deserve.

And yet, as this book will show, Anglo-Canadians emigrated at rates similar to those of their French counterparts; they exhibited a comparable demographic profile; and, as in the case of French Canadians, their migration relied significantly on networks of kin and friends. Equally significant, their presence was inseparable from the growth of states, cities, and towns in New England, the Great Lakes region, and the West Coast. The skills and the technical resources they brought made them key actors in the history of several U.S. regions.

The serious gap in our knowledge of the two movements has largely resulted from cultural and linguistic factors. The presence of Anglo-Canadians in the United States, unlike the presence of French Canadians in the United States, did not give rise to the kinds of ethnic institutions or residential clusterings that historians normally associate with immigrant settlement. This was largely the case in the nineteenth century; it became even truer in the twentieth. Anglo-Canadians entered the mainstream of industrial and urban America, as we shall see, but the historian looks in vain for prominent symbols of group identity and self-protection: the national parish, the ethnic press, the mutual benefit society. And so their reduced visibility in the American sociocultural landscape has made it difficult to identify those institutional markers that might give us access to the particular universe of this immigrant group and open up paths of research on its composition and inner dynamics.

This book seeks to fill this gap in both Canadian and U.S. historiography. After devoting many years to the study of French-Canadian emigration to the United States, I found it increasingly difficult to resist the urge to enlarge my field of inquiry to the rest of Canada. I wanted to assess the significance of a continent-wide movement for both the history of Canada and the history of North America.

Canadian historians, I believe, need to know what basic factors resulted in a significant and protracted loss of their country's population and human resources. Moreover, a study that encompasses both English and French Canada could help break the mutual isolation that has produced essentially two narratives within the same nation-state. Hence my major concern has been to identify the different regional and cultural contexts that produced out-migration from Canada, to reconstruct the variety of patterns emerging from those contexts, and to shed new light on the significance of migration for both English and French Canada—and thus for the country as a whole.

I also believe that U.S. historiography, both national and regional, can benefit from knowing those northern neighbors who crossed the border. Whatever their degree of visibility in American society, especially in the eyes of historians, they became real neighbors, bringing to numberless rural and urban districts their youth, their distinctive traditions, and a variety of work skills that turned most of them into agents of American progress.

This book does not follow Canadian immigrants through their settlement and acculturation into American life, though in many ways it projects the basic socioeconomic parameters within which their insertion into a new society occurred. This aspect of the migration process would make for a separate study—one based on other kinds of sources and requiring a different analytical focus. Yet, it could hardly be conceived without a knowledge of the places from which those immigrants came and the variety of patterns that shaped their movements across the border.

Not since Marcus Hansen's *The Mingling of the Canadian and American Peoples* appeared—more than fifty years ago—has an attempt been made to encompass in one single volume the continent-wide migration of Canadians.[1] Hansen's work remains today a historiographical milestone for its wealth of information on population movements that crossed the border in both directions. In many ways, however, his work was conceived more as a history of Canadian-American relations than as a history of migrations. It belongs to an era when the analytical tools enabling social historians to explore the various dimensions of migration had not yet been developed. Despite Hansen's attempt to situate the various population movements within specific time frames and regional contexts, ultimately much of the mobility he found was a response to environmental and continental forces flowing from east to west, reminiscent of the Turnerian paradigm from which Hansen drew much of his inspiration. Not surprisingly, with the exception of a short section on the industrial era, Hansen's migrants move predominantly through and across a nineteenth-century North American agrarian universe, and farmland is as much the historical actor as is the migrant.

Yet, as *Crossing the 49th Parallel* will show, in the history of Canadian out-migration the agrarian context coexists with a growing industrial one, and urban labor markets increasingly play a much larger role than do home-steads and virgin land. These labor markets could be found a short distance across the border, just as they could be reached after a one-day railroad journey into U.S. territory—eastward as often as westward. Moreover, as the twentieth century set in, the free movement of Canadians across the boundary line—so much stressed by Hansen—became a controlled movement, and the border itself increasingly acquired the role of separating, rather than joining, two distinct nation-states.

Such is the context within which the narrative of this book unfolds. It was a period when Canada and the United States came out of the long depression of the 1890s, consolidating their place as industrial societies, significantly expanding their productive bases, and affecting in new and dynamic ways the movement of population and labor both continentally and intercontinentally. This is also the period that has received the least attention from historians of Canadian emigration to the United States. Yet although the movement underwent a decline in relation to its late-nineteenth-century peak, it continued relentlessly through major socio-economic changes and world events, and in some years it turned Canada into the leading supplier of population and labor to the United States, before migration was brought to a stop by the onset of the Great Depression.

But Canada also holds a special place in the history of international migrations, not only for its contribution to the demographic and economic growth of the United States, but also for having been an important receiving society. Throughout its history, first as a British colony and then after confederation, Canada resorted significantly to immigration to promote the peopling of its vast territory and to ensure its demographic and economic development. Much of the new population came first from the British Isles, and some from the United States; but as industrialization and the exploitation of its vast natural resources became the leading priority, Canada increasingly turned to central-eastern and southern European countries, often by means of aggressive recruitment campaigns; to such an extent that during the early decades of the twentieth century, the number of foreign-born in Canada was proportionately greater than it was in the United States. Although the history of immigration to Canada has produced a substantial literature, historians have shown no interest in studying the country's double role as both a sending and a receiving society or its significance for international migrations—as if a tacit division of labor had prevailed among migration historians, leading specialists of out-migration to ignore immigration and vice versa.[2] I confronted this issue in a previous book;[3] but further research has allowed me to describe one important aspect of Canada's role in international migration when I discovered the significant number of European migrants who had chosen Canada as their destination but who, after a more or less lengthy period of residence, decided to remigrate and moved to the United States—a pattern that has often been alluded to in the historical literature but that has never been subjected to systematic study. In the emigration flow from Canada to the United States, in fact, nearly one out of five individuals belonged to this category. Although they were responding to personal and family circumstances and basing their decision on their subjective assessment of the opportunities available, their migration trajectories placed Canada at the center of the international circuits of population and labor. This is the theme I address in the last chapter of this book. My concern is not only that of identifying these European remigrants in terms of their ethnolinguistic affiliations and their demographic and occupational profiles; by switching the scale of analysis, I also seek to go beyond aggregate data, focusing on specific subgroups and individuals who composed that movement.

A variety of qualitative sources—from oral life-histories to newspaper accounts and public reports—has proved essential to my narrative. Yet, a study on such a spatial scale has largely been made possible by one archival source that to my knowledge has never been systematically used by migration historians. The *Soundex Index to Canadian Border Entries to the U.S.A.* contains the original information entered on manifests by U.S. border officials posted at the many points of entry along the entire boundary, information pertaining to every person entering the United States, whether that person originated from overseas or was a Canadian crossing the border. (The appendix gives a more detailed description of the *Index* and the sampling method adopted.) This source provides a rich variety of information on each migrant's social, ethnolinguistic, demographic, and occupational background, shedding new light on the migration patterns among Canadians and Europeans. It has also provided the empirical backbone for the reconstruction of the various movements in all their sociodemographic, occupational, and regional dimensions—without ever losing sight of the individual migrant, the ultimate actor in this narrative.

Although the main objective of this book is to throw original light on one of the major continental and transcontinental migration movements, it will also open new paths of research on a number of aspects that still await in-depth analysis.

The research on which this book is based was made possible by a three-year grant from the Social Sciences and Humanities Research Council of Canada. My colleagues in the Groupe de Recherche Société et Ethnicité

(GRES) showed their generosity by providing some financial aid at a critical moment. The research was enormously facilitated by the Bibliothèque Municipale de Montréal, holder of a copy of the main archival sources used in this book. I thank in particular Mr. Daniel Olivier, supervisor at the Salle Gagnon, for graciously allowing me to work out a special loan arrangement with the Bibliothèque.

This work would still be in the making had it not been for Yves Otis. He stuck to the project even after the grant ran out, participating in the design of the book and making sure that the data bank would speak to the issues I wanted to treat.

Several students of mine worked at one time or another at the tedious task of retrieving the data from the microfilm collection and computerizing them. I thank them all: Nelson Ouellet, Sophie Jacmin, Johanne Roussy, Mylène Desautels, and Chantal Cuillerier. I also thank Gillian Leitch and Mélanie Fortin for their assistance in the preparation of the final version of the manuscript. My thanks also to the several friends and fellow historians who either read portions of the manuscript or offered criticism and encouragement during presentations I made at seminars or on other occasions: René Leboutte, Ewa Morawska, and Nicole Malpas during my stay at the European University Institute; François Weil, Jean Heffer, and Catherine Collomp during my stay at the École des Hautes Études en Science Sociale; Fernando Devoto, Donna Gabaccia, and Ira Glazer at a special seminar on nominative sources at the University of Buenos Aires; Mary Blewett, Dirk Hoerder, Fraser Ottanelli, and Marian L. Smith, during various informal discussions and exchange of letters. I am also grateful to the two anonymous scholars who evaluated the project for Cornell University Press, and to John LeRoy for his excellent and perceptive copyediting. Donald Avery, Paul-André Linteau, and Rudolph Vecoli have read the entire manuscript. As with previous works, they have proved generous with their time, their invaluable insights, and their encouragement. And as with previous works, their response as scholars and as friends remains blurred in my mind.

Only two other persons read the entire manuscript: Christiane "Bée" Teasdale, instigator of the most tenacious kind, who knows why I dedicate this book to her; and Roger Haydon, my editor at Cornell University Press. Roger's professionalism, sensitivity, sense of humor, and commitment proved truly essential in transforming an ill-defined project into the book it is and in making this publishing experience a more humane one.

BRUNO RAMIREZ

Montréal, Québec

*Crossing the
49th Parallel*

Fig. 1. En route toward the U.S. border, Manitoba, 1872.
Courtesy of the National Archives of Canada, PA 74679.

CHAPTER ONE

◈

Societies in Motion in
Nineteenth-Century North America

In 1857 the Legislative Assembly of the Province of Canada issued its *Report of the Special Committee on Emigration*. The report contains the following remark:

> When a people still in the early youth of their national existence, weak in numbers, though distinguished for sobriety and hardihood, inhabiting a vast territory of an extent and fertility sufficient for the residence and abundant support of fifty times their number, abandon their homes, emigration is an evil, a public calamity to be deplored, and, if possible, averted. An exodus like this, without legitimate cause, must of necessity be the consequence of a radical social defect, which it is the business of society, to detect, and, if possible, to cure, by the application of timely remedies.[1]

Canadians who happened to read this passage may have found the word *exodus* exaggerated and puzzling. Even in a moderately religious culture, that biblical expression conjures up visions of a people fleeing from oppression, crossing rivers and valleys in search of a promised land. Were not Canadians living under the benign protection of British economic and military power, their lives nurtured by the Empire's civilizing influence? And why cast the country into a land of oppression when so many people had risked their lives crossing the Atlantic and had found in Canada their promised land?

Yet, in the years and decades to come that word *exodus* would echo throughout numberless counties across the country, and many who had reacted skeptically to the report would become part of a swelling south-ward stream. In the decade of the 1850s, more than 150,000 Canadians moved permanently to the United States.[2] During the decade that fol-lowed, that number would double, and momentous political events such as the reorganization of the colonies into the Confederation and later the launching of a national economic policy would have little or no effect in slowing the movement. By the turn of the century, the number of Canadi-ans working and living in the United States had grown to over one mil-lion—no less than 22 percent of the Dominion's population. By then, their presence and that of their U.S.-born children had become a perma-nent feature in the landscape of many American regions and districts.[3]

In retrospect, the alarmist tone of the committee's report was only partly justified, since what the authors called an exodus was part of a wider and more complex population movement that encompassed much of North America and had their roots in various parts of the North At-lantic economy. For one thing, the evidence on which the committee based its report was almost entirely drawn from Lower Canada (Quebec) and made little mention of emigration from the other two regions of British North America, namely, Upper Canada (Ontario) and the Mar-itime colonies. Moreover, a reader of the report could hardly realize that while tens of thousands of Canadians were migrating to the United States, an equally significant number of foreigners, mostly from the British Isles, were entering Canada, most of them to settle permanently, others to seek their ultimate destination in the American republic. By mid-century, in fact, these parallel population movements had become a firmly estab-lished pattern. As we shall see in subsequent chapters, they would confer on Canada, during much of the nineteenth century and until the 1920s, a special role in the continental and transatlantic circuits of population and labor.

A reader could hardly deduce from the wording and the tone of the report the extent to which the phenomenon it addressed was part of a continent-wide population movement westward. If in the North American historical literature this movement has been largely associated with the national history of the United States, geographical, legal, and economic factors made Canada—both its territory and its people—an integral part of the "settling of the West."[4] Local reports submitted to the special com-mittee by Lower Canada spokesmen pointed clearly to the significant number of French Canadians who had left their villages along the Saint Lawrence to seek more fertile and more easily accessible land in the Ohio Valley and in the Great Lakes region, some even as far west as California.[5] And in their move, these French-Canadian migrants were not acting much differently from New Englanders or Maritimers who had joined the great westward movement.

I

Nowhere in British North America were these population movements more integrated into this continental phenomenon than in Ontario. With its southwestern section located in the heart of the Great Lakes region and separated only by bodies of water and boundary agreements from the American Midwest, Ontario became an important step in the great westward movement, first as a frontier for American settlers from the east in search of new land in the early 1800s, and later as a point of departure for Ontarians seeking cheaper and more fertile land farther west. It may be a historical irony that Ontario was first settled by American migrants and that the early settlement of Michigan was the work of Canadians, but it is an eloquent indication of how political, physical, and topographical factors could interact with the desire for material betterment to produce a peculiar human geography.[6] Ontarians, of course, had their own frontier—the thickly forested territory that extended from the shores of Lake Erie and Lake Ontario northward to that vast natural barrier that has become known as the Canadian Shield. And during the following decades, this territory would transform a significant portion of the Ontario population into settlers to such an extent that by mid-century the frontier had been pushed to its northern limits, and a forbidding and inhospitable forest land had been turned into one of the most important agricultural regions in British North America and in the entire continent.[7]

But until a new Canadian agricultural frontier—the western prairies—became accessible by rail transportation, and until industrialization in the United States created new migration routes, Ontarians and indeed Canadians from other regions kept turning their eyes toward the measureless, fertile lands of the American West.

Geographical proximity and similarity of climate, vegetation, and soil explain why Michigan became the state attracting the largest number of Ontarians. In significant numbers, they joined the "Michigan fever" of the 1830s. Most of them originated from the coastal counties along Lake Huron and settled across the lake in Michigan's lower peninsula, especially in Huron, Sanilac, and Saint Clair Counties, where by 1850 they represented about two-thirds of the foreign-born population.[8] A writer from the *Detroit Free Press* seemed impressed by the number of Ontarians transiting his city in the summer of 1838 and by the quality of their belongings: "The emigration to the new states from our neighboring province of Upper Canada in the present season is immense. A large number of families, well provided with money, teams, and farming utensils, have crossed over to this place within the last few weeks. Twelve covered waggons *[sic]*, well filled and drawn by fine horses, crossed over yesterday."[9]

Although hunger for land was the main factor feeding this population flow, it was not the only one. Samuel Edison, for instance, was one of many Ontarians who in the late 1830s crossed the border to escape arrest and possible execution. The son of a New Jersey Loyalist who during the American Revolution had exiled himself and his family in Canada, he was one of twenty-one Middlesex County men named by a November 1838 royal proclamation calling for their arrest. Like thousands of Ontarians, Edison had taken part in the political insurrections that shook the Canadas in 1837–38.[10] Their unsuccessful struggle against what they believed to be a tyrannical rule, and in favor of republican principles of government, brought about political instability, repression, and turned the United States into a land of exile. The exact number of Ontarians who, like Edison, sought a safe haven south of the border will probably never be known. But when one considers that during those two years of turmoil total arrests amounted to 1,031, one may safely argue that for every rebel caught by authorities several more were able to cross the nearby border and find logistic help and ideological support. Even more difficult is it to know the number of those who left Ontario towns and farms not as political runaways but as ordinary citizens, men and women who were concerned about developments that, in their eyes, foretold an uncertain future for themselves and their children. Although a number of exiles eventually returned to Ontario once peace and order were reestablished, many others settled permanently in the United States.[11] Samuel Edison, for instance, managed to get his wife and children to join him in Milan, Ohio—a town that soon afterward would become the birthplace of one of the world's greatest inventors.[12]

By mid-century, Ontarians, along with a significant number of French Canadians and smaller groups of Maritimers, had become Michigan's most numerous foreign-born population, a position they retained for the remainder of the century.[13]

Historical and geographical factors also explain the choice of the American Midwest as a destination for significant numbers of French Canadians. Their familiarity with the region dated back to the New France regime, when *coureurs de bois* and *voyageurs* in the service of fur trading companies had penetrated every corner of the region; but neither the British Conquest of that portion of the continent nor the American Revolution had erased their presence. Indeed, French Canadians constituted the dominant white population when Michigan became a territory in 1805. Other French-Canadian settlements that had grown out of the fur trade survived elsewhere in the region, most of them in Illinois and Wisconsin but some as far west as Montana.[14] Actually, the fur trade route, that network of rivers and streams which had long interconnected scores of villages along the Saint Lawrence Valley to the Midwest, continued to be traveled by thousands of French-Canadian out-migrants, who swelled existing settlements and formed new ones. Many of them were attracted by a trade that had long traditions in the French-Canadian culture and economy. The historian Allen Greer has shown the important role that *engagés* and *voyageurs* continued to play in the 1820s and 1830s, many of them recruited in the Sorel and Trois-Rivières districts. The reorganization that the fur trade underwent in the 1820s did not affect the positive attitude toward French-Canadian workers and employers. The American Fur Company, one of the main products of that reorganization, relied heavily on French Canadians.[15] But increasingly, French Canadians moved to the American Midwest as agriculturalists, pursuing the dream of independent yeomanry, often creating farming communities such as the Bourbonnais colony south of Chicago or, also in Illinois, the better-known colony founded by Father Charles Chiniquy, well remembered for his skill in recruiting large numbers of parishioners from his village in Quebec.[16] By the time the railroad revolution disrupted long-standing communication routes and began to transform the economic and social geography of the region, French-Canadian settlements and enclaves had become firmly established in various parts of the Midwest, especially in Michigan, Illinois, and Wisconsin.[17] They would serve as important terminal points for new migration networks developing throughout the remainder of the nineteenth century and into the early twentieth.

To a much smaller degree, the pull exerted by the American Midwest was also felt in the Maritime colonies. According to U.S. census data, for instance, in 1850 Maritimers made up 16 percent of the Canada-born residents of Michigan.[18] The little information we have about these migrants suggests that they were mostly agriculturalists attracted to the upper Midwest by the possibility of combining lumbering and farming—a practice that had a long tradition in many agrarian districts of Nova Scotia and New Brunswick. The desire "to re-establish his farming-lumbering way of life" was the main reason that led A. Sinclair and a group of fellow Nova Scotians to settle in Wisconsin in the 1840s.[19] Many Maritimers had, of course, taken other, more popular migration routes to the United States, ones that reflected the regional reality of a coastal economy and oceanic

transportation. The Maritime colonies had made New England their natural trading and cultural neighbor, and ambitious men and women found
easy access to the commercial economy of the "Boston state," both on a
seasonal and a permanent basis.[20]

II

By mid-century, then, all three regions of British North America contributed to the population flow into the United States. These movements,
however, grew out of socioeconomic conditions that varied considerably
from one region to the other. These conditions determined not only
which populations were more likely to move but also what motivated their
move. Whereas in Ontario and in the Maritimes out-migration took on
the character of the mobility associated with a growing regional economy,
in Quebec it emerged as the symptom of a society caught in the grips of a
severe economic crisis.

Despite the heated debates among historians as to its magnitude and its
root causes, a basic consensus has been reached on a number of key interrelated factors.[21] Central among them was the dramatic decline of
wheat—the cash crop that until the turn of the nineteenth century had
fueled much of the agrarian economy of the colony. Whereas in the late
eighteenth century wheat had represented 60 to 70 percent of total harvest and the leading export crop, by 1827 it had declined to 22 percent. In
some important ways, this was a trend that Quebec shared with much of
the northeastern continental region. Much as in New England, soil exhaustion and the increasing competition from the more fertile wheat-
producing midwestern districts were key factors discouraging the growing
of that crop. In Quebec, these difficulties were compounded by a series of
natural calamities in the 1830s when poor climatic conditions, and the
devastation caused by the wheat midge parasite and by wheat rust, dealt
the final blow. By 1844 wheat represented only 4 percent of the total harvest and had virtually disappeared from export markets. Faced with ad-
versities largely beyond their control, most Quebec farmers had turned to
substitute crops, primarily potato and oats. Although these crops had
some limited commercial value in local markets, high production costs
kept them out of export markets.[22]

Unable to find a substitute cash crop capable of generating surplus income and stimulating technical innovations, much of Quebec's agrarian
society fell back on subsistence agriculture. As a consequence, alarming
numbers of smallholders and farm laborers left their parishes in search of

land and wages. Their search took some of them to the backcountry, to fringe areas within their seigneuries, or to the few towns and cities whose labor markets offered opportunities for employment. But an increasing number headed south and west, beyond the confines of their colony.

The alarm signaled by the 1857 report had already been voiced in the 1830s and 1840s by two other government inquiries. In what was to become one of the most important official policy pronouncements in Canadian history, Lord Durham submitted in 1839 a report on the state of British North America. In it he expressed concern for the "exodus of young people" from Lower Canada and made reference to the two major political concerns of the time: the fear that the rebellions the country had suffered in 1837 would be rekindled, and the fear of an annexionist movement to the United States, which at the time was drawing support from both sides of the border. He pointed to another danger, which he considered still more ominous for the future of the country. "I dread, in fact, the completion of the sad work of depopulation and impoverishment which is now rapidly going on [which could have] a much more speedy and disastrous result."[23]

The phenomenon Lord Durham had observed and deplored had intensified during the 1840s, to such an extent that a select committee of the Legislative Assembly had been created with the specific task of inquiring into "the Causes and Importance of the Emigration from Lower Canada to the United States." A phenomenon that in earlier years had been confined to a few districts—mostly around the Montreal plains, the city of Quebec, and a few counties near the U.S. border—had now spread throughout the string of parishes along the shores of the Saint Lawrence River, reaching some of the most remote districts of the province.[24]

By that time, much of Quebec rural society was bearing the consequences of two concomitant developments that had heightened the crisis. One was the significant growth of its population, due mostly to an unusually high fertility rate that had brought it from about 340,000 in 1815 to nearly 900,000 by mid-century.[25] The other was the limited arable surface for a population of that magnitude. Much of the arable land of Lower Canada had in fact remained circumscribed in the seigneuries and become filled by the 1830s. Here, proprietors exacted a variety of levies from censitaires and imposed increasingly high rents on prospective farmers wishing to take up land.[26] And by 1851, 66 percent of the entire Quebec population, and 83 percent of the rural population, lived within the confines of seigneurial territories where indebtedness and landlessness had become endemic.[27] In 1831, for instance, in the old and overpopulated district of Ile d'Orleans, 41 percent of the heads of families were landless farmers or laborers.[28] The natural outlet for this rural population, which had overfilled the old established parishes, was the vast forested back-country. Hard-pressed Quebeckers had begun venturing outside the seigneuries even before the seigneurial landholding system was legally abolished in 1854. Moreover, a 1848 provincial law had incorporated several colonization societies, thus signaling the beginning of what in subsequent decades would grow into a significant population movement.[29] But as the legislative reports of both 1849 and 1857 made amply clear, prospective settlers were discouraged from venturing into the interior by the lack of the most basic road network. Indeed, the failure to undertake adequate internal improvements was the most frequent grievance voiced by local spokesmen who submitted information to the legislative committees—a grievance that was eloquently summarized by the authors of the 1857 report:

> A considerable number of the sons of farmers, at this moment unprovided with land, would be ready to settle on lands of the Crown, if access to them were made easy. How is it to be expected of young people, or fathers of families, all, or nearly all of whom have but scanty means, perhaps none, that they can resolve to plunge into the recesses of a boundless forest, made aware as they are by the experience of those who have gone before, that they must give up all hope of intercourse in their new locations with their relatives and friends, otherwise than on the hard condition of traversing miles of trackless swamps and mountains intersected by rivers and stream-lets, and a thousand obstacles which defy human courage and energy to surmount them.[30]

This problem had been compounded by the government's policy of granting vast tracts of crown land to individuals or companies who were expected to transform their concessions into bustling lumber chantiers. But, as the report pointed out, "such individuals or companies almost invariably neglect their lands until the Government have opened roads and built bridges in the neighborhood, or until the lands are occupied by settlers who, for the most part, suppose them to form part of the Crown domain."[31]

The result of these policies was that Quebec's vast frontier stood largely unexploited except by lumber barons; and the multitude of landless farmers swelling the old parishes were prevented from becoming the agents of the expansion of the province's agrarian economy. Only during the second half of the century would colonization societies and the clergy organize a vast campaign among landless farmers aimed at "conquering" the forest. In the meantime, much of this surplus population had begun to spill over into the bordering states of New England or had taken the route west, selling their labor to lumber companies or seeking land in the American frontier.

◧

If the 1857 report made no mention of the thousands of Ontarians who yearly crossed the American border, this is largely because their departure was seen as the geographical mobility engendered by a bustling agrarian economy that afforded them the choice of seeking better working and living conditions elsewhere.

The fortunes of Ontario hinged on its success in developing a staple product, wheat, the sale of which to continental and imperial markets would bring capital into the economy and turn farming into a commercial enterprise for both the large farmers of the old townships and the pioneers who were pushing the frontier farther north. By the 1840s Ontario had become "the granary of two continents," its net exports of wheat rising by about 500 percent in that decade and doubling during the following decade.[32] The promises of the wheat trade provided the main impetus for pioneers who ventured into the backwoods, cleared forest land, established productive farms, and built the necessary road connections to reach market centers.

By the end of the 1850s, the line of settlement had almost reached the Canadian Shield, drawing into its swift march not only Ontarians but also thousands of immigrants from the British Isles. To most established farmers and new settlers the promise of wheat farming was fulfilled, since during the era of the wheat boom nearly three-quarters of their cash income came from wheat sales.[33]

The wheat trade was responsible not only for the expansion of Ontario's agrarian base but also for the transformation of its economy, which it accomplished by favoring the creation of a variety of productive activities that historians associate with protoindustrialization. The magnitude of the trade, the widespread participation of the farming population, and its insertion in the continental and transatlantic commercial routes required a set of operations designed to ensure ongoing production and efficient marketing. Consequently, the era of the wheat boom witnessed a dramatic acceleration in the construction of roads, in the expansion of the water and rail transportation networks, and in the creation of activities needed to service the farming population. Gristmills and shops that manufactured or repaired agricultural implements and transportation and loading equipment sprang up throughout the province and constituted the infrastructure supporting the agrarian economy.[34]

It is not surprising, then, that by mid-century Ontario's economy had given rise to an industrial workforce that was more than twice as large as that of Quebec despite their comparable populations.[35] Perhaps more significant was the distribution of the working population in the two provinces. Whereas in Quebec nearly one-third of that workforce was concentrated in metropolitan areas (mostly Montreal and Quebec City), in Ontario less than one-fifth worked and lived in metropolitan areas, the overwhelming majority belonging to the new universe of small and medium-sized commercial centers which had largely been brought into existence by the wheat-export economy.[36]

The emergence of these centers foreshadowed an urban configuration that was consolidated during the remainder of the century and affected the pattern of spatial and occupational mobility both provincially and internationally. Rural Ontarians who wanted to try their luck in the city could choose their destinations from a variety of local and intermediate urban agglomerations offering an increasing variety of jobs and trades. This pattern of urbanization accompanied by a diversification of labor markets also acted as a powerful pull for British immigrants with commercial and craft experience, making Ontario the most important immigrant-receiving region in British North America.[37]

Spatial and occupational mobility were in mid-nineteenth-century Ontario—as in most capitalist societies undergoing rapid growth and expansion—tightly intertwined phenomena, separable only by the conceptual rationale of social scientists. Most people relocated because they believed they could improve their material condition or find the security they lacked in their present circumstances. For many, the move occurred within the confines of the province; for others it entailed crossing the ocean and settling either in the burgeoning towns of Ontario with fellow British immigrants or in the isolated backwoods; yet others moved in a direction they perceived as the logical extension of their economic space, but which lay beyond their southern border.

Migration is also a question of public perception, and this is true both in mid-nineteenth-century Canada and in earlier and later periods. It is therefore quite conceivable that the extraordinary prosperity that Ontario was experiencing in those years entirely overshadowed the out-migration phenomenon, stripping it of its potential to become a social problem and turning it into what most contemporaries saw as a free choice that out-migrants made among the options the local economy offered, rather than, as was the case in many Quebec parishes and counties, a movement forced upon them by impoverishment and even near-starvation.

◆

Just as the character of Ontario's agrarian economy affected the patterns of spatial mobility and migration of its population, so did the peculiar geographical and economic configuration of the Atlantic provinces. Throughout the first half of the nineteenth century, the region had experienced a steady growth, largely due to its role in the North Atlantic market. Some historians have characterized the particular economic configuration of the region with the expression "wood, wind, and sail economy"—an expression that stresses not only the predominance of shipbuilding, lumbering, and fishing but also their high degree of interrelation, which ensured the region a steady growth and propelled it by mid-century into what some authors have called its Golden Age.[38] The most important of these sectors in terms of investments, output, and technical resources was shipbuilding. Thanks to the abundance of good timber in the region and to the steady demand of ships by Britain, the industry had undergone a progressive expansion since the early decades of the century, reaching its peak in 1864 when 586 ships were produced.[39]

But the centrality of the industry rested also on the impact it had on the regional economy. Besides requiring a large variety of specialized crafts, shipbuilding also absorbed a great many workers from farming districts, mostly for unskilled operations that were seasonal in nature. The industry also provided the opportunity for rural craftsmen to exercise their versatility—a quality that in the view of a contemporary Halifax observer had become a tradition in the local rural landscape: "persons who, having acquired the alphabet of a mechanical education, attracted to the city by cash payments, traveling like birds of passage from place to place, with an abundance of assurance and a measure of modesty, who would as readily engage to construct a locomotive or a watch, as a ship, provided they had some persons to show them how."[40] Some would find work in the shipyards on a temporary basis; for others, the journey to the yards could mean the beginning of a lifetime career as shipwrights, caulkers, or other tradesmen.

The relationship shipbuilding had with the other most important Maritime industry, lumber, is obvious: shipbuilders could rely on a steady supply of quality wood locally produced and quickly transported. Timber producers, on the other hand, had a ready outlet for their product; it was an industry that had become firmly entrenched in the regional economic landscape and continually increased its output. Although, as a local Nova Scotia newspaper observed, this interdependence was a leading cause of the "circulation of a large amount of capital" engendered in the region, lumbering was central to the region's economy and its people for other reasons. Mostly concentrated in New Brunswick, where in 1852 it was responsible for 82 percent of its exports, the timber industry was an important generator of jobs both in the logging operations and in the hundreds of sawmills that sprang up in the region.[41] As late as the 1860s, it was natural for young New Brunswick farmhands like John Nelligan to turn to lumbering as a vocation. The son of a Northumberland County smallholder, Nelligan joined his first lumberjack crew when he was fifteen, aware that the first couple of seasons would provide more experience than earnings. Those early winters in the New Brunswick woods proved in fact crucial, not only for learning the skills of the trade, but also for developing the physical endurance demanded by the harsh working and living conditions. Besides the lack of basic sanitary facilities, winter nights got so cold that the men "would pull the one big blanket over them and pack themselves together as a housewife packs and ties her spoons, back to breast, all facing in the same direction and covered with the same blanket." Nelligan must have been surprised to learn firsthand that in those forbidding conditions even sleeping had its own hard-fought rules and traditions. "When one of the jacks would become tired of lying on one side, he would shout 'Spoon!' and everyone would promptly flop over on the other side, eventually landing in the same compact position as before, but facing in the opposite direction."[42] By the time he was nineteen, Nelligan felt he could tackle any lumber camp in North America. As he recollected in later years, "[after] four years of experience in the woods I was an accomplished camp cook and had worked as both woodsman and riverman. All in all, I felt that I was able to take care of myself almost anywhere."[43]

But if for people like Nelligan lumber work constituted a lifelong occupation, many rural Maritimers saw its advantages in its seasonal character, since the industry offered winter jobs to farmers who would have otherwise remained idle during their dead season.

Here, then, were two dynamic sectors of activity responsible not only for inserting the region's economy into some of the major routes of international trade but also for creating a symbiotic relationship with a predominantly rural population practicing largely subsistence farming. A similar relationship had come into being in the third most important sector of activity—fishing. Though never a major industry, either in terms of the quality and size of its fleet or in terms of the revenues produced, fishing was nevertheless the main occupation in hundreds of coastal villages, from the most remote, wave-battered shores of Newfoundland to the quieter fjords of the Bay of Fundy. But its local, artisanal character made it a seasonal activity, practiced by fishermen who combined it with subsistence farming. Just as the lumber industry had produced the farmer-lumberman, so many of the coastal villages had produced the farmer-fisherman, perpetuating a way of life that for the Acadian population of the Bay of Fundy was a century-old tradition, which many of them had taken to the marshes and swamplands of Louisiana.[44] The diverse occupations of the Maritime farmer was caught by a Nova Scotian contemporary observer who, after noting that "farming [was] the principal occupation," added that "many of the population are engaged in lumbering and shipbuilding. In summer, numbers are engaged in the shad and other fisheries of the Bay of Fundy; and in winter in cutting timber for ship building and foreign markets."[45]

The migration that developed in the Atlantic colonies bore the marks of this particular socioeconomic configuration. Except for the relatively small proportion of Maritimers who journeyed west, selling their labor in the logging camps of Michigan or starting a farm in the Ontario frontier, much of the migration grew out of the mobility patterns engendered by the "wood, wind, and sail economy," expressing the degree of integration of the Maritimes into the larger North Atlantic region. As the perimeter of that mobility enlarged, it became increasingly frequent for Nova Scotians to take up work on American fishing vessels, for naval craftsmen to join a building crew in the yards of Rhode Island, or for New Brunswick farmers to seek high wages in a Maine lumber camp. When John Nelligan at the age of seventeen decided to migrate, he did so simply because, as he put it, "the time had come for me to strike farther afield." He thus left his New Brunswick rural district and traveled to the port city of Saint John, where he embarked on a steamer that took him to his first American job, in Eastport, Maine. Like many migrants of his trade, Nelligan would follow the westward movement of the lumber industry, working in the pine forests of Pennsylvania and then moving on to the lumber frontier of Wisconsin.[46] For many others, the long-established coastal trade linking the colonies to New England provided easy access to the growing urban labor markets of what Maritimers called "the Boston state."[47]

As long as these migrations, whether seasonal or permanent, grew out of mobility patterns that were part and parcel of a stable sea-oriented economy, they did not arouse much concern either in the Maritimes or in New England. These movements become part of a migration phenomenon only for the scholar intent on stressing the crossing of an often invisible legal border. Soon, however, these movements would grow to such numbers as to attract the concern of local politicians and community leaders, whose denunciations and outcries frequently invoked the biblical expression they considered most apt to describe the phenomenon, "exodus." By that time, the population flow across the border revealed—to use the expression of the 1857 report—"a radical social defect," and needed to be treated as "an evil and a public calamity"—as it had been in Quebec for quite some time.

III

Two major economic and political developments of the 1860s had crucial repercussions on the economy of British North America and on population movements both within the country and across the U.S. border. One was the abrogation in 1866 of the Canadian-American Reciprocity Treaty, and the other, the following year, was the merging of the various provinces and colonies into the Confederation. With the end of reciprocity, much of British North America saw its exporting capabilities drastically reduced, and much of its agrarian economy was thrown into uncertainty as it was forced to grapple with new domestic and international realities.[48] Many of these realities became paramount in the agenda of the newly constituted Confederate state, as the Canadian political class sought to integrate a highly decentralized country and in the process ensure its economic growth and social stability.

Of the three British North American regions, Quebec was the least affected by the abrogation of reciprocity. For while it is true that efforts at diversification and the growing practice of mixed farming had helped to pull Quebec agriculture out of its long crisis, very few of its new markets had been assisted by reciprocity.[49] The still predominantly subsistence nature of its agrarian base, and its relatively minor dependence on export trade, made the province much less vulnerable to the negative economic repercussions engendered by the loss of American markets.

Whereas, as we shall see, the economies and populations of Ontario and to a lesser extent the Atlantic provinces were forced to confront major dislocations, commercial farmers in Quebec continued to search in their own milieu or local universe for the financial and technical resources necessary to consolidate their position. It was a slow and uneven process, but one that by the end of the century had changed the geo-economic and social configuration of the province considerably.

It was in the commercial farming sector that these efforts produced some of the most conspicuous results. Aided by an aggressive educational movement conducted within the rapidly proliferating agricultural societies (*circles agricoles*), and stimulated by a growing domestic urban market, farmers who had the necessary land resources and financial means found in diversification a way out of their impasse; others specialized their operations, raising crops targeted to specific sectors of both the domestic and international markets; most of them undertook more efficient cultivation techniques, such as crop rotation and the use of fertilizers and mechanical implements.[50]

A symbol of this class of commercial farmers was Prosper Allard, on whose ingenuity and talent depended much of the agrarian development of his Berthier County. In 1871 he held all his 210 acres under cultivation, except for forty acres he used for pasturage. Like most farmers of his scale, Allard made diverse use of his land, cultivating over a dozen types of produce but at the same time specializing, in his case with oats and hay. Livestock was another of his major activities. In that year he had sold five head of livestock to local butchers, produced wool from half of his herd of sheep, and turned some of the milk produced by his thirty-six cows into 560 pounds of butter. In order to carry out all these activities, he certainly needed the help of local farmhands—other farmers who could not compete with his mechanical implements, which included three plows, a horse rake, a thresher, and a sifting machine.[51]

Thanks primarily to the progress made by farmers like Allard, the gross value of crops in Quebec doubled between 1851 and 1861. Even greater was the increase in agricultural cash income, which jumped from an estimated $1.8 million in 1851 to $5.2 million in 1861, and almost doubled ten years later.[52]

The most drastic reorientation of activities occurred, however, in the dairy sector. The dairy establishments in Quebec grew from a handful at mid-century, producing mostly butter and cheese, to 162 in 1886 and to more than 1,000 ten years later. Dairy production, of course, not only entailed sufficient investments in livestock but also encouraged many farmers to turn hay into one of their major cash crops. It did not take long before dairying became the leading specialized activity, rapidly expanding its domestic market and finding in Britain its leading importer.[53]

The other agrarian sector that witnessed a major expansion was forestry. Stimulated by a growing demand for sawn lumber, forest products became the single most important export, dominating the agrarian economy and providing seasonal work for farmers in newly settled regions such as the Mauricie, the Saguenay, and the Outaouais.[54]

However important these developments were in boosting the performance of Quebec's agrarian economy, they had little positive impact on the province's rapidly increasing rural population, much of which had to confront subsistence farming and landlessness. Several studies have shown that the increasing commercialization of farming set off a process of land concentration, rendering smallholders vulnerable to the acquisitive drive of commercial farmers.[55] Lacking sufficient financial means and acreage to enter commercial farming, they had no choice but to continue living off their smallholdings, resorting to wage labor when they could. It was a precarious condition; adverse circumstances, or an additional mouth to be fed, could entail hardship and impoverishment, forcing smallholders to sell their plots and take the colonization route, or resign themselves to a life of wage labor. In 1871, for instance, in the same agrarian landscape in which Prosper Allard operated, nearly one-third of the holdings were of a size that could only allow subsistence farming, and in the best of cases enable a smallholder to use a portion of his crop for petty local exchange. A closer look reveals that a significant minority of these smallholders were listed by census takers as *journaliers*—individuals whose main source of income was wage labor. In the long-established parish of Saint-Cuthbert, one out of three smallholders were journaliers—a number whose significance should be assessed in conjunction with the large proportion of journaliers who owned no land.[56] A similar socioeconomic landscape emerges from research done on the Richelieu district—an area southeast of Montreal where commercial farming was more developed.[57] Moreover, much like the myriad villages and parishes brought to historical attention by the impressive research done by Serge Courville, Saint-Cuthbert had long developed the infrastructure of petty craft production and services that historians associate with protoindustrialization; but its range of activities had remained too limited, absorbing only a tiny minority of tradesmen and laborers.[58]

Of course, the coexistence of commercial and subsistence agriculture was a feature of Quebec's rural society that had its origins in the earliest seigneuries. But as commercial farming and its byproduct—land accumulation—became the dominant force of a parish economy, and as demographic pressures drastically reduced the access to land ownership for growing numbers of young people, the equilibrium that had existed between these two sectors of the economy was upset, making subsistence synonymous with proletarianization, and landlessness the lot of growing numbers of families.

As the century progressed, several options became increasingly open to this rural proletariat, ones that could have helped extirpate "the evils of emigration": finding wage labor in the existing urban centers, clearing forest land in the hope of establishing a family farm, and, after the 1870s, jumping onto the newly built Canadian Pacific Railway and becoming a homesteader in the new Canadian frontier. All of these routes were taken, and to such an extent as to transform, by the end of the century, the social and economic space of the province. But another option, already tried during the long agricultural crisis, proved more promising and ultimately attracted the largest number of out-migrants: moving south of the border. It too helped transform the social and economic landscape of much of the province, and also that of scores of industrial towns and cities in the United States, some in the Midwest but most of them in New England.

◈

These demographic and economic factors interacted to produce in Quebec a classic case of rural surplus population, marked by high levels of proletarianization and a generalized lack of industrial skills. This scenario had already emerged and consolidated during the long agricultural crisis and, as mentioned earlier, had been responsible for significant out-migration. But neither the progress made in commercial agriculture during the 1850s and 1860s nor the increasing industrialization of the province slowed the growth of the rural surplus population. Although commercial farming and the timber trade helped create a local demand for agricultural laborers, they proved insufficient to absorb the growing number of subsistence smallholders and landless young men. Insufficient, too, was the increasing industrialization of the province during the last third of the century, much of it occurring in the Montreal region. The availability of capital in this city, Canada's leading commercial center, acted as the major localization factor.[59] Investors and industrial entrepreneurs could, moreover, draw significant benefits from the ample supplies of cheap labor in the surrounding districts. A prominent feature of the city's potential for industrial development, according to the authors of *Montreal 1856*, was the existence of "cheap and abundant labor . . . [among] the rural population of the surrounding districts"—mostly smallholders or landless Quebeckers "unwilling to leave the older settlements in the valleys of the Saint Lawrence and Richelieu." Investors and prospective manufacturers should therefore take advantage of the fact that "no where are there found people better adapted for factory hands, more intelligent, docile, and giving less trouble to their employers, than in Lower Canada." The qualities imputed to this rural population put Montreal in a special position, since "hands can be obtained to work in the factories at more reasonable rates [than in the rest of Canada]."[60]

Montreal's industrialists were indeed able to draw from this surplus rural population to such an extent that the Quebec metropolis became by far the major pole of urbanization.[61] The past agrarian and commercial developments in the province had in fact failed to produce more than a handful of urban centers capable of triggering industrial growth and attracting significant numbers of rural people. For every rural person willing to move to Montreal or Quebec City from the surrounding districts, many more, both in the Montreal hinterland and in overcrowded parishes further up the Saint Lawrence Valley, chose to sell their labor to American midwestern lumber and mining companies or, increasingly, to New England mill owners.

Some of this population pressure was alleviated by an aggressive colonization movement developing during the last third of the century, largely under the moral incitement of the church. Ultimately the movement would be responsible for the creation of major settlement areas, in addition to those that grew in the Saguenay-Lac-Saint-Jean and the Mauricie regions.[62] But the forbidding topographical and climatic conditions, the lack of adequate internal improvements that might have decreased the isolation of settlers, and the particularly demanding land-granting policies of the government meant that only the most heroic souls participated. One Mauricie settler who had cleared a tract of forest and turned it into a cultivable smallholding expressed quite eloquently the precarious conditions he now confronted: "The main problem with our townships is the lack of work. It is evident that a young household that settles on new soil, most often without any resources, cannot live right away from the products of the land. The man must then find ways to earn something, and clearly it is not the few sawmills we have here and there that can provide sufficient employment for these new settlers."[63]

The "ways to earn something" were increasingly found in the unprecedented development of manufacturing production in New England and in its insatiable demand for unskilled labor. Earlier population movements from Quebec to New England had largely been limited to borderland areas, especially in Vermont, and had occurred within an agrarian context. As late as 1850, 65 percent of the entire French-Canadian population of New England resided in Vermont, mostly concentrated in the Lake Champlain and Burlington districts. Thirty years later, the population flow to the south took on a radically new configuration, when 70 percent of all French Canadians in New England resided in the southern portion of the region and worked in an urban-industrial environment.[64] The rapid development of the railway system on both sides of the border had linked many new Quebec counties and districts to the American network, making the move much easier. So did the recruiting activities of New England mill owners, who frequently sent agents to Quebec rural districts to advertise jobs. Later, railroad ticket agents often of French-Canadian origin, whose income depended on the number of Quebeckers they could convince to travel on the railways they served, added their voice to the recruitment chorus. By the end of the century, French Canadians had become the leading immigrant group in most textile centers of New England, their number in the region having jumped from 103,500 in 1870 to 573,000.[65] The creation of one of the most "complete" institutional networks to be found among immigrant groups played a major role in encouraging prospective migrants and in facilitating their insertion in the new society.[66] It was a role that can hardly be overlooked in assessing what proved to be one of the major population shifts in the history of North America.

But if rural Quebeckers responded in such large numbers to the appeal of southern New England, this was largely because textile mills offered employment not only to adults but also to their children. Thus, the exodus of Quebeckers toward that region was made up overwhelmingly of family units. For instance, 81 percent of the French-Canadian population residing in Rhode Island in 1880 belonged to nuclear families. And the children of those families contributed significantly to the household revenues. In that same year, in fact, children aged fifteen and under made up a quarter of the total French-Canadian workforce. The extent of child labor within that population is also shown by the fact that 80.4 percent of children aged eleven to fifteen had been listed as working by census enumerators.[67] Studies done in other New England textile centers show comparable rates of child participation.[68]

Research done at both terminal points of one of the numerous "migration fields"—out-migration from Berthier County, Quebec, to Rhode Island—confirms some of the characteristics of this surplus population mentioned earlier. The overwhelming majority consisted of subsistence farmers and farm laborers, who belonged to the same social class the authors of *Montreal 1856* had praised. They had little to offer in terms of skills, but they brought with them a willingness to work and, of course, the labor power of their children.[69]

Agrarian Berthier County and industrial Rhode Island constituted one of the many migration fields through which rural surplus population flowed to industrial capital. Other such fields—though in a smaller proportion—were oriented westward, reactivating migration routes that had been traveled by previous generations of French Canadians.

Next to New England, in fact, the Midwest region was the most important destination for French Canadians. By the end of the century the region

contained approximately one-quarter of all French Canadians residing in
the United States. Although the dream of taking up farming in the ad-
vancing American frontier motivated some of them, the majority sought
work in urban and industrial districts. Nearly half of them chose the state
of Michigan, where long-established French-Canadian enclaves and communities facilitated the initial economic and cultural adjustment. As Jean
Lamarre's study has shown, the largest concentrations of newcomers occurred in the Saginaw River Valley and in the Keweenaw Peninsula. In the
former district, one of the leading centers of the lumber industry, French
Canadians became an important component of the workforce employed
in forestry-related activities. In the Keweenaw Peninsula, French Canadians participated in the development of one of the country's most important copper-mining districts. But the lack of specialized skills relegated
them to the lower occupational rungs; most of them worked as surface
laborers.[70]

As we shall see in a subsequent chapter, Michigan would continue to be,
well into the twentieth century, the leading destination outside New England, feeding old migration networks and developing new ones as the
state's industrial base underwent major transformations.

◈

If in Quebec the increasing commercialization of its agriculture, coupled with the overcrowding of its parishes, set off a process of proletarianization that rendered several strata of the rural population candidates for
out-migration, in the Atlantic provinces what soon became known as the
"exodus" resulted from more complex forces. The region entered a period of important economic change whose effect was the disruption of
long-established ways of life and work. The delicate balance on which the
resource- and shipbuilding-based economy had rested ultimately disinte-
grated, producing major dislocations in all sectors of society and making
out-migration the solution to which growing numbers of Maritimers
turned. By the 1870s, journeying to the United States had ceased to be
viewed as an integral part of a growing Atlantic economy; it was seen instead as the sign of an impending crisis. *Exodus*, the word that the 1857 report used to describe Quebec's leading social calamity, began to be heard
throughout much of maritime Canada as local politicians and commentators raised their voices to denounce the migration unfolding under their
eyes. Hopes that the national political union would confront the problem
and find adequate solutions were soon shattered; the economic policies
implemented by federal politicians and the investment decisions made by
a powerful sector of Maritime businessmen did little to contain—let alone

prevent—the exodus, their long-term effect being rather that of letting the Atlantic provinces slide into a subordinate economic role from which they never recovered.[71] From 1871 to 1901 the Maritimes suffered a net population loss to the United States of approximately a quarter of a million, much of it during the 1880s and 1890s. During each of these two decades, the losses amounted to 10.5 percent of the region's total population, the highest experienced in those years in Canada.[72]

Historians of the Maritimes have made a considerable effort since the 1970s to explain the forces that led to the rapid economic decline of the region and its marginalization within the new political and economic union. Although the debates are still raging, largely because of the variety of interpretative models adopted, a basic consensus has been reached linking the widespread migration from the region to the new economic configuration of the post-Confederation era.[73]

Central to the socioeconomic transformations experienced by the region during the last third of the century was the rapid decline of two industries—shipbuilding and the timber trade—that had been the major players in the export market and, more important, had acted as crucial integrative forces for the regional economy. Historians, however, are less certain about the impact that the decline of these two industries had on the sectors that depended on them—on farmers, timber workers, craftsmen, and urban white-collar workers and their households. In part, the uncertainty is due to the fact that the decline of these basic industries was not as synchronic as previously thought and that it followed a different tempo in each of the three provinces. The difficulty is compounded by the concomitant emergence of new industrial sectors that—at least for a while—ensured the region a sustained economic growth.[74] Coal mining, for instance, saw a rapid expansion that led to the construction of large iron smelters in Nova Scotia and to the emergence of Cape Breton as one of Canada's leading sites of industrial expansion. During the 1890s, the county's population doubled, and local centers of steel production such as Sydney and Glace Bay attracted thousands of workers, mostly from the rural hinterland.[75] Manufacturing made significant inroads in a variety of other sectors, sugar refining and textile production in particular. As T. W. Acheson has observed, after Confederation and during the initial stages of the National Policy "the Maritimes experienced a dramatic growth in manufacturing potential, a growth often obscured by the stagnation of both the staple industries and population growth. In fact, the decade following 1879 was characterized by a significant transfer of capital and human resources from the traditional staples into a new manufacturing base."[76] The coming of the railroads culminated with the completion of the Intercolonial Railway in 1876, making Halifax its eastern terminal point and linking the region with central Canada. Although it did not engender a classic railway boom, it had a significant impact on the region's communication network. It stimulated the economy of some towns and cities and it favored the emergence of new industrial and commercial centers, but it also spelled the decline of others.

The 1860s to the 1890s could then be more aptly characterized as a period of economic conversion, entailing the restructuring of some sectors, the creation of new ones, and the elimination or disappearance of still others. The overall effect was continuing growth.[77] Yet, it was a growth engendering considerable dislocation, occasioned by, among other things, changes in the utilization and processing of natural resources, the introduction of new technologies, the penetration into the countryside of factory-produced consumer goods, and, most important, the localization of new productive activities. These dislocations could not but disrupt local labor markets and established occupational patterns, such as the relations a subsistence farmer in New Brunswick or Nova Scotia had developed with the forestry industry or with shipbuilding, or the relations a rural or urban craftsman had established with various manufacturing sectors, or yet again the place that women's domestic production occupied in the local rural economy. One of the most immediate consequences of the dislocation was widespread mobility.

The extent of this mobility and of the major tendencies it expressed emerges from Patricia Thornton's estimates of population variations at the county level in the Atlantic region. During the last three decades of the century, with very few exceptions, all counties experienced net population losses. But this general trend was marked by significant spatial and temporal variations in the timing and the volume of losses. Important commercial and industrial centers, such as Halifax or Cumberland County, suffered population losses at a more gradual pace than was the case with most rural districts. Although suffering net population losses, Halifax and Cumberland Counties most likely experienced a certain degree of in-migration, mostly from surrounding districts. Moreover, a striking aspect of this movement was the significant overrepresentation of the young of both sexes among the migrating population, denoting the primacy of work-related moves, especially when coupled with sustaining levels of economic activity in both the Maritimes and the greater Atlantic region.[78] As we shall see, the occupational characteristics of Maritimers residing in the leading U.S. area of in-migration, Boston, points to a workforce strongly represented in the skilled trades, in commerce, and in white-collar sectors.

The transformation to an economy of iron, coal, and rail had opened new opportunities in a number of cities and other centers of development, and many Maritimers tried their luck there, thus putting an end to their migration. But these labor markets proved too limited in number to absorb the large numbers of people on the move. For many Maritimers, they functioned as a step in an ongoing migration which ultimately took them outside their region, and for the majority this meant the United States.

Of course, the available sources do not allow us to distinguish between migrations that ended (if only temporarily) at a nearby district or province and those that ended in the United States. They suggest, nevertheless, a high level of step migration, first to commercial and industrial districts and then beyond the region to Ontario, the Canadian West, and the United States.

When due consideration is given to this variety of factors, the exodus from the Maritimes emerges as a phenomenon inextricably linked to dislocations in a regional economy undergoing substantial transformation. Mobility was the most immediate consequence, as growing numbers of people sought to confront change and uncertainty. The nature of the change, its timing and articulation in the region's economic space, created multiple patterns of mobility: intraregional, transprovincial, and transnational. For reasons that are more than simply economic, transnational migrations prevailed over the other two.

Margaret Pottinger, a working-class woman from Pictou County, Nova Scotia, viewed the mobility of Maritimers from the perspective of her family circumstances: "When we look back it seems but a little while since we was all children together and now we are growing old and are scattered over the world."[79] Margaret wrote these lines to her sister Jessie after having remigrated to Fall River, Massachusetts, in 1876 with her husband and daughter. She had good reason to choose those words, for three of the six children in the Pottinger family had left their county—two of them moving to a Fall River textile district and one to Boston. Moreover, two of the children who remained in Nova Scotia must have contributed to her image of a scattered household, for one was a sailor and the other a railway employee, who was able to put his administrative skills to the service of his country and eventually become general manager of the Canadian Government Railways.[80] When Margaret wrote those words she was thinking not only of her family but also of many of her childhood friends, whom she often mentioned in her letters.

The trend toward transborder migration had already become visible in the early stages of the exodus. In 1880–81 three out of four Maritimers residing outside their region were in the United States.[81] As the exodus progressed this trend underwent little change despite the pull that the opening of the Canadian prairies exerted on some Maritimers. The old routes

Fig. 2. Women workers leaving a Lynn, Massachusetts, shoe factory, ca. 1890s. Courtesy of the Library of Congress.

established during half a century of continental migration served to channel the massive new population flow. Geographical proximity produced much transborder migration, becoming a pattern mainly for New Brunswickers and a limited number of Nova Scotians who resettled in Maine.[82] But a significant number of migrants, particularly from New Brunswick—John "Spoon" Nelligan among them—took the route west, finding employment in the Great Lakes region where the lumber industry was going through its boom years; others sought homesteads in the American agricultural frontier. Still, by far the largest proportion of Maritimers chose industrial New England.

For young Maritime women, much as for Quebeckers, the rapid growth of the textile and leather industries after the Civil War provided ample job opportunities. Many of these women had seen their role in the household economy increasingly undermined by cheaply produced consumer goods. When Hannah Richardson left Yarmouth, Nova Scotia, in 1871 and moved to Lynn, Massachusetts, out-migration had not yet reached exodus proportions. Yet, nearly each one of the more than 150 shoe factories operating in the city employed some women from the Atlantic provinces. By 1885 their number had grown to nearly 1,900, making Lynn the U.S. city with the largest concentration of Maritime women, next to

Boston and on a par with Cambridge. Along with domestic service, shoe production was the leading sector of employment, with four out of five single Maritime-born women working in one of these sectors.[83] Twenty-seven-year-old Hannah had no problem finding work at the P. P. Shoe Factory, where several of her Maritime friends and acquaintances worked. She must have had previous work experience in that field, or else she must have been particularly gifted, for within a few weeks she held one of the elite jobs in the factory; as a "lady stitcher," she was assigned to operate one of the new Singer sewing machines, which paid a daily wage of $3.40 and a yearly income of over $500. The Lynn job allowed Hannah to save money and assist both her father, back in Yarmouth County, and her brother in Boston. She even managed to do what many Maritime immigrant women wished to do but could not afford: take a vacation and visit their folks back home.[84] In her skillful study of Maritime-born women in industrial Lynn, Betsy Beattie has shown the variety of family contexts leading to the migration of these "working girls." For some, migration was clearly a family strategy that sent the more mobile members of the family to earn cash, some of which would be remitted to support the household economy. For women who, like Hannah, came from a family less hard pressed, working in the "Boston state" afforded them revenue for an eventual marriage or for greater autonomy in their living conditions. We have only fragmentary knowledge of the economic conditions of these working girls' families in the Maritimes, but Beattie found considerable variety in the occupations of their fathers. Of the hundred such cases she studied, forty-four were daughters of farmers, indicating the predominantly agrarian context of out-migration; of the remaining cases, nineteen of the fathers were artisans, seven were mariners, seven were merchants, six were fishermen, and five were laborers—figures suggestive of the varied economic context that characterized the Maritimes during the last third of the century.[85]

But it was the greater Boston district that became by far the leading destination. The New England metropolis had long been for Maritimers a crucial reference point, both for its economic opportunities and its cultural attraction. As with those who had previously sojourned or settled there, Boston proved true to their expectations. In his 1903 study done for the American Economic Association, Frederick Bushee placed Canadians on a par with native Americans in terms of their rank within Boston's occupational hierarchy—a trend that a few years later would be confirmed by the nationwide findings of the Immigration Commission (see chapter 4). Bushee found that only 4 percent of them were classified as unskilled laborers. Craftsmen and tradesmen found in Boston the

opportunity to put their skills to profit, to such a point that they soon became the dominant force as carpenters in the local building industry and
the shipyards, and made inroads in a variety of commercial and white-
collar sectors. Equally important, Boston afforded ample opportunities to
Maritime women migrants, who, in the above-mentioned study, outnumbered men. The majority of them found employment as domestics, but
significant numbers of them turned to nursing, sales, and office work.[86] If
one is allowed to use a term currently associated with the departure of
highly trained technicians and professionals and apply it to the late nineteenth century, one could legitimately say that to a great extent the exodus resulted in a "brain drain" whose adverse consequences for the Maritime economy, society, and culture would be felt for a long time.

But the pull that New England and in particular Boston exerted on
Maritimers cannot be explained merely in economic terms. Another reason lies in the history of the relations between the Maritimes and New
England. A traditional isolation from central Canada, coupled with the
seagoing "vocation" of the provinces, had made contacts with New England more frequent and tangible than with the rest of British North America.[87] To use an anthropological concept, the Boston state figured more
prominently in the "psychic map" of Maritimers than the mostly French
Lower Canada or the distant Upper Canada. By the time the Intercolonial Railroad linked the Maritimes to central Canada, it was too late, not
only because the link came with heavy economic and political strings attached, but also because migration fields based on generation-long traditions had become well consolidated. The road to the south had long been
safer and more promising than that to Ontario or the Prairies. And it continued to be so.

Ontario too lost a significant portion of its population to the United
States during the last third of the century. As in the Maritimes and Que-bec,
out-migration was part of wider and complex population movements set off
by rapid and profound changes in Ontario's economic base and
society. In Ontario historiography, these movements have not received
the attention they deserve, since their significance has usually been associated with demographic growth or with the urbanization of the second
half of the century. Even more conspicuous is the lack of research into the
reasons that led tens of thousands of Ontarians to emigrate to the United
States.[88]

Basic for an understanding of these population movements is the
transformations that occurred in the two major sectors of Ontario's econ-

omy, namely, agriculture and industrial manufacturing—transformations that propelled the province to its undisputed role as Canada's leading center of economic development.

During the last third of the century, the region that had been "the granary of two continents" had to face new challenges due to developments in international trade and the domestic market. Most momentous of these was the abrogation, in 1866, of the Reciprocity Treaty with the United States, which resulted in the loss of what for over a decade had been the major market for Ontario's agricultural products. This, coupled with a period of severe instability in the international price of wheat, spelled the end of the wheat boom era. After the 1860s the wheat trade never regained the role it had played in the local agrarian economy. Crop failures, soil exhaustion, and the growing scarcity of new land also brought chaos and insecurity to many rural counties and districts.[89]

At the same time, however, the unprecedented accumulation of agricultural capital that the wheat trade had made possible enabled many farmers to turn to new branches of agriculture and to develop new markets for their products. In addition to the necessary financial resources, Ontario farmers could benefit from the most advanced transportation and service infrastructures, with important positive consequences not only for their marketing operations but also for the required technological advances. The ensuing decades, therefore, witnessed the most important structural transformations in Ontario agriculture. Mixed farming, already practiced in many districts even during the wheat boom, became the rule, allowing farmers to adjust their production to changing market demand and to shelter themselves from sudden declines in the price of some products.

The diversification of farming activities culminated in the widespread switch to livestock and dairy production. Even before the century came to a close, dairying had surpassed all other branches of agriculture, becoming by far the leading export. Indeed, the preeminence of dairy production, coupled with new technological developments, led to the rise of butter and cheese manufactures, a prime illustration of the degree of integration between agriculture and industry.[90]

A major repercussion of these transformations on the rural population was the degree of mechanization that occurred in the province. As a leading agricultural historian has concluded, "Ontario farmers turned enthusiastically to mechanized farming after 1870."[91] Thanks to the financial resources available to them, and spurred by the need to save on labor costs, the closing decades of the century witnessed the spread of farm implements that technological inventions made available. The mechanization of harvesting operations may serve to illustrate the magnitude of the shift toward capital-intensive agriculture. In the wheat boom era a relatively common and rudimentary implement such as the reaper required the labor of about eight men to harvest twelve acres of grain a day; but with a harvester (which both reaps and ties the grain) the same work could be performed by one man in a single day. When, by the end of the century, steam-powered tractors made their appearance in the province, labor requirements were further reduced by four or five times.[92] With the total acreage under cultivation remaining nearly constant through the turn of the century, the widespread mechanization could not but result in the freeing of a considerable volume of farm labor—whether performed by household members or by locally hired hands—and thus became one of the main factors contributing to rural depopulation.[93]

Population pressure was another such factor. As mentioned earlier, by the 1850s the Ontario farming frontier had been pushed to its physical limits, with only a few tracts of marginal crown land left for settlement. The relatively high fertility rate among rural Ontarians, coupled with the constant arrival of land-seeking immigrants, could not but make land availability a major problem in both long-established farming districts and areas of new settlement. When farmers wanted to establish their sons on the land, few could do so through land accumulation. For every such case, as the historian David Gagan has documented in his now classic study of Peel County, there were many more cases of farmers who passed their family holdings to one son, which left the other children with the prospect of seeking land elsewhere or finding some other line of work. Another common practice in several counties was the division of family land among all the children—a practice that resulted in fragmentation to such an extent as to preclude viable commercial farming. In the most thorough demographic and occupational study done to date of nineteenth-century central Ontario, the extent of mobility induced by land scarcity emerges unambiguously. During the years 1861–71, in any given district only 16 percent of the sons of farmers remained in their district and became farmers. When mortality and uncountable cases are discarded, the rest of the cohort either turned to some other occupation in the district or simply moved away.[94] Much of this decennial period occurred during the wheat boom, suggesting the hypothesis that a portion of these farmers' sons, in the best of cases, possessed the financial means to acquire cheaper land elsewhere or to establish themselves as independent craftsmen. Still, they had to resort to strategies that took many of them out of their districts, especially in the post-1871 years, when the agrarian sector faced new challenges posed by the decline of the wheat trade.

Still another, though less studied, mechanism of rural depopulation brought about by the new agricultural age was the wedge that these economic and technological developments drove between commercial and subsistence farming. If, during the wheat boom era, the distinction between commercial and subsistence farming had been somewhat blurred (since even smallholders could participate in the production and marketing of wheat), commercial farming increasingly required significant financial resources. Farmers needed to keep up with technological modernization, and they had to adopt a more rational approach to husbandry than was necessary earlier in the era of predominantly extensive agriculture. As a leading Ontario agrarian publication, the *Farmers' Advocate*, concluded after surveying forty years of agricultural practices and methods, the Ontario farmer had evolved "from the rank of a strenuous toiler to the more complex status of a business proprietor."[95] In the absence of an easily marketable cash crop, and faced with the unequal competition from commercial farmers, most smallholders who wished to supplement their home-produced means of subsistence had no alternative to wage labor, and increasingly that meant moving to where the jobs could be found.

The extent of rural depopulation at the provincial level emerges eloquently from census statistics. During the last three decades of the century, despite an increase in the province's population from 1.6 million to 2.5 million, the total number of rural Ontarians remained constant, its proportion declining from 78 percent in 1871 to 57.1 percent in 1901.[96] When proper weight is given to the rates of natural growth and rural in-migration, it is clear that the increase that the rural population would have normally experienced from 1871 onward was offset by out-migration.

As the century advanced, rural depopulation touched most regions of the province. It was pronounced in the more populous sections of southern Ontario, where virtually all counties had suffered population losses by the end of the century, and less so in the more peripheral counties situated in the northeast—where the growing in-migration of French Canadians, mostly attracted by the developing mining industry, offset the losses. In the southeastern region studied by R. Widdis—a region marked by economic decline during much of the closing decades of the century—the widespread depopulation was accompanied by a generalized decline in the size of farm holdings along with an increase in the number of landholders. These indicators suggest a sharp change in the man/land ratio, the result of widespread land subdivision. This practice was so frequent that, as Widdis concludes, by the closing decade of the century the smallholdings had become "no longer economically feasible, and more and more young people were leaving."[97] A similar scenario emerges from a study of Middlesex County, at the other extreme of southern Ontario. Ex-

cept for the main urban center, London, all subdistricts in this area experienced population losses between 1881 and 1901.[98]

The economic and demographic mechanisms inducing growing numbers of Ontarians to leave their rural districts acquire their full meaning
once they are inserted in the context of the wider transformations occurring in the social and economic universe of the province—and beyond.
And one of the distinctive features of the evolving Ontario universe, when
compared to Quebec and to the Atlantic region, was the high degree of
interpenetration between agriculture and industry.

Indeed, the particular character of industrialization in nineteenth-
century Ontario can hardly be understood without taking into account
the role played by the region's agrarian economy, especially in making financial resources available and in providing labor and technical know-
how, both of which had a determining impact on the localization of industrial activities. The seeds of industrialization in Ontario were provided
by the myriad villages and small commercial towns spread across much of
the province's countryside, most of which had come into being during
the wheat boom era. It is here that artisans, flour mills, merchants, and
transportation facilities supplied the services needed by the farming population of their district. As agriculture entered its new age of commercialization and diversification, with their corollaries of mechanization and
processing of agricultural produce, many of these centers came to constitute the basic structure that triggered more specialized and technically
advanced forms of industrial production. It should not be surprising,
then, if already by 1870 three out of four persons engaged in industrial activity belonged to this universe of small towns, servicing primarily a farming population whose estimated average cash income was more than
three times higher than that of its Quebec counterpart.[99] It is in these
towns that small manufacturing and commercial enterprises began to
cluster and in time, but by no means uniformly, gave rise to regional centers of industrial development. The typical early industrial center has
been described by historian Craig Heron as "a small, multi-factory town
serving a nearby (and, it hoped, growing) agricultural hinterland. . . . One
could expect to find in these places some combination of agricultural-
implement works, woolen mill, stove foundry, furniture or woodworking
factory, wagon shop, brewery, tannery, and eventually perhaps a knitting
mill."[100] Although most of these enterprises were small, employing only a
handful of workers, some of these towns, such as Oshawa, Galt, and Dun-
das, had by the 1870s given rise to large-scale enterprises, whereas others
had become specialized in specific manufacturing sectors, such as metalworking, woodworking, furniture, and musical-instrument production.

Along with this type of industrial center there emerged others which, due primarily to their location within the transportation network, developed a more complex urban economy, one in which commercial and transportation services were as important as manufacturing. Towns of this type were well distributed along the highly populated southern belt of the province, and to the mixture of industrial activities described above, they added "metalworking shops turning out heavy transportation equipment, and the first large-scale producers of light consumer goods."[101] It is out of this type of town that eventually the metropolitan centers of Toronto and Hamilton would develop.

This was, to a large extent, the counterpart of the rural depopulation that occurred in Ontario during the second half of the century. Although this process has often been subsumed under the broad categories of urbanization and industrialization, the trajectories taking a rural Ontarian to a town and to an industrial work site could be complex and far from linear, and they could lead beyond the province's borders.

The interpenetration of agriculture and industrial activities, and the particular spatial configuration that industrialization took in Ontario, therefore had a crucial impact not only on the making of an industrial working class but also on the patterns of mobility and on the range of opportunities available to out-migrants in their own region.

More than in the Maritimes, and much more than in Quebec, in Ontario sons and daughters of farmers, clerical workers, and skilled craftsmen and industrial workers did not have to travel very far to find the wages and the career opportunities they sought. Many of them could conduct their search in nearby districts, or in towns or industrial centers just south of the border. It should not come as a surprise, then, if a fast-growing industrial district such as Detroit, located just on the other side of the Detroit River, would become the most important single destination for Ontarians, and attract Canadians from other provinces as well. In 1860 Canadians already made up 14.5 percent of the city's foreign born; twenty years later their proportion had risen to 23.6 percent, making them the third largest foreign-born group after the Germans and the British.[102] By then, their presence had become firmly established in the city and was felt in all sectors of the labor market. Although half of the heads of household worked in unskilled and semiskilled occupations, as many as 31.8 percent of them had found their way into a variety of skilled trades, and another 17.1 percent into white-collar occupations. In the ensuing two decades, their presence within the city's population continued to grow. Despite the massive arrival of immigrants from southern and central-eastern Europe, Canadians made up 30 percent of all the foreign born (French Canadians accounted for 3.6 percent), and the percentage rose progressively toward the top of the occupational structure. By the end of the century, in fact, the proportion of unskilled and semiskilled heads of families had declined to 23.9 percent, while that of skilled workers had grown to 35.4 percent. The most dramatic change, however, had occurred in the white-collar occupations, whose proportion had more than doubled since 1880, rising to 38 percent—thus revealing an occupational trend that would intensify during the twentieth century.[103] This large population influx also consolidated patterns of settlement that—despite the proximity to Canada—contributed to making the English Canadians (mostly Ontarians) little visible as a group in Detroit's public and social spheres. In his study of Detroit, Olivier Zunz sought in vain for residential clusters comparable to those of recent European immigrants or even of a long-established group such as the Germans. The few small clusters of English Canadians he did find were in areas largely populated by native white Americans and, to a lesser extent, by British immigrants. Equally revealing of the English Canadians' rapid entry into the mainstream of American life were the marriage patterns they practiced. Only 21.4 percent of the English-Canadian males in Detroit who married during the 1890s chose an English-Canadian spouse. A larger number, 29.3 percent, chose native white Americans as spouses, and the other half married women belonging to a wide variety of ethnic groups. Quite significantly, English Canadians were the most frequent partners chosen by native white Americans who married foreigners.[104]

Why should the boundary line stop these men and women from heading to nearby states such as New York, Michigan, Ohio, or Illinois, where they could chose among industrial metropolises and countless medium-sized and smaller centers whose productive structure, level of technology, and work habits were not much different from those they might have left in Sarnia, Hamilton, or Toronto? Why should their search end within their own borders when, just beyond, there were plenty of employers and office supervisors ready to welcome these neighbors from "the other side" who spoke the same language—some of them descendants of American settlers and Loyalists—and, perhaps more important, who knew how to handle their tools. A few years after the turn of the century, the U.S. Immigration Commission would find in its survey of midwestern industries that English-Canadian immigrants—most of whom had emigrated before 1900 and undoubtedly from Ontario—occupied the top levels of the work hierarchy, often outranking native white Americans (see chapter 4). If by crossing the border these migrants had taken a calculated risk, for many of them the risk had paid off.

The waves of population that during much of the nineteenth century flowed across the border, replenishing the labor resources of countless American districts, lose much of their historical meaning if looked at merely in aggregate figures, or through the public outcries of Canadian politicians, or as a sort of population balance sheet in the relations between two nation-states.

As this chapter has sought to show, out-migration was first and foremost a local affair. People left from farms, small towns, and industrial districts—not from a nation. True, they were all Canadians, whether they spoke English, French, or some other language. Much as their future might have been influenced by decisions taken by their national government, they considered their options in the light of local concerns, and it is through these same realities that they assessed the outer limits of their universe. Out-migrants made those universes expand—from New Brunswick to Maine, from Nova Scotia to Massachusetts, from Quebec to Vermont and down to Connecticut, from Ontario across the lake to New York or to Michigan.

By the end of the century, what historians call euphemistically "the flood" had become a population movement that ran along well-delineated streams; but unlike natural streams, they could suddenly change course, flowing upward across mountain ranges, linking opposite lake shores, or converging into a large river; yet in most cases drawing human maps that were regional in scale. To most Maritimers, what happened in the "Boston states" was more relevant and likely more meaningful than what happened in English Canada, which lay much farther away on the far side of French Canada. And those Ontarians who cared to look eastward saw little to attract them in a backward French people or in an Atlantic population they knew little about. For most of them, their future lay in their province—the richest, most dynamic, and most diversified of their country. And for many of them, the outer limits of their province overlapped the borders of neighboring states, drawing a region that transcended legal boundaries.

The pattern had been set, and it would undergo little change as hundreds of thousands of new out-migrants would cross the border from coast to coast.

Fig. 3. Building a boundary mound on the Canadian prairies, 1872.
Courtesy of the National Archives of Canada, C 73304.

◆

CHAPTER TWO

The Rise of the Border

Many Canadians celebrated the coming of the new century not in Canada but in the United States. How many of them were south of the border, Canadian authorities did not know, for no count was taken. But in rural parishes, small towns, and metropolitan neighborhoods throughout the land, many of those "missing"—their names and much more—were not only well known but likely also a topic of much discussion.

For some of those who lived just on the other side of the line, the coming of the new century must have provided an occasion to celebrate with dear ones and friends on both sides of the border. But in most other cases, only prayers, remembrances, and wishes helped connect people that had been separated by hardship or ambition.

When the decennial 1900 U.S. census figures were made public, the number of Canadian-born living in the United States became officially known: it amounted to 1,179,922, corresponding to 22 percent of the Dominion's population.[1] If their U.S.-born children and other descendants were added, their number more than doubled, equaling 54.8 percent of Canada's population.[2] The Dominion had undergone an important demographic growth during the previous decades, but equally important was the expansion that had occurred among Canadians on the other side of the border.

Whether they viewed the missing as a loss for the nation or as a fact of life in a continent blessed with opportunities, many Canadians had reason for optimism: their country had now taken a new path, which would make it unnecessary to cross the border in order to improve one's material conditions. The long and troubling depression that for a good portion of the 1890s had taken a heavy toll on their country seemed now well behind them. The recovery had done more than merely set off a new cycle of growth. It became evident to many national and international observers in the early years of the new century that Canada—much like her southern neighbor—had entered an irreversible process of transformation, one that touched all sectors of the economy and society. The optimistic pronouncement of the newly elected premier Sir Wilfrid Laurier, that the twentieth century would be "Canada's century," became the motto of the era.[3]

In many ways the bet that a generation earlier the "fathers" of Confederation had made with the future of their country was finally being won. The Dominion could now boast a national market, rendered possible by a growing transcontinental railway system that perhaps more than anything else made Canadians feel part of one country—a national market, moreover, serving a fast-growing population whose number would double to ten million people during the first two decades of the century. Canada, of course, reaped the benefits of new economic world trends that set in from 1896 onward: a sharp rise in the price of grains and natural resources and a constantly growing demand for foodstuffs in Western countries undergoing rapid urbanization. But much of the self-confidence expressed by Canadians during the Laurier era stemmed from a belief both in the inestimable natural resources lying unexploited in the west and north and in the fast-growing manufacturing sector. It also grew from the ability of the political and economic élite to protect the Canadian home market while firmly inserting the country in a pattern of international exchange in which its exports significantly exceeded its imports, while attracting the investments and labor resources necessary to transform this potential into real wealth.

By the eve of the Great War, the economic geography that would last for decades was in place: the rapid settling of the Prairies and West had transformed that region into the country's wheat basket; hinterland districts, in both western and central Canada, as well as in the Maritimes, yielded growing amounts of minerals and lumber, much of it for export. The industrial manufacturing heartland of the country became well entrenched in central Canada—largely Toronto and its many satellite towns, and the Montreal region. Though on a smaller scale, industrialization also developed in cities ranging from Winnipeg, Manitoba, to Sydney, Nova Scotia, and in scores of small towns across the country engaged in the processing of agricultural and mineral resources. But inevitably the new geography

Fig. 4. Lumbermen during lunch, North Shore, Ontario, 1905.
Courtesy of the National Archives of Canada, PA 51818.

of a fast-growing national economy produced new regional disparities and consolidated old ones—inequalities that would have an important impact on the mobility of labor and on migrations, at both the domestic and international levels.[4]

So powerful was the economic drive and so swift the ensuing transformations that Canada had to resort massively to immigration. Immigrants were needed to people the vast vacant lands in the prairies and transform them into productive homesteads; they were needed in new mining districts and lumber camps, on railroad lines, and in the construction of urban infrastructures; as both unskilled and skilled labor, they were also needed in the factories and mills that radiated eastward, westward, and increasingly northward from central Canada. From 1897 to 1914, when the outbreak of the Great War temporarily interrupted the transatlantic influx of immigrants, close to three million people had entered Canada—the greatest concentration occurring during the years 1907–14. And there is no question that their contribution proved crucial to the country's doubling of its railway mileage, to the tripling of its mining output, and to the staggering increase in wheat and lumber production.[5] In 1911, for instance, 57 percent of the workers in the mining industry were immigrants, and in the mines of the western provinces of British Columbia and

Alberta (the fastest developing mining region) the proportion was 84 and 88 percent. Moreover, American farmers from northwestern states were attracted in such numbers to what became known as "the last best West" that they became the largest immigrant group in the provinces of Saskatchewan and Alberta.[6]

A Canadian nationalist viewing the country's socioeconomic development—whether informed by Malthusian criteria or motivated by patriotic fervor—might have recommended that empty regions be peopled by Canadians from overpopulated districts, and that industries suffering shortages of labor be manned by Canadians suffering from unemployment and job uncertainty. In part this did happen, as significant population shifts took place between provinces and toward both agrarian and industrial developing districts. Yet this nationalistic perspective did not square up with that of many other Canadians who by crossing the border seemed to give priority more to concrete and personal considerations than to their sense of national obligation. Canadians in fact kept crossing the border from every province. Much as in the nineteenth century, for some it was a way of escaping hardship; for others it was a way of putting to better profit the skills they already possessed. Still others migrated prompted by the desire to pursue a new vocation among family members, kin, and friends who could assist them in their search for jobs and housing and familiarize them with the new economic and cultural environment. And by the end of the 1920s, the number of Canadians who had settled in the United States since the turn of the century surpassed one million.[7]

But for all the elements of continuity, one important change had occurred in the relations between the two nation-states. Transcontinental developments that were beyond Canada's control sent repercussions westward along the boundary, forcing Canadians to reassess their migration projects and changing forever the meaning of their southern border.

I

When in October 1869 John "Spoon" Nelligan boarded a ship in Saint John, New Brunswick, and journeyed to the small coastal town of Eastport, Maine, he probably did not even realize that at some point he had left one national territory and entered another, because no one was there at the docks to inquire about his health, his criminal record, his occupation, and the purpose of his trip. Similarly, the Jones family, who in the 1850s had entered Wisconsin on a horse-drawn wagon, may have not even

Fig. 5. Building a bridge over the Souris River near the U.S. border, Manitoba, 1874.
Courtesy of the National Archives of Canada, PA 74644.

noticed the mound—if one had been built—that served as boundary marker. This was hardly the case for a Canadian immigrant like Wilfrid Desmarais. When on 26 January 1908 his train stopped at Swanton, on the Vermont border, immigration officials were there to make sure that he complied with admission regulations.[8]

During the 1890s and the first few years of the new century, the Canada-U.S. border had undergone a major transformation, both as a symbol and as a legal/geographical reality. It was no longer a mere line drawn by international agreements to mark the end of one national territory and the beginning of another; it had also become a system of controls to prevent the entry of unwanted persons into U.S. territory.[9]

The free circulation of Canadians and Americans across the border had reflected the lack of concern by authorities of both countries about what

Marcus Lee Hansen has called "the mingling" of the two populations.[10] But it also meant that the number of those who crossed the border in either direction was left to guesswork and estimates. As late as 1896, for instance, the U.S. commissioner-general of immigration admitted that the lack of statistics prevented him from reporting on the number of Canadians entering the United States. All he could say was that "it is known that many of the citizens of Canada annually come to the States across our northern frontier, as well as by rail and water routes."[11]

By that time, however, figures on Canadian entries into the United States—or the lack of them—had acquired a nasty political character. The massive exodus of Canadians during the 1880s led to a fierce controversy between U.S. and Canadian authorities. The issue started when John Lowe, the Canadian secretary of agriculture, charged that the figures published by the U.S. Treasury Department were highly inflated. He set out to produce his own figures and meanwhile continued to investigate the flawed inspection procedure followed by U.S. border officials.[12]

Lowe had been compiling a study of the Canadian population that he was to read before the prestigious British Association of Economic Science and Statistics meeting in Montreal. With the help of statistical tables and graphs, he would describe the main characteristics of that population, from the founding of New France to the most recent wave of continental European settlers. But the figures did not always speak for themselves, and so he would extol the virtues of this multiethnic population, its attachment to the land and to the promises that the Dominion held for the present and future generations.[13] When the U.S. figures arrived on his desk, he must have been deeply troubled and unwilling to tolerate the idea that so many of the people he described in such laudatory terms were leaving Canada and moving south.

In his zeal to add credence to his assertions, Lowe stepped down from his chair as a top government bureaucrat and did some fieldwork. He boarded a train bound for the United States, sitting in a car with immigrant passengers so he could observe firsthand the work of U.S. border officials. In so doing, Lowe left historians a rare description of the admission procedure followed by U.S. authorities at the border check of Port Huron, Michigan—the leading inland port of entry from Canada. His description says much about the degree of free circulation Canadians enjoyed at the time.

During his crossing from Sarnia, Ontario, to Port Huron in a second-class car, U.S. customs officers examined his hand baggage and those of the other passengers but did not ask any questions. "After crossing the river," Lowe explained, "my checked baggage in common with that of other passengers was taken out of the train and placed in a large shed for the purpose of being opened and examined. . . . Everything was conducted with apparent efficiency and dispatch. But here again no questions were asked," neither to him nor to the five or six passengers traveling in his car.[14] To make sure that this inspection procedure had not occurred on an unusual day, Lowe went through the crossing procedure some weeks later, and satisfied himself that what he had observed on both occasions was standard: "The passenger's or immigrant's name is taken and the value of his effects, but he is asked nothing with regard to his age, or calling, or number of his family, or his destination, and there is nothing in the printed form of entry, a copy of which I have in my possession, which calls for any further information."[15]

It is very likely that Lowe's observations were accurate, for a few years later a customs officer on duty at the Detroit border checkpoint—though motivated by different concerns—expressed his disapproval about the lack of controls on passengers entering the United States.[16] His criticism was echoed soon after by a special congressional committee inquiring into the importation of contract laborers. Committee members expressed disbelief that so many people could cross the border into the United States without being subjected to inspection.[17]

Whether the procedure described by Lowe was also common in the few other existing border points, we do not know. What seems certain, however, is that U.S. authorities were much more concerned about Canadian goods and customs revenues than they were about the Canadians, who in any case were exempt from the head tax charged to overseas immigrants. It would not be a surprise, then, if the approximation in numbers of immigrants contrasted with the precise statistics on duties exacted on the northern border.

◈

This system of inspection might have continued had it not been for the sudden explosion of a problem thrust on the border by transatlantic developments. By the early 1890s, in fact, the issue was no longer the number of Canadians entering the United States but that of Europeans who used Canada as a backdoor to gain entry to the industrial giant to the south. The alarm had been sounded by U.S. labor organizations and newspapers mostly in states and cities adjacent to the Canadian border. But when another special congressional committee inquiring on immigration and naturalization procedures made its report known, the magnitude of the problem gained national attention. "It is believed," stated the report "that 50,000 European immigrants have landed in Canada and reached the United States by this circuitous route within the past six months, and have avoided inspection."[18] The figure was in itself dramatic, accounting as it did for approximately 22 percent of the total immigrants admitted to the United States.[19] But perhaps more dramatic was the committee's skepticism about the capabilities of American authorities to face the challenge: "It appears to be practically impossible to place a sufficient number of inspectors on the border to entirely preserve us from this class of immigrants."[20]

If this indictment had been meant as a call for action, the results were not long in materializing. Through the Immigration Act of 1891 and a subsequent 1893 law, jurisdiction on immigration law enforcement was transferred from states to the federal government. The centerpiece of this reorganization was the creation of an Immigration Bureau headed by a superintendent (later a commissioner-general) who reported yearly to Congress, as well as the creation of a corps of immigration border inspectors. Where no such inspectors could be assigned, customs officers were given immigration inspection duties.[21]

In dealing with the pressing problem posed by the northern border, the U.S. Immigration Bureau decided to concentrate its resources on the major Canadian ports. A subsequent inquiry had revealed the staggering movement of U.S.-bound passengers transiting through Halifax, Quebec City, Point Lévis, Saint John, and Vancouver. In its estimate, 40 percent of all passengers disembarking in those ports were immigrants who then traveled inland—through the Saint Lawrence waterway or by rail—thus evading the entry inspection set up in U.S. ports.[22]

Clearly this tide of potentially illegal overseas immigrants called for the cooperation of the Dominion. In 1894 the U.S. Immigration Bureau therefore entered into an agreement with Canadian authorities as well as Canadian steamship and rail companies. As result of what became known as the "Canadian Agreement," U.S.-bound overseas immigrants disembarking in Canadian ports had to undergo inspection by U.S. officers stationed there before being allowed to proceed to a U.S. destination. Those who passed the inspection were issued a certificate of admission to be presented when entering the United States.[23]

In his 1896 annual report, the U.S. commissioner-general of immigration expressed satisfaction with the system, which in his view had discouraged immigrants "to seek this mode of entry into the United States in greater numbers to evade inspection at our own ports."[24] American authorities were aware, however, that overseas immigrants who did not pass inspection might remain in Canada and later find their way into the

United States; others might try to circumvent the system altogether by declaring a Canadian destination and later slip into the United States. Authorities sought to gain control over such evasions by providing that any immigrant unable to produce such a certificate would be refused entry into the United States and handed over to Canadian railways, which were bound by agreement "to return [one such immigrant] to as remote a point from our borders as he is willing to go."[25]

Satisfaction with the working of the system was again expressed the following year. In his 1897 report, the commissioner-general of immigration praised the work of U.S. inspectors placed in Canadian ports and also expressed confidence that the system was "more effective and less expensive than an attempt to guard against immigrants subsequently entering points on our frontier."[26] Moreover, and significantly, potentially deceitful overseas immigrants were contrasted with the "large number [of Canadians] who arrive and depart along our northern frontier and the eastern or maritime provinces of the Dominion." In his view, these immigrants were "thrifty, industrious, and belonging to all trades and occupations, and are both skilled and unskilled laborers."[27]

But by 1898 optimism and confidence in the system had given way to concern that the fight against illegal entries through the northern border was far from won. No estimate was available of people entering illegally "at any point on the border which is not on the regular line of travel between the two countries," but the commissioner-general expressed "no doubt that violations of the law occurred . . . and that they will continue to increase as the laws are more carefully and successfully enforced here." He cited the special report of a U.S. inspector referring to a British immigration agent who "boldly declared that anyone who really wanted to go to America could scarcely be kept out, no matter how vigilant the United States authorities may be."[28]

The alarming situation called for a change in strategy; the commissioner now believed that controls had to shift from Canadian seaports to inland border locations to be designated as "the sole points of entry to this country of trans-Atlantic and trans-Pacific immigrants, and of all [foreign-born] Canadians who shall not have resided in Canada for at least five years prior to their migration to the United States."[29] Clearly, the gravity of the situation had led him to reverse the position he had so confidently held in previous reports.

A year later no action had been taken on the recommendation. The concerned commissioner reiterated his fear that overseas immigrants who entered legally via Canada "represented only a part of the number actually coming into the United States" evading inspection. To stress the urgency of the situation he added that he was in possession of "voluminous evidence . . . accumulated from day to day confirming that . . . efforts to enforce the laws and regulations are in a great measure nullified by the open door through the Dominion and across our northern boundary lines."[30]

We do not know whether these signals of alarm were falling on deaf ears or whether the implementation of new regulations ran into political and bureaucratic wrangles. But clearly the commissioner did not like to be in command of a losing platoon, for the tone of the 1900 report was as decisive as professional language permitted it to be. The commissioner could not "too strongly" reiterate the recommendations submitted in the two previous reports, and referred outright to the "ineffectiveness of the present system." It was now urgent, he went on, "that exclusive ports of entry be designated along our northern and southern boundaries for the admission of aliens, and that such ports be properly equipped with the requisite buildings and a sufficient corps of officials, including a marine hospital surgeon." In the face of a possible resistance by "Canadian transportation interests," the commissioner maintained that "the interests of the entire people of the Union . . . were much more important than those of such companies."[31]

Finally the recommendation received the green light, but border inspection points were set up too slowly to prevent illegal entries. When in 1902 an immigrant inspector was stationed at Sault Sainte Marie, immigrants headed west to Winnipeg, where another inspector had to be assigned in February 1903. As the historian Marian Smith has formulated it, "Each time an Immigrant Inspector took control of a new land port, the immigrants simply moved further west or to some other unguarded point."[32] By 1908, however, a string of entry posts dotted the northern boundary line from east to west; moreover, following repeated recommendations, the new corps of inspectors—separate from customs officers—was increased in the face of the growing flow of transatlantic immigration. For instance, the Detroit district, which during the 1890s had operated with only one immigration inspector, was assigned a second one in 1902, and by 1907 it was staffed with thirteen officers.[33]

The U.S. Immigration Bureau was now satisfied, at least for the time being, that the new system of controlling the northern border was complete and fully equipped to protect the national territory from illegal entries.

◆

And so, unlike John Lowe, who only got his luggage checked by a customs agent, Wilfrid Desmarais had to undergo a careful inspection and supply answers to a string of questions an immigration agent asked. And he answered them all. He was twenty-three years of age, single, and traveling alone; he was born in Milton, Quebec, and was emigrating from that same parish. When asked about his race and nationality, he answered "French" and "Canadian." He knew how to read and write; the name he gave as a reference was that of his father, who lived in Milton; he was a laborer and had previously spent several years in New Bedford, Massachusetts. His new destination? Providence, Rhode Island. When the inspectors asked if he knew anyone in Providence, Desmarais gave the name and address of one of his sisters, adding that he intended to move to the United States permanently. He then declared how much money he was carrying in his pockets and that he had contracted no job with any American employer.[34]

Desmarais was one of the earliest representatives of a new generation of Canadian immigrants for whom the crossing of the border was more than a mere reminder that they were about to leave their country behind. It was also their first encounter with the American state and their entry into an administrative apparatus that inspected and certified their admissibility to American civil society. The information that Desmarais and the hundreds of thousands of other border crossers provided has resulted in the wealth of data that has made this book possible.

The need to protect the northern border from overseas immigrants seeking to evade U.S. inspection had now put an end to the regime of "free circulation" that Canadian neighbors had enjoyed ever since a legal boundary between the two countries existed. In some important ways, Canadians continued to constitute a separate category of entrants compared to overseas immigrants. They were, for instance, exempted from the head tax—a sort of "human duty" the United States exacted from the importation of immigrant labor and population. This exemption made Canadians part of a de facto "free trade" agreement, as far as the movement of citizens between the two nation-states was concerned. Moreover, the border inspection system was also meant to benefit Canadian entrants who subsequently would apply for naturalization—a procedure that, as reformed by a 1906 act, required an official record of their entry into U.S. territory.[35]

Still, however favorable the attitude of U.S. inspectors may have been, Canadians had to satisfy all the admission requirements of U.S. immigration law. It is thus likely that when Desmarais was declared admissible by his inspection officer and free to resume his journey to Providence, he let out a sigh of relief—aware as he probably was that the inspector might have found an infraction preventing his entry. And infractions that most likely had gone unnoticed when border inspectors were interested only in the luggage Canadians carried with them, now were caught and certified, and Canadians declared inadmissible.

Thus, people like Hatty L., James S., or Rachel F. experienced firsthand how the legal crossing of the border could hold unpleasant surprises. For Hatty, this happened at the inspection post in Port Huron, Michigan, on 7 July 1910. An eighteen-year-old waitress from London, Ontario, Hatty was headed to Detroit with the stated intention of migrating permanently. Her inspectors, however, found her undesirable and she was declared debarred; the reason is stated in their manifest: "prostitute."[36] James received his surprising response the same year on the Pacific coast, after he left Vancouver heading for Seattle. Born in Manchester, England, James had migrated to Canada in 1896 at the age of eighteen, leaving behind his father and possibly the rest of his family. Unmarried and a laborer, he had previously been in Montana and Washington, but now in 1910 he was met by inspectors who cared less about his Canadian nationality and more as to whether he could sustain himself without becoming a public charge. Their decision was that he could not, and so the gate to the United States closed in front of him.[37] Rachel had traveled from her parish of Saint-Émile, Quebec, to Montreal where she would have boarded a train taking her to Manchester, New Hampshire, where she had an uncle. Aged eighteen like the others, single, and a domestic by occupation, Rachel would have treaded the path that had taken thousands of French-Canadian women to the large Manchester textile mills had it not been for the medical inspection that revealed a "heart disease." Fearing that once in the United States her health would deteriorate and she would become a public charge, the inspectors debarred her, and on 25 May 1909, her migration project came to an end.[38]

II

But for every Rachel F. who was denied entry by a U.S. immigration inspector, more than ninety Canadians were admitted and reached their destinations. Although the border turned into a sort of gigantic administrative filter ensuring that only people judged capable of contributing to the economic and moral growth of the American Republic would be admitted, most Canadians who went through the inspection procedure met those requirements.

At the same time, one can only speculate to what extent the new system of border inspections served to restrain the traditional freedom of Canadians to move south; obviously this restraint would not show on the data recorded by inspectors—except for the small numbers of debarred immigrants. The answer could only come from individual and family histories of prospective immigrants—hard-pressed parents, sons, daughters, widows, or men and women who had run into trouble with the law—who, after assessing the likelihood of being sent back at the border, never set forth.

Subsequent changes in U.S. immigration regulations affecting the admissibility of Canadians were few, and their impact on the flow across the border unequal. For instance, the passing in 1917 of the controversial literacy test had few repercussions on a migrating population that was overwhelmingly literate. More consequential, instead, were the public debates accompanying the enactment of the immigration quota legislation and, in 1924, the institution of a visa system applying to Canadians as well. In the former case, the impact was essentially psychological, a result of the uncertainty produced on prospective Canadian migrants by discordant views being voiced in the United States. Canadians had been exempted from the 1921 quota restrictions, but as the debate on more stringent measures heated up, proposals that Canada be included among the countries with quotas sent shock waves throughout the Dominion. As we shall see, this brand of anti-Canadian sentiment was essentially a form of labor protectionism spearheaded by the powerful American Federation of Labor, whose corporatist concerns found an attentive ear in the U.S. Labor Department. Fear that the gate to the south would significantly narrow lasted until the passing of the 1924 quota law reconfirmed Canada's special status as a Western hemispheric country. But until then, it is likely that persisting fears of a quota, fueled when the controversy spilled into the Canadian media and traveled like lightning through the many cross-border migration networks, pushed many Canadians to head south while the opportunity lasted.

Particularly apprehensive were Canadians living in border districts, whose ties to the U.S. economy were a matter of daily life. The mayor of Windsor—Canada's largest border city—reported "serious alarm" in all municipalities along the American boundary and expressed concern for his city's four thousand residents who daily commuted to work across the border. The imposition of quotas on Canada, he felt, would not only create "an alarming labour situation" but also "strain the present cordial relations between Canada and the United States."[39] This could be one of the several factors explaining the dramatic rise in the flow of Canadian entrants, which in 1923 and early 1924 reached levels comparable to the peak years of the nineteenth century.

Ultimately the passage of the 1924 quota law came as a relief to many Canadians. Still, the provision and enactment of a visa regulation, part of the same 1924 law, did result in more stringent immigration controls and had an immediate impact on Canadian migration patterns. Before the enactment of the new provisions, U.S. border inspectors had not been concerned whether a Canadian intended to move to the United States permanently or temporarily—a decision left entirely to the entrant once residing in the United States. Now a Canadian desiring to work and live in the United States had to decide beforehand whether he or she intended to move permanently or temporarily. And in the former case, the candidate had to go through the bureaucratic procedure of obtaining a visa from a U.S. consular office in Canada, and no doubt be subjected to more careful controls. This procedure may have discouraged people unable or unwilling to spend one or two days in a Canadian city hosting a U.S. consular office—a sojourn some may have seen as expensive, and its outcome uncertain. Ovila Lafrenière, a worker at the Scoville Manufacturing Company in Waterbury, Connecticut, was sent back to Saint-Élie, Quebec, at his company's expense to help family members and co-villagers to go through the immigration procedure at the U.S. consular office in Montreal. "I could speak English and I knew the ropes, so they could go through quickly instead of having to sleep in Montreal sometime up to three nights; that was quite expensive. . . . So my company could get new workers right away."[40]

Canadians could also declare that their migration was temporary, and if found admissible, they were issued a permit extending for no longer than six months. There is no way of assessing the precise extent to which the temporary permit provision may have discouraged prospective migrants, but as we shall see in the following chapters, it had a definite impact on the demographic and occupational composition of the Canadian population allowed through the border.

Canadians had won the fight over the quota issue; yet, if the goal of U.S. authorities was to slow down or limit Canadian immigration, they succeeded through these administrative measures—witness the sharp decline of the flow in the months and years following the enactment of the visa provisions.

More importantly, although not visibly in either administrative records or public debates on cross-migration, these measures altered profoundly the relations that Canadians had entertained with the United States ever since the creation of a legal boundary. Ever since French-Canadian *engagés* had traveled the streams and lakes of midwestern forests in the employ of American fur companies until the turn of the century, when factory workers, office clerks, and professionals joined the labor force of

American cities and towns, their trip—whether temporary or permanent—reflected the freedom of movement across the border they enjoyed as neighbors of the American republic. It was a freedom of movement that allowed them to choose if and when they would return to Canada, if and when they would settle in the United States, if and when they would take up American citizenship.

The new regulations took this freedom away. To some they may have come as an indication that permanent residence in the United States and naturalization were a much more serious matter than they might have believed. Canadians had to confront this decision thoughtfully before taking the road to the south, and if they did not feel like committing their future to the new nation-state, their sojourn could not last longer than six months.

That Canadians had used that freedom of decision emerges in part from the large proportion in our sample of border crossers who had previously lived and worked in the United States at least once.[41] More compelling evidence comes from 1913–14 data showing that Canadian-born immigrants waited an average of 16.4 years before filing a final petition for naturalization—thus significantly outdistancing the other nineteen nationality groups included in the inquiry.[42]

But fluctuations during the decades covered by this book (see chart 1) did not result merely from admission criteria. The Canadian population, spread largely along the southern border of the country often near major U.S. centers of economic development, responded readily to specific economic conjunctures. Canadians profited from their proximity to the border, their knowledge of conditions to the south, and the measure of assistance they could rely upon in their migration. But as the following chapters will show, fluctuations in migration also reflected the regional socioeconomic realities that made migration a more compelling option for some Canadians than for others (chart 2).

World War I and its aftermath were the most important of these conjunctures for their immediate impact on population movements both continentally and transcontinentally. As is well known, transatlantic traveling and migration came to a virtual halt when U.S. military preparedness and the subsequent intervention made labor shortages the most acute the country had ever experienced. Along with Mexicans in the Southwest, African Americans in the South, and women throughout most of the states, Canadian immigrants were crucial in meeting these shortages while at the same time taking advantage of the conditions U.S. industries offered them. It should not come as a surprise, then, if during the

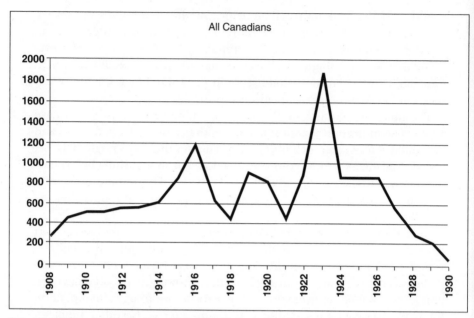

Source: Sample drawn from *Soundex Index to Canadian Border Entries*, Record Group M1461 and M1463. U.S. National Archives (Washington, D.C.). Computed by the author. All charts and tables in this book are based on this source.

Chart 1. Emigration of Canadians to the United States, 1908–30 (yearly fluctuations). Adapted from *Soundex Index to Canadian Border Entries*, hereafter cited as *Index.*

years 1915–18 Canada contributed 31 percent of all immigrants entering the United States despite comparable shortages experienced in its own labor markets.[43]

The war also intensified American restrictionist sentiment toward a variety of European nationality groups, resulting in the 1921 Emergency Quota Act. Once again, Canadians could compensate, at least in part, for the drop in the number of immigrants originating from central-eastern and southern Europe. During 1922 and 1923, Canadians made up nearly 20 percent of the immigration flow into the United States.[44]

But if Canadians were excluded from the quota provisions, they were not entirely spared the restrictionist animosity that swept American society in the early 1920s. American hostility toward Canadian immigrants had only occasionally surfaced in the past, most often in protests from trade unions and advocates of labor reform. Probably the best-known example is the negative image of French-Canadian immigrants found in the

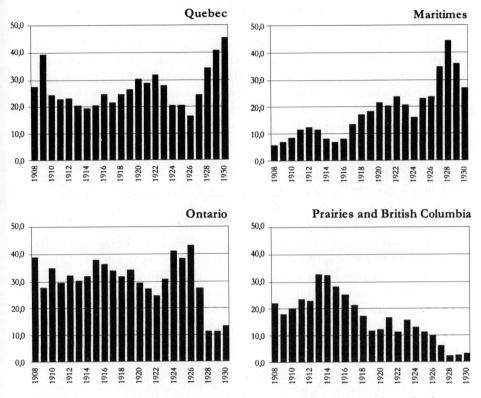

Chart 2. Emigration of Canadians to the United States, 1908–30 (by yearly share of each province or region in the national movement).

annual report for 1881 of the Massachusetts Bureau of Labor Statistics. The bureau portrayed these Canadians as the "Chinese of the East" because of their alleged willingness to accept lower living standards and their lack of interest in American institutions—an unfortunate public stereotyping that provoked angry reactions from Franco-American leaders throughout New England.[45]

Though not couched in ethnic terms, Anglo-Canadians had been accused of similar antirepublican behavior. Thomas Klug has documented the hostile attitudes of the Detroit Knights of Labor toward Canadian immigrants, who were accused of accepting lower wages, acting as strikebreakers, evading the contract-labor provisions of the U.S. immigration law, and weakening organized labor's efforts.[46] True, American labor leaders tended to address these accusations to transient as opposed to permanent Canadian immigrants—though one is not so sure how their behavior in local labor markets could have differed from that of American workers pulled to Detroit from a variety of counties and states.

In his 1896 annual report, the commissioner-general of immigration, while not identifying any specific district or region, drew attention to the problem caused by Canadians who entered American labor markets on a temporary basis and in so doing "evoke urgent protests from our trade unions, labor societies, and individual workingmen against the employment of these transitory aliens."[47] Moreover, judging from the testimonies presented to the 1901 U.S. Industrial Commission, it is likely that studies of other American industrial border cities would reveal similar attitudes by local labor organizations.[48]

But as the 1900s progressed, bringing unprecedented numbers of southern and central-eastern Europeans to the American shores, U.S. labor spokesmen in border districts had to worry more about overseas immigrants reaching their factories and workplaces from the eastern states than about their neighbors from the north. Moreover, the massive arrival of European newcomers in most U.S. industrial centers coincided with a decline in Canadian immigration compared to its nineteenth-century levels. If this did not necessarily reduce the visibility of Canadians, theirs had become the visibility of stable communities that had become integral parts of the cultural and institutional landscape of scores of American cities and towns.[49]

It did not take long, however, before the war and the wave of nativism it set off would bring Canadian immigration back to public scrutiny. As Canadians crossed the border in numbers that had not been witnessed since the 1880s, they too became the target of restrictionist sentiment.

Catherine Collomp's comments on American organized labor's stance on immigration could not be more appropriate when looking at the context of the early 1920s. "In its pursuit of legislation, organized labor set itself up as a guardian, or rather a censor, of the ethnic composition of the American people, a concern that was more a national than strictly a labor interest."[50] As the national voice of American labor and as defender of American democracy, the American Federation of Labor (AFL) took the lead in the struggle for immigration restriction during the early 1920s. It unleashed its rhetorical weapons both against the "reactionary" stance of those business interests bent on keeping the gates open and against those "racial groups who want the doors left open for an influx of their countrymen regardless of the menace to the people of their adopted country."[51] It also lent its full support to the various bills introduced in Congress demanding a stricter application of the quota criteria.[52] In so doing, it made full use of racialist discourse to dramatize the impending disaster

awaiting American civilization unless nationalities and races deemed inferior and unassimilable be prevented from contaminating republican institutions and corrupting democratic life.

Yet, a closer look at the AFL's stance toward Canadian immigration
shows that in its restrictionist discourse, the theme of nativism was closely
interwoven with the theme of labor protectionism and thus with the age-
old concern with trade union control over the labor market. Just as the
nation had to be sheltered from the danger of racial and moral degener-
ation, so American workers had to be protected from unfair competition
originating in foreign lands and making its evil impact felt in American
factories and workplaces. The AFL was resorting to the same protectionist
demand that in the 1870s and 1880s had led organized labor to launch
and pursue the struggle against contract labor; but now the expansion
and complexity of international migrations required new and more efficient means of protection, including a reassessment of relations with the
northern neighbor.

Thus the AFL campaigned for the restriction of Canadian immigration
by giving its support to bills demanding that quotas be extended to Canada;
but it refrained from using against Canadians the same nativist rhetoric unleashed on southern and eastern Europeans. In calling for the restriction of
Canadian immigration the AFL was speaking less as a guardian of the nation's ethnic integrity and more as a protector of the interests of the American worker. As the supreme head of a federation composed largely of "international" unions reaching into most industrial centers of the Dominion,
Samuel Gompers knew only too well how to distinguish Canada from Italy,
Poland, or Mexico.[53] And as the leader of a movement whose locals—particularly in border states—included significant numbers of Canadian immigrants, he knew the limits that prudent labor diplomacy imposed on him.
During the heated congressional debates leading to the passage of the
Johnson-Reed Quota Law, Gompers gave his support to the bill while acknowledging that it was the most the restrictionist forces could expect. The
ideal solution, Gompers stated, would be "to replace the three per cent
quota law with a law absolutely forbidding immigration into the United
States for the next five years; that would be the most advantageous thing
that could be done."[54] This was the voice of absolute protectionism, where
distinctions between Canadian, Turkish, or even Scottish nationalities were
secondary in the face of the danger that American workers "be overwhelmed" by alien labor. True, in a major article on the principle of quota
restrictions, the paper reproduced a one-page graph drawn from a U.S. military study in which Canadians had been ranked seventh in intelligence
after various Anglo-Saxon nationalities.[55] Only on one occasion did the

American Federationist specifically refer to Canada as one of the countries to seek protection from. Its author, however, was not an AFL leader but the government's major spokesman for the interests of American workers. In its April 1924 issue, in fact, the paper hosted a long article written by Secretary of Labor James J. Davis in which the government's view on immigration restriction was presented and its protectionist philosophy explained. Much as Gompers had argued, the question was not which countries should be subjected to quota restrictions, but rather how should those restrictions be applied. Davis's answer : "Any quota limitations imposed shall apply to all countries from which we permit aliens to come." The 1921 Emergency Quota Law, Davis went on, was more than inadequate; it was "manifestly wrong" because it "exempted from the quota restrictions British North America, Mexico, Central and South America."[56] Davis made his argument rest, at least in part, on the fact that during the previous fiscal year Canadian immigrants had made up 22 percent of all immigrants admitted into the United States. Unless a quota were imposed and strictly enforced, this trend was bound to continue, Davis believed, because that northern flow contained significant numbers of "aliens from any country in the world" who by means of acquired citizenship, required residence, or "fraud" can gain legal admission to the United States.[57]

One implication in Davis's argument was clear. His real concern seems to have been not "true Canadians"—however he might have defined them—but aliens who used Canada to gain entry, legally or illegally, into the United States. And that he had some difficulty in defining them is shown by the nationality breakdown of those pseudo-Canadian entrants he mentioned in his article. One large group, which he listed as "French," were in fact French Canadians, whose ancestors were the first Europeans to settle in North America.

Still, by subjecting the Dominion to a quota, immigration inspectors would have to worry only about filling the allotted number of admissible immigrants without concern for their legal or ethnic background in Canada. Once again, the northern border had become the thorn in the flesh of Canadian-American relations, as well as a socioeconomic space drawn into the ever expanding circuits of transnational migration and labor.

Both the American secretary of labor and organized labor had to succumb to the superior will of Congress, which refused to disregard the Dominion's status as a Western hemispheric nation and force on it a fixed number of entrants; perhaps because by this time the problem had become less the number of real or pseudo-Canadians passing through border inspection posts, and more the multitude of aliens from all over the world who crossed along rivers, through wooded valleys, and over remote farmland. In the fight between the immigrants and the American nation-state—the former seeking to reach the promised land, the latter trying to close its doors tighter and tighter—immigrants were again proving they could be one step ahead. Moreover, if the restriction battle had been fought mainly among Americans, the war against "immigration bootleg-ging" was being fought against a flagless army whose real strength no one could guess. A 1923 Immigration Bureau report coming from the Seattle district could not be more eloquent: "The [1921] quota law has increased the surreptitious entries across the land border. There has been, too, an increase in the number of apprehensions of aliens who smuggle across the land border."[58] But Seattle was not the only problem area; from infor-mation received from other districts, the bureau concluded that "it is clear that far too many inadmissible aliens have successfully smuggled across the land border and reached the interior of the country." A con-sensus now existed among "all our border officers in charge [that] the smuggling in of these Europeans has already become a quite serious problem, and there is general agreement that it will become increasingly serious as time goes on." In the same report, the commissioner-general complained that "mobile inspectors" appointed to perform surveillance duty along the border had been forced to work "at fixed stations" because of the "never-ending stream of applicants who seek legal admission at es-tablished ports of entry." It must have been a bitter admission of defeat, coming from the man who in previous years had repeatedly called atten-tion to the problem, bringing several federal agencies to work together with a view to creating a border police force.[59]

When it came to Canadians and to the possibility that they might par-ticipate in that illegal behavior, the commissioner-general's logic was quite different from the one displayed by Secretary of Labor Davis—one that reversed the relationship between enforcement and violation of the law. It was wise, he felt, that Canada (and Mexico) remain exempt from quotas, for it ensures the "rather wholesome respect for our immigration laws that exists among the people of Canada and Mexico"—implying that they might be tempted to resort to smuggling if "a limit is put upon the numbers who may come from those countries."[60]

Just as at the turn of the century, once again the legal and administra-tive measures deployed to protect the sovereign territory from unwanted aliens had proved inadequate. The urgency of the situation called for quick action, and so the commissioner-general reiterated his recommen-dation, speaking also for the corps of border inspectors: "The bureau and its officers in charge of the various districts concerned are united in the conviction that the creation of a force of well-paid men, especially quali-

Fig. 6. International border on the Vancouver-Seattle road near Blaine, Washington, ca.
1930. Courtesy of the National Archives of Canada, PA 49848.

fied for police work of the peculiar nature involved, is the only solution of
the border problems."[61]

The majority of Congressmen must have realized that it had become
both politically and morally humiliating to let the situation degenerate
further, and by an appropriation act signed on 28 May 1924 they author-
ized an expenditure of one million dollars to create a land border patrol.
Additional funds were provided in early 1925, and by that time a force of
472 men was operating along the northern and southern borders trying
to stem the flood of illegal entrants.[62] Although in the following years the
number of patrol officers would be raised—to 805 men by 1930—one
may legitimately doubt whether this new protective measure could truly
prevent illegal entries. Still, the creation of the patrol force had a strong
symbolic meaning, for in the long and frustrating attempts to safeguard
the integrity of the national territory, the border had now entered into its
final phase: policing.

The more stringent 1924 quota measures along with the creation of a border police must have quieted fears regarding the legal and cultural vulnerability of the United States. But probably not the fears of Secretary of Labor Davis, nor his concern about the kind of men and women Canada was sending through the border; for, in his view, the Dominion's socializing influences on immigrants who had resided there at least five years, or who had qualified for Canadian citizenship, were not deemed sufficient to meet U.S. admission standards.

North of the border, a leading Canadian social scientist was observing the same migration phenomena but reaching quite different conclusions. According to R. M. Lower, "wholesale immigration" to Canada had turned his country "into a training ground for American citizens. We instruct our new-comers in the ways of the continent, teach them, often at considerable pains, to fit themselves into our social structure; we educate their children at great expense to the state and then send them across the border. When they become American citizens, they are welcomed as highly manufactured products, finished at the expense of another country."[63]

III

The fear of an invasion from the north voiced in the United States had its dissonant counterpart in denunciations arising in various Canadian milieus: the exodus across the border was doing irreparable damage to the Dominion. Never before—with the possible exception of the 1880s—had spokespersons and commentators from both English and French Canada been so attuned in addressing an issue of national import.

Before the surge in out-migration of the early 1920s and the animosity set off by restrictionism, the loss of Canadian population to the south had hardly attracted the same degree of concern in the two sections of Canadian society. Whereas in French Canada this issue kept popping up in public debates, in English Canada—with the possible exception of the Maritimes—it was overshadowed by the more controversial issue of overseas immigration.

In Quebec, where immigration from Europe had been largely confined to the Montreal region, *le mirage américain* pulling French Canadians southward had given rise to a loud chorus of concerted voices that had become a permanent feature of public controversy. The strong sense of peoplehood that marked French Canadians (compared to their English counterparts) did much to dramatize the loss of population and provide precious ammunition to those who raised the specter of national extinction.

"If our population keeps on abandoning the land for a few more years," an editorialist had written in 1892, "the French Canadian nationality will be transported to the United States."[64] Though at a slower pace, as the twentieth century progressed, French Canadians continued to abandon the land, and variants of the alarm kept ringing in the province, often replacing the term "nation" with "race." For every word or sentence that a Henri Bourassa or Lionel Groulx contributed to their vision of a French-Canadian nation, a trainload of Quebeckers headed south across the border.[65]

But far from merely indulging in jeremiads, French-Canadian leaders had taken concrete steps to try to contain the problem. They had sent repatriation agents to the United States to convince expatriates to return to their homeland. More important, colonization societies—often inspired by the church, when not under direct clergy leadership—had sprung up throughout Quebec, sending representatives to New England mill towns to extol the virtues of agrarian life and to elevate colonization to a supreme gesture of nation building. The provincial government had jumped on the bandwagon and created in 1888 a Department of Colonization that used public money and a staff of newly appointed agents to facilitate the repatriation and settlement of frontier districts.[66] The Franco-American press of New England constitutes a rich and eloquent record of the interminable procession of Quebec prelates and government agents preaching colonization to their brothers and sisters living in exile. Despite disappointing results, the flame of colonization was kept alive throughout the era. Eugénie Savoie-Coté recalled when in the late 1920s "Missionary Fathers" stopped at the Connecticut town where she was working while living with her family. "They came down to push people to return and settle on the land—they did not want to give up on the land." In this case the message fell on receptive ears, for shortly afterward the Savoie-Cotés packed up and resettled on a Quebec farm, thanks in part to the dollars they had earned in the United States.[67]

But while French Canada was trying to rescue the race from extinction, much of English Canada confronted the dilemma posed by a tide of immigration that, although deemed essential to ensure the growth of its natural resource industries, increasingly included nationalities seen as threatening to the cultural and civic makeup of the Dominion. In many ways, the Laurier era stands as an ongoing tug of war between two large opposing coalitions: the large railroad companies and immigration authorities, on the one hand, and a variety of civic groups and restrictionist associations, on the other. The former's pragmatism and determination to pursue an open-door policy was countered by accusations that special interests and their economic greed were threatening the cultural and social fabric of Canadian society.[68]

Thus, as the policies making possible the arrival of three million immigrants were pushed through parliamentary debates, political scandals, and fears of invasion, few Canadians expressed their concern with the loss of population to their southern neighbor. Certainly few did in Ontario, the province that received the largest contingent of newcomers, and even fewer in the Prairies and the West, where growth and expansion became inextricably dependent on the immigration of Europeans and Americans.

A sharp decline in immigration to Canada in 1914–18 (down to 23 percent of the 1909–13 annual average) was certainly responsible for taking much of the steam out of the issue.[69] Moreover, the war economies of the two neighboring countries, with the differing roles played by regional labor markets, produced reverse population movements across the border that puzzled even the most attentive observer. A migration student of the stature of Marcus Lee Hansen saw in those movements "a great variety of often conflicting influences," growing out of "frenzied developments [that] were complicated in the extreme."[70]

Once that frenzy ended, the return to normalcy in Canada took much longer than in the United States; and the postwar surge in out-migration across the border was accompanied by widespread unemployment and by a renewed activism on the part of the powerful immigration lobby.[71] Despite significant regional disparities, Anglo-Canadian and French-Canadian observers saw similar developments unfolding under their eyes. It was one of the rare contexts in Canadian history that brought the two major opinion movements to converge into a truly pan-Canadian outcry; it also brought to the fore what observers in both parts of Canada saw as a perplexing and nonsensical contradiction: opening the gates to massive immigration while the country kept losing its own population to the south.

John A. Stevenson was one of those writers who sought to tackle this issue head on. When in early 1923 he set out to write on it for one of Canada's leading national magazines, he was immediately confronted with the lack of statistical data. His information on what he called "a southward exodus on an alarming scale" came from reports of "families hurrying in concert from Alberta to California," of parliamentarians up in arms because "half of their ridings' populations" had been lost to out-migration to the south, and of similar reports from Winnipeg, Calgary, Vancouver, and the Maritimes. One report from Edmonton claimed that "the loss of population [had] changed landlords from supercilious tyrants to gracious suppliants."[72]

However eloquent Stevenson may have found those reports, lack of data made it "difficult," he admitted, "to keep track of our lost citizens because Ottawa, unlike Washington, does not indulge in emigration statistics."[73] He then turned to a report from the U.S. Treasury Department and found "the most disconcerting novelty." It contained figures on customs returns as of 31 December 1922, showing that "the value of imports under the head 'settlers' effects' total[ed] $6,195,569 against a total of exports amounting to $7,832,052." With the aid of other data—and some guesses—he managed to estimate the approximate number of effects-carrying Canadians who had emigrated to the United States in 1922, as against the number of Americans crossing in the opposite direction.[74]

Stevenson lamented the fact that the superior economic and professional conditions in the United States were draining "the flower of our national stock," and he conceded that it was "difficult to blame young men who succumb to the lure." He also warned that if the flow continued "the results were bound to be disastrous." Among those who crossed the border, however, there were significant numbers of European immigrants who had found that conditions were better farther south. Unlike the early Ontario settler who seemed to have a stake in his new homeland, Stevenson explained, the latter-day immigrant was more adventurous and mobile "and too often he moves before he has given the new life a fair trial." Why then try to bring over more of these immigrants ? His answer was "obvious": "while the exodus on a serious scale is in progress, expenditure on immigration schemes is a sheer waste of money."[75]

The charge against Canadian authorities for wanting to bring over immigrants who would then find their way south of the border was voiced by several other Anglo-Canadian critics—as well as in Parliament.[76] But Stevenson must be credited with having been one of the first commentators, if not the first, to apply the term *sieve* to Canada for a role the country had long played in intercontinental migrations. If his article reached the desk of Secretary of Labor James Davis, it is likely that he drew from it precious ammunition to argue his case in favor of quota restrictions.

In Quebec, commentators did not use the corresponding French term but exposed the same paradox, directing a barrage of accusations against the government, against big business, and against the immigrants themselves. Much as in English Canada, Quebec readers were treated to articles containing lists of estimates of the number of out-migrants, the population growth the country would have attained if Canadians had stayed within their borders, and the waste of money for importing immigrants. "Fraud" (*duperie*) was the term used by *Le Devoir*'s leading immigration editorialist, Georges Pelletier, to characterize the government's record in the area of migration. In surveying the past twenty years of population movements in and out of the country, Pelletier raised a cry that had become a litany in the Quebec press: "We should have encouraged our own people to remain in the country, to establish themselves on the land, to have children, rather than inviting strangers to take that land." Then came the list of the culprits: "the owners of trans-oceanic fleets, of railroads, of land for sale, of factory owners who have sought the cheapest workforce—and the rest. This group then went on making more money by bringing immigrants back to Europe, or by transporting more than half of them to the United States."[77]

Despite the dubious arithmetic contained in the above statement, Pelletier conceded that government policy had resulted in a substantial number of European immigrants remaining in Canada. But in Pelletier's misguided logic, they were a sort of human residue, "much of it refuse that ended up in hospitals, in prisons and penitentiaries"[78]—however hard they sought to make Canada their new homeland.

Here was then the basic theme of an argument that resounded in the Quebec press with only slight variations. For the founder of the Société de Colonisation de Montréal, for instance, the disastrous immigration campaign was the work of "imperialists" from both England and Canada acting in concert with "international financiers who had no motherland and whose only god was the golden calf." And here, too, the immigrants were the inevitable part of the equation—"the coveted prey" pulled "from the bowels of all the motherlands of the world." The man who pronounced these words in front of the Montreal Chamber of Commerce was also a medical doctor, le docteur T.-A. Brisson, and he prefaced his impassioned speech by saying that he was going to treat the subject as a "surgeon who must delve deeply into the plague so that he can come up with the necessary remedy." And thus, in his surgical logic, the immigrants easily turned from "prey" to part of the "plague"; as such they constituted a grave danger to the health of Canadian society, which was now confronted "with garbage, with despicable leftovers who crowd our courts, our prisons, our hospitals, our asylums."[79]

While applause was filling that sanctuary of civic responsibility and moral rectitude, in another part of Montreal Michele Marcogliese—illiterate but smart as a fox—was going from house to house speaking to fellow immigrants from Casacalenda, Italy, trying to convince them to set up a mutual benefit society; they had to find on their own a measure of protection against unemployment, illness, and death—though their immediate task was raising enough money so that on the day of their patron saint each villager back in Casacalenda could have "one kilo of meat and two kilos of potatoes." And in a movie theater not far from the Chamber of Commerce, Antonio Funicelli, his violin tight under his chin, was helping entertain Montrealers while they watched a silent movie.[80]

Dr. Brisson, Georges Pelletier, and the others who raised their voices in the public square were smart enough to know that hardly any immigrant went to settle in those agrarian districts that sent French Canadians across the border; meanwhile they stubbornly stressed that most of their fellow citizens who left their parishes had been attracted by "luxury, an exaggerated love for enjoyment, and the taste of adventure."[81]

Ultimately, then, the only hope of finding a remedy was to address the migrants themselves, to make them understand the gravity of their actions, whether they were departing from the timber district of Saguenay, the fertile parishes of Bas-Richelieu, or the recently settled region of Abitibi. And who else had a greater moral authority and power of conviction than the church? Who else in the province had such an elaborate outreach, making it possible to address the faithful not merely through publications and associations but directly from the pulpit? And so, on the first Sunday of June 1923 hundreds of thousands of Quebeckers sat on their pews, their eyes turned toward the altar, listening to the pastoral letter sent by Archbishop Bégin and cosigned by the province's bishops. The letter could be read in a calm, solemn tone, as part of the liturgical ceremony. But it could also be read passionately, with emphasis on carefully chosen words and expressions, with fist-waving and finger-pointing.

It was not the first time—ever since mass migration had begun in the nineteenth century—that this medium of communication had been used to call French Canadians to their national responsibility. Now once again, in the face of an "intense migration movement that pulls out of our farmland and industrial centers thousands of our fellow countrymen," the Quebec prelates felt they had "to raise [their] voice" and denounce a "danger that threatens again our national expansion." It was not sufficient to remind the faithful that "migration weakens the living forces of our race"; it was necessary to stress that migration amounted to an act of desertion—all the more reprehensible as people were "deserting their place at the very moment when, in order to rescue it, they had to double their sacrifices and their devotion." And deserting one's nation in the face of "circumstances of an exceptional gravity" amounted to "a sort of betrayal and the forfeiting of those duties that bind every citizen to his motherland." It was then the church's duty to remind to every French Canadian that "the land you are deserting is the same one that through sweat and blood your forefathers wrung from barbarism in order to pass it on to you as sacred heritage."[82]

But 1923 was a record year in the flow of French Canadians to the United States (see chart 1). No one will ever know how many of those migrants represented by that sharp peak crossed the border carrying with them the moral wounds of their act, and how many were able to make the distinction between rhetoric and facts. The curé of Manseau, a parish in rural Quebec, certainly understood that in the light of his parishioners' harsh existence, it was inappropriate to condemn them. As Bruno Noury recalled, "he did not scream at us for leaving—he was not blind! He saw that there was no work."[83] And so did the pro-labor journalist Jean Syndical who brought to public attention facts he had gathered as a lone researcher; he showed that about half the people who lived in Quebec rural districts were not farmers but *emplacitaires*—rural dwellers who drew from their tiny plots just enough to survive. Why then scream that "the land is being deserted, that productive farms are being abandoned," he asked. And what about the half of Quebec's rural population that was made up of "sons of merchants, public employees, storekeepers, craftsmen, and day laborers." Why wave at them the flag of "colonization, which they don't recognize; or that of farming, which they know even less about and cannot contemplate, not even if they wished to; for they don't have the means to acquire a piece of farmland." These facts, and others, gave this lone researcher the courage to raise his voice and aim where few others dared to: "Stop beating on the people who leave; stop telling them that they have forgotten the providential mission of French Canadians, that they have no faith, that they are not patriotic; stop throwing the responsibility on their shoulders," for the real responsibility lies with those who run the government and the economy.[84]

Voices such as this, likely submerged by the turbulent tide of patriotism, help us appreciate the distorting effect that nationalism and racialism could have on social and economic realities; and we understand how the alleged homogeneity and the sacredness of the nation could efface local differences, banalize international dynamics, and drag the individual struggle for betterment in front of the altar of national purpose.

English-Canadian commentators did not slip into these emotional and rhetorical excesses. Their arguments suggest a more rational and calculating frame of mind, one that in later years would be termed a "cost-benefit" approach. Yet, once the sieve metaphor took hold of their imagination, the terms of the equation were not much different from those of French Canadians. And immigrants were part of the equation, not only because they played the game of misguided politicians and greedy corporations, but also because they forced Canadians out of their country.

Few commentators managed to articulate this logic more fully and sci-

entifically than Professor R. M. Lower, in later years one of Canada's leading historians. In discussing the issue, he did not resort to the supreme
design of Providence, but to "Gresham's Law of Immigration," which he
redefined as "cheap men will drive out dear." Lower went on at length
displaying a series of demographic calculations meant to prove that immigration had prevented the Canadian population from growing. By constantly displacing Canadians and pushing them beyond their borders, immigrants had prevented the nation from fully exerting its mechanisms of
natural growth. Using a logic not unlike that of Samuel Gompers, he pro-
posed that in the competition for economic betterment Canadians lost
out to the aliens because "the man with the higher standard of living cannot compete with the man with the lower. In this sense," Lower continued, "virtually all immigrants are 'cheap' men for on arriving in this
country they are not in a position to bargain for the sale of their
labour."[85] Lower could resort to compelling metaphors as easily as he
could handle elaborate historical statistics; and thus he likened Canada
to a ship, one that

> can carry only a fixed number of people, crew and passengers. If she takes a
> number of passengers in excess of her complement, there is only one way of
> compensating for it, some of the crew must be left behind. We in Canada
> for sixty years past have been taking on so many passengers, that is immi-
> grants, that we have had to keep leaving many of the crew behind. To pro-
> vide room in the ship of state for immigrants we have had to embark a large
> proportion of our own children for the voyage of life in another vessel, the
> good ship *United States*.[86]

In his zeal to apply rigorous demographic and economic laws, Lower
did not care to look closer at his country's population, at its ethnic and
linguistic composition, at the length of residence that had turned many of
the foreign born into Canadian citizens. His sharp distinction between
"crew" and "passengers," between "our children" and "the immigrants,"
and between Canadians and non-Canadians could only be predicated on
an idea of nation which he did not spell out, but which ultimately made
his argument not so different from the one expounded by French-
Canadian nationalists. But unlike French Canadians who could so easily
graft the idea of a nation into concrete historical, linguistic, and religious
developments, Lower's nation arose by default—by contrasting his ideal
Canadian to the foreign and the alien. And his nation, much like that of
French Canadians, had to be protected from those who infused it with
new blood, for "much evil must come out of this constant renewal of

blood generation after generation." Lower's sieve was more complex than the one described by John Stevenson. It kept immigrants within the Dominion, and it let Canadians filter through the border, and as long as this went on, it was difficult "to see Canada [as] a nation and possessed of all best attributes of nationhood."[87]

◆

While Lower and other commentators were deducing and judging through population statistics the behavior of both newcomers and native Canadians, migrants such as Michele Delforno, Eli Mason, and Almira Lusk had long disproved their theories.

Michele Delforno had arrived in Halifax in early April 1913 with the SS *Campaniello*. A fifty-six-year-old married man, he had left his family behind, and like thousands of Italian sojourners he had sought in Canada the wages that would enable him to improve his situation back in Carpino. His stay only lasted six months, for on 29 September he crossed the border at Niagara Falls headed to a U.S. port city and a ship that would take him across the Atlantic. It is very unlikely that while in Canada Delforno displaced native workers, for Canadians were hardly interested in the unskilled jobs that laborers like Delforno filled, most often in remote work sites or towns. Delforno's last job was in one of these towns in Northern Ontario, Fort William, which largely owed its development to immigrants from Italy, Finland, and several central European countries.[88]

Nor were Eli Mason and Almira Lusk likely to have been displaced by immigrants. Before heading to South Boston in December 1922, the twenty-seven-year-old Eli had worked as a fisherman in his native village of Voglers Cove, a Nova Scotia rural district few immigrants would be able to find on a map.[89] Almira Lusk headed south of the border from a Canadian city, Toronto, that had attracted large numbers of immigrants. But as a graduate nurse, her professional universe was totally separate from that inhabited by immigrants. Young, single, and educated, Almira very probably migrated out of professional ambition, heading in 1918 to the New York City Woman's Hospital, where a job awaited her.[90]

The experience of thousands of migrants like these, however fragmentarily it emerges from our data, reveals the full variety of local and regional contexts that received and sent migrants across the border. It helps us put national and political discourses in their proper perspective. It also allows us to go beyond aggregate population data and reach individual migrants, their families, and their networks of friends and associates, the men and women who ultimately changed the social and economic geography of North America.

Fig. 7. French-Canadian weavers, Lowell, Massachusetts, 1905.
Courtesy of the Lowell Museum.

CHAPTER THREE

➤

Emigration from French Canada

to the United States

In the summer of 1903 the *Gazette de Berthier* proudly announced to its readers that the town's factories were in full production to such an extent that it was difficult to find enough workers in the area. Berthierville was the administrative seat of a county that during much of the second half of the nineteenth century had seen a significant portion of its population join the migration flow southward, mostly to New England. The economic revival that started around the turn of the century had strengthened the county's largely agrarian base, producing in Berthierville a small but significant concentration of industrial manufacturing. This did not end out-migration, it only slowed its pace. New England continued to be the leading destination, although some migrants were now heading for the fast-growing industrial and commercial activities of the nearby Montreal metropolitan region, whereas others were joining the colonization movement and settling in the interior.[1]

I

In many ways, Berthier County exemplifies the variety of population movements that marked Quebec during the ensuing decades as the province partook in the transformations occurring throughout much of Canada. These multidirectional population flows had been part of the socioeconomic landscape of the province in the nineteenth century, but in the twentieth century their course modified somewhat as new centers of economic development emerged or as old ones expanded within and outside the province, offering opportunities to prospective newcomers.

A key factor in the modification of these population shifts was the increasing pull exerted by cities, large and small, on the rural population— a reflection of the province-wide process of urbanization. Between 1901 and 1921 the province's urban population grew from 36.1 percent to 51.8 percent.[2] Although the Montreal metropolitan area absorbed by far the largest share of the increase, other cities consolidated their role as regional commercial/industrial centers, while new ones came into being, often associated with the exploitation of natural resources. For instance, the city of Sherbrooke, the industrial and commercial center for the Eastern Townships region, saw its population grow from 11,675 in 1901 to 23,515 in 1921. At the same time, a district in a mostly forested area of northern Quebec that had not even been enumerated in the 1901 census became in the ensuing years the village of Jonquière because of the rapid emergence of wood-pulp processing plants; by 1911 it counted 2,354 inhabitants, and ten years later it had become a town of nearly 5,000 and was one of several centers in that region specializing in pulp and paper production.[3]

It was thus the growing urban economy, much more than the colonization movement, that acted as the prime factor in reducing the population flow south of the border. Still, the United States continued to be the leading destination for French Canadians who left their parishes, towns, and cities. Between 1900 and 1930 the number of French Canadians who went to work and live in the United States grew to 320,000.[4] Despite a decline compared to the peak years of the exodus, the movement was so widespread as to touch virtually all regions of Quebec and involve nearly all social classes. Moreover, U.S.-bound French Canadians did not leave exclusively from Quebec. By the turn of the century, significant numbers were living and working in Ontario. Another substantial portion of departing French Canadians consisted of Acadians who had deep roots in the Atlantic provinces, particularly in the neighboring province of New Brunswick and in the many rural and fishing districts of the Bay of Fundy. Smaller settlements had also come into being in the Prairies, mostly in and around Winnipeg and in Saskatchewan. They hardly figure in the historiography of French-Canadian emigration to the United States. Taken all together, their contribution to the migration flow south of the border was significant if one considers that throughout the years under investigation they represented approximately 23 percent of the entire French-Canadian movement (table 1).

Thus, people kept moving from farming districts, cities and towns, and

Table 1. *French Canadian Emigration to the United States by Provinces of Departure and Major States of Destination, 1906–30 (in percentages)*

	Nova Scotia	New Brunswick	Prince Edward Island	Quebec	Ontario	Prairies	British Columbia	Province Unspecified	Total N	Total %
Massachusetts	74.4	42.8	35.0	24.9	5.3	9.2	7.1	8.8	1,027	25.5
Maine	6.7	38.8	52.5	18.5	0.7	3.8	3.6	14.7	698	17.3
New Hampshire	2.2	3.7	—	17.6	1.2	3.1	—	12.7	536	13.3
New York	8.3	4.0	5.0	8.1	28.9	—	3.6	11.8	390	9.7
Michigan	1.7	3.3	2.5	4.2	45.6	10.8	—	24.5	361	9.0
Rhode Island	1.7	0.3	5.0	8.4	1.7	3.8	—	6.9	263	6.5
Vermont	—	0.7	—	8.4	2.9	0.8	—	3.9	256	6.4
Connecticut	2.8	4.3	—	5.0	0.7	—	—	1.0	163	4.0
Minnesota	—	0.7	—	0.5	2.9	11.5	—	1.0	45	1.1
California	0.6	0.3	—	0.4	0.5	13.1	10.7	—	36	0.9
Washington	—	0.3	—	0.1	—	6.9	71.4	2.0	35	0.9
Illinois	—	0.3	—	0.8	1.7	3.1	—	1.0	35	0.9
Montana	—	—	—	0.2	0.5	12.3	—	2.9	27	0.7
Other states	1.7	0.3	—	2.9	7.3	21.5	3.6	8.8	155	3.8
Total	100	100	100	100	100	100	100	100		100
N	180	299	40	2,836	412	130	28	102	4,027	

Source: Sample drawn from the *Soundex Index to Canadian Border Entries*, Record Groups M1461 and M1463 (Washington, D.C.: U.S. National Archives). Computed by the author. All the tables in this book are based on this same source.

Note: Cases dismissed (last permanent place or destination in United States unknown): 369.

colonization areas. For some, migration occurred in steps, for others it was a direct move from their villages or towns to their U.S. destinations. Some moved in family units, others moved to reunite with their families, still others moved as unattached young adults in search of a new life in a land that promised more than just steady employment and high wages. For some people, their move was their first border crossing; for others it was a return to the United States after one or several previous migrations, often years apart.

How can the historian make sense out of the enormous variety of individual and group experiences? Felix Albert, for instance, was among those who migrated after a considerable period of often painful assessment of their future as marginal farmers. Before leaving Quebec for good, he had sought a solution to his economic hardship by selling his smallholding in Ile Verte and acquiring a large parcel of land in a colonization district. Turning forested land into arable fields soon proved more arduous than he had foreseen. When, moreover, bad weather ruined much of his crop, he was forced to move temporarily to Maine to earn some much needed cash. Resumption of his farming activity did little to improve his situation, and after losing another crop to wheat rust he and his wife decided to give up. For this couple, the planning of their migration must have been all the more careful as they had nine children and were heading for a city—Lowell, Massachusetts—where they had no relatives or friends.[5] Bruno Noury, on the other hand, decided to emigrate because in those years in his parish "going up to the States" (*monter aux États*) was what most unemployed young people would do. "I remember, in front of the church, those who couldn't leave would tell us 'lucky you, lucky you.'" When in 1921 this eighteen-year-old, single farm laborer migrated, his small village of Manseau, Quebec, offered so little opportunity that the scene of young people saying farewell to their dear ones had become a familiar one. Lack of work and the resignation of his parents made Bruno's decision to leave and choose Mainville, Rhode Island, an easy one. "When I left, I wasn't sure whether it was temporary or to stay. I had two of my older brothers there, so I said, 'I'll do like them.' I wanted to try what they had done." It is very likely that this is how two of his younger brothers arrived at their decision, for soon after Bruno left, they too headed south in search of work, and never returned.[6]

Written and oral accounts of family and individual migrants such as the Alberts and the Nourys help us understand the micro-universes in which present conditions and future perspectives were assessed, decisions were made, and strategies enacted. However, this kind of documentary source— though much more substantial than is the case with Anglo-Canadian migrants—offers only fragmentary evidence of a vast movement that grew out of a great variety of local conditions and particular family circumstances, and that responded to specific economic and political conjunctures.

Still, the main corpus of data used here allows us to adopt various scales of analysis in such a way as to capture, out of the multitude of experiences, the most important patterns that gave the movement its spatial, temporal, and social configuration. Through the reconstitution of such patterns, the challenge for the historian is to assess the significance of a truly continental phenomenon while at the same time penetrating the universe of the individual migrants who, alone or in small groups, were the ultimate protagonists of the movement.

When at the turn of the century Béatrice Mandeville and her family left their parish in the lower Saint Lawrence River and moved to a Massachusetts textile town, or when in 1913 Marie Hetu quit her job as a stenographer in Sydney, Nova Scotia, and headed for Detroit, they were pursuing paths that had been traveled by tens of thousands French Canadians before them and that would be traveled by many thereafter.[7] Although they would not have formulated their trip in these terms, they were linking points of departure and destination within a "migration field."[8] This geographer's term provides a useful conceptual framework, not only because it helps circumscribe a physical space, but also because it allows us to "fill" it with economic, social, and cultural content. This space acquires historical meaning when we see how, over the years, it was crossed and often recrossed by people bringing with them their hopes for a better life, their labor power, and their values and traditions. The concept of migration field is also useful because it allows us to observe the migration phenomenon at different spatial scales.[9] Migration fields may be reconstituted by circumscribing as a point of departure a single parish, a town, or a county, and then following the process that channeled migrants toward a given destination, whether a U.S. city, county, or state. One can best visualize this concept by using the metaphor of a river that is fed by many tributary streams and, at its mouth, divides into channels in a delta.

Our task is not that of identifying the multitude of migration fields that shaped the movement. We want to understand the most important itineraries followed by out-migrants, without, however, ignoring other movements that could be considered marginal owing to the small size of the population involved. This enables us to reconstitute the spatial configuration of much of the movement, to shift from larger to smaller spatial scales, and to provide answers to one of the most basic questions concerning the formation and reproduction of migration fields: Why were certain destinations chosen while others excluded or simply ignored?

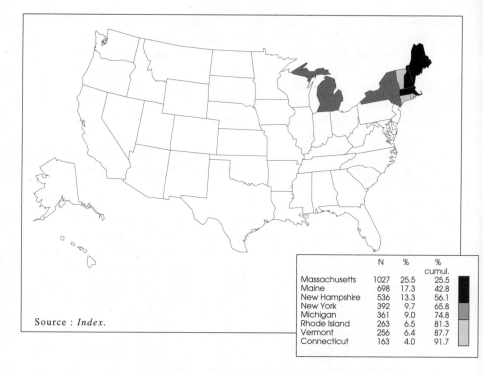

	N	%	% cumul.
Massachusetts	1027	25.5	25.5
Maine	698	17.3	42.8
New Hampshire	536	13.3	56.1
New York	392	9.7	65.8
Michigan	361	9.0	74.8
Rhode Island	263	6.5	81.3
Vermont	256	6.4	87.7
Connecticut	163	4.0	91.7

Source : *Index.*

Map 1. Main U.S. destinations of French Canadians, 1906–30

Before the Great Depression virtually shut the border, migration movements were to a large extent a continuation from the previous century,
when migration fields operated largely within the confines of specific continental regions. Thus, French Canadians overwhelmingly chose New England, with Massachusetts ranking first throughout the era. Outside New
England, smaller but significant flows linked Quebec to New York State and
Michigan. Thinner and hardly perceptible streams brought French Canadians to places as distant and far apart as Florida and Washington State.

A combination of three major factors explains this broad spatial configuration. One was physical proximity. Of course, this factor was less
important than it had been in the earliest stage of the movement, when,
because of the agrarian context and difficult travel conditions, most migration fields extended no further than the northern portions of neighboring states. A notable exception had been the flow toward the Great
Lakes region. But here again, fluvial transportation along the Saint
Lawrence River made the traveling easier than an inland move on foot,
on horseback, or in horse-drawn wagons.

By the turn of the century the consolidation of an elaborate continental railway system widened considerably the choice of destinations for prospective migrants. Still, physical distance must have been a consideration—albeit not the most important one—influencing the choice of destinations. This emerges clearly as one correlates places of departures and places of destination (table 1). Thus, those departing from the Atlantic provinces chose above all New England. French Canadians in Nova Scotia, for instance, chose Massachusetts at a rate of 74 percent. Three out of four French Canadians living in Ontario made the bordering states of New York and Michigan their leading destination. On the other hand, French Canadians residing in Quebec, a province that extends from Maine to upstate New York, exhibited a more varied geographic pattern: while New England absorbed the majority, a significant minority (14 percent) chose either New York State or midwestern states as far west as Minnesota.

As we shall see, economic changes and especially sociocultural phenomena relativized the importance of physical distance in the choice of destination, producing a variety of scales. Such scales ranged from the short distance that linked communities in eastern Quebec or in New Brunswick with locations in neighboring Maine, to the considerably longer distance traveled by northwestern Quebeckers to destinations in southern New England. It should also be added that in the twentieth century French Canada, unlike English Canada, produced very few "transborder districts," that is, small migration fields extending from one city or district to another across the border. Cross-border migrations of this sort were more frequent among small groups of French Canadians living in Ontario border towns such as Sault Sainte Marie, Niagara Falls, or Windsor. T. Benoit, for instance, a forty-nine-year-old married bricklayer whose migration in 1914 entailed crossing the border to Sault Sainte Marie, Michigan, had lived and worked in the Ontario city of the same name, which held a sizable French-Canadian community.[10]

◆

But geographic proximity was strictly related to another important factor, economic opportunity. Although this aspect will be discussed later, one cannot but notice that the two leading receiving regions, New England and the Midwest, were major areas of industrial concentration and economic growth in the United States. As mentioned in the previous chapter, the pull that the New England textile industry exerted on French Canadians dated back to the post–Civil War era, and for the remainder of the century the resulting population shift provided a leading illustration of the concentration of one ethnocultural group in a single industry. During the first two decades of the new century, textile mills continued to be the single most important supplier of jobs for French-Canadian newcomers. In its 1908–11 investigation, the U.S. Immigration Commission documented the widespread presence of French Canadians in the various branches of textile manufacturing.[11] And as late as 1922, as Eugénie Savoie-Coté recalls, French Canadians were in such high demand in textile mills that those who left their jobs for family or personal reasons had no problem being rehired when they showed up again at the factory gates several weeks or even a few months later. Eugénie had migrated to Springvale, Connecticut, from an eastern Québec parish at the age of fifteen, and after a brief experience in a shoe factory she switched to a textile mill, where she became a spinner. For two consecutive years she and her sister left their jobs and got them back after spending part of the spring and summer in Quebec helping their father with farmwork. She also recalls that French Canadians were "everywhere" (*partout*) in Springvale, both in the mill and in the town—to such an extent that she did not feel any pressure to learn English, for, as she put it with a smile on her face, "most people there spoke French, ah, ah!"[12] It is not surprising that the most frequent destinations chosen by the population in our sample were major centers of textile manufacturing: Fall River, Lowell, Lawrence, and Holyoke, Massachusetts; Lewiston, Waterville, and Jackman, Maine; Manchester, Nashua, and Berlin, New Hampshire; and Woonsocket and Central Falls, Rhode Island.

Moreover, to many prospective immigrants from Quebec, choosing cities such as these meant more than textile employment. It also meant moving to places where French Canadians often constituted the largest ethnic minority and had developed one of the most elaborate institutional networks in the United States. The French-Canadian presence not only translated into employment opportunities in ethnic services, ranging from private hospitals and schools to various branches of the retail trade, but also produced a distinctive sociocultural universe that minimized for newcomers the feeling of being in a foreign land. It would be only in the second half of the 1920s that, due to a major structural crisis affecting New England textile manufacturing, the relationship between French-Canadian immigration and the textile industry would be significantly altered, without, however, undermining the region's position as leading destination.

Similarly, French Canadians leaving for the midwestern states chose most frequently industrial and commercial districts that offered a variety of job opportunities, mostly in manufacturing, construction, and services. In New York State, for instance, among the destinations most frequently chosen were Buffalo, Niagara Falls, Cohoes, Watertown, and Massena. And in

Michigan, Sault Sainte Marie and especially Detroit overshadowed all other state districts as preferred destinations. We know that Cohoes had been an important destination for French Canadians since the post–Civil War era, when large numbers of them had found employment in the city's textile industry.[13] In Detroit their presence went back even farther, to the fur trade era, and their presence was constantly reinforced when Detroit emerged as a leading manufacturing center of the Great Lakes region and subsequently became "Motown," the center of the nation's automobile industry.

Yet, geographical proximity and employment opportunities provide only a partial explanation for the choice of destination. A third factor was the presence of kin or fellow villagers who facilitated the recently arrived migrant's entry into the new, highly urbanized and industrialized context. In many ways, the choice of destination was enhanced by the previous existence of well-delineated migration fields, most of which had either emerged or consolidated during the exodus of the latter part of the nineteenth century. It was as if during those years the major routes of north-south population flow had become firmly established, providing the spatial parameters within which successive generations of French-Canadian out-migrants would move. Illustrations from three different Quebec regions should throw more light onto this historical phenomenon.

Of the eight Quebec districts that the historian Yves Frenette identified as birthplaces of French Canadians having migrated to Lewiston, Maine (most of the eight are in the province's central-eastern region), one district in particular, situated on the south shore of the Saint Lawrence River and centered on Arthabaska County, had sent by 1880 about 42 percent of all out-migrants who had chosen that New England city.[14]

In Champlain County, an agrarian district located between Trois-Rivières and Québec City on the north shore of the Saint Lawrence, one may observe the working of these fields at the parish level thanks in part to the fieldwork undertaken in the early 1890s by E.-Z. Massicotte. A researcher who visited most parishes of the county, Massicotte compiled lists of individuals and families who had migrated, including their year of departure (mostly in the 1880s and early 1890s) and their cities of destination in the United States. Two parishes in particular provide striking evidence of the existence of migration fields. From the parish of Saint-Prospère radiated two major fields —one southward, the other westward. Of those who left that parish during a twelve-year period, four out of five headed to either of two destinations in separate regions of the United States, namely, Woonsocket, Rhode Island (44 percent), and unspecified locations in Michigan (35 percent). At the same time, in a nearby parish situated only some fifteen kilometers to the south, Saint-François-Xavier, nearly half of the out-migrants chose as their destination the city of Meriden, Connecticut.[15]

Raising the scale to the county level also allows one to observe the emergence of migration fields and their persistence over time, in this case, one stretching from Berthier County to the tiny state of Rhode Island. A systematic analysis of all deeds notarized in that county between 1875 and 1905 in which one of the parties resided in the United States shows that 40.5 percent of these individuals worked and lived in Rhode Island at the time of the transaction; the rest were spread over a dozen states mostly in New England and the Midwest. This county-to-state field encompassed in turn a number of specific fields joining a given Berthier parish to a specific Rhode Island city. One was the parish of Saint-Cuthbert. Of all those who were born in that parish between 1845 and 1900 and who married outside the Province of Quebec, 60 percent had done so in Woonsocket (only 3 percent married in other Canadian provinces). One has good reason to argue that by the turn of the century the migrants from Saint-Cuthbert had created a link with Woonsocket that was even more solid than the one existing with the nearby metropolis of Montreal, where a smaller number of marriages had been performed than in its Rhode Island counterpart.[16] Montreal had long been in the mind of Lucien Dumontier, a Berthier County resident who had studied accounting and was hoping to find a white-collar job in that Quebec metropolis. But the presence of several of his co-parishioners in Woonsocket made him change his plans, and in 1922 he joined the stream that—much like the one originating in Saint-Cuthbert—for generations had linked Saint-Barthélemy to the largest Rhode Island textile center.[17]

It should not come as a surprise then if throughout the first three decades of the new century the majority of French Canadians chose a U.S. location in which they had a member of their immediate family, a relative, or a friend waiting for them (table 2).

The historical literature on French-Canadian out-migration has underlined the central role played by kinship relations in a movement largely made up of family units.[18] But the data provided by the Soundex Index to Canadian Border Entries allow us to observe as closely as possible the working of this phenomenon, as entrants to the United States were asked by border officials to provide the name and location of a contact person at destination, as well as the relationship existing between the two.

Thus, for instance, when Frederick Chaussé, Pauline Guthro, and Oscar Brunelle decided to leave their parishes and head for the city of Woonsocket, they moved through migration fields that had long become con-

Table 2. *French-Canadian Migrants, by Type of Relationship with the Reference Person(s) at Destination, 1906–30 (in percentages; N = 4.396)*

Spouse/son/daughter	11.0
Parents/brother/sister	27.2
Other kin (uncle, aunt, cousin, in-laws)	26.7
Friend	8.3
Board/hotel	0.4
Institutions (including companies)	3.2
Other	10.6
Undetermined	12.6

solidated by the back-and-forth traveling of their predecessors and by a constant flow of information across that space. Chaussé, an unmarried twenty-nine-year-old butcher, left Saint-Cuthbert in 1924 and was received in Woonsocket by his brother-in-law.[19] Guthro left from the county seat, Berthierville, in 1926; an unmarried twenty-two-year-old factory operative, she also headed to Woonsocket, where a brother-in-law was waiting for her.[20] The case of Oscar Brunelle, like several others, is interesting because he departed not from Berthier County but from a parish in another Quebec region where he had moved sometime earlier, Saint-Didace. But this forty-one-year-old married laborer was a native of Saint-Cuthbert, and when in 1909 he decided to move to the United States, he joined a stream that through the years had brought hundreds of his previous parishioners to the city of Woonsocket.[21] The case of George Marion is even more revealing. He left in 1921 his Saint-Gabriel-de-Brandon parish heading for Fall River with his parents, who had previously lived there. Both his mother and father had parents living in that same Massachusetts city. For three generations Fall River had thus been a crucial part of the Marion family's life. When a few years later his mother and father returned to Quebec, George was hardly left alone. He went to live with his paternal grandparents, though he might as well have chosen one of several uncles living in the city.[22] Illustrations of this sort can be multiplied many times in most counties and parishes of Quebec.

The picture that emerges then is one of a migration movement in which people moved within specific family and kinship networks—networks that, besides linking departure points and destinations, reproduced themselves in time through subsequent births and marriages. Thus, although migration fields help us delineate the spaces within which French Canadians moved, family and kinship relationships gave vital social and cultural content to the pattern of chain migration.

It is important to add that migration fields were not static but dynamic entities. As the number of French Canadians in the United States increased over time, it was far from unusual for a portion of them to move from their first destination to a new location, whether for economic reasons or personal circumstances. The new location would in turn act as new pole of attraction for newcomers, thus engendering new migration fields.

Migration fields, then, call for the observation both of starting points and of destinations. In the French-Canadian case, such fields could protract themselves in time largely because the social space that these immigrants created in urban America was rapidly filled with institutions, associations, and communal networks devoted to preserving as long as possible their language, their religion, and their culture. When in December 1918 twenty-year-old Eugène Audette arrived in Fall River from his Saint-Damien parish, he did not find just his wife there; he also found a city whose twenty-eight thousand French Canadians made up 24 percent of the city's population, constituting its largest ethnic minority. For the past forty years, this leading textile center had seen its French-Canadian population grow progressively into an elaborate institutional network, which in 1909 included six parishes, eleven parish schools, a college, and more than 150 societies and associations ranging from mutual benefit societies to religious congregations to cultural and leisure organizations—a population that no doubt played an important role in the election in 1922 of the city's first Franco-American mayor, Edmont Talbot.[23] Eugène was far from surprised to find in Fall River a community of compatriots larger than most Quebec towns, and he knew quite well how to go about his business. He had in fact previously lived in the city for eleven years, and like many youngsters of his ethnic cohort he had found employment in one of the several textile mills, ascending to the enviable position of loom-fixer. Though to varying degrees, the urban-ethnic landscape that Eugène Audette found in Fall River was common in most centers of French-Canadian concentration.

◁▷

If these urban spaces acted as a magnet for potential newcomers as well as returnees, it is because those distant and not-so-distant *petits Canadas* had entered the psychic maps of many Quebeckers, becoming "appropriated spaces" kept alive in the imagination by the constant flow of people and information across the border. Migrants might return home to attend family events, participate in religious pilgrimages, and show off their newly acquired economic status to fellow villagers; but then they frequently set out again. This practice of repeat migration did not merely re-spond to economic need; it also reflected familiarity with the southward path to be pursued. Our data show that during the period under study, the majority of adult male migrants had made at least one previous mi-gration to the United States.[24] And this was true of French Canadians liv-ing in Quebec, in Ontario, and in the Maritimes, both men and women. Anthony Le Blanc, for instance, a thirty-two-year-old laborer, left his na-tive parish in Nova Scotia in September 1922, headed for Gardener, Mass-achusetts, where he had a sister. This small New England town was well-known terrain for this Acadian, since he had lived and worked there from 1914 to 1916.[25] Laura Charbonneau, a waitress from the northern On-tario community of Sudbury, crossed the border at Sault Sainte Marie in November 1916 along with her sister; they were heading for Ludington, Michigan, where one of their aunts was waiting for them. In effect, Laura's was a remigration, as she had lived in the United States from the age of nine to fourteen. Now she was migrating as an adult.[26] Joseph Al-bert Forcier, a priest from the Quebec parish of Sainte-Clothilde, had likely sojourned several times in Woonsocket, a city where the Franco-American community could boast a half-dozen national parishes. He de-clared to border officials that he had lived there from 1914 to 1918, and now in January 1919 he was heading back to the same Rhode Island city, answering "permanent residence" when asked about the purpose of his entering the United States.[27]

The knowledge of "Franco-America" among Quebeckers, Franco-Ontarians, or Acadians grew also from the constant coverage that the press—from the large-circulation city newspapers *La Patrie* and *La Presse* to the smaller parish dailies and weeklies—gave to immigrant communi-ties in the United States. In virtually every issue, for instance, the weekly *L'Étoile du Nord* in Joliette reported on community events occurring among French Canadians in the United States. The articles might deal with the closing or the opening of a mill in a given New England location, with the efforts to erect a national parish, with the return to Joliette of fel-low parishioners, or with the creation of a new association in some *petit Canada*. This was the case during the 1880s, the peak period of out-migra-tion; it was still true forty years later.[28] On the other side of the border, the Franco-American press—perhaps the most extensive among all ethnic groups in the United States—reported constantly on Quebec and other French-Canadian communities, from developments in provincial politics to events in remote parishes.[29]

Fig. 8. President Taft visiting the Association Canado-Américain in Manchester, New Hampshire, 1911. Courtesy of the Manchester Visual History Project and *Ovo Magazine*.

II

With this understanding of the geographical configuration of the movement and the key factors determining the choice of destination, we can now take a closer look at the migrant population, at its main demographic and social attributes, and at the variety of patterns it assumed.

On 23 November 1922, Hervé Aubry left his native parish of Nemachiche, Quebec, and crossed the border, heading for Woonsocket. This twenty-eight-year-old factory worker was accompanied by his wife and their two children. In Woonsocket, Hervé's father and perhaps some relatives were waiting for them.[30] The Aubrys were representatives of a substantial portion of French Canadians who migrated in family units. At the peak of the exodus during the 1880s and 1890s, family moves predominated, particularly because the flow was largely toward New England textile manufacturing centers, where children able to withstand factory labor could readily be put to work.[31] In the twentieth century, however, migration in family units, while still widely practiced, became progressively less frequent. The majority of French Canadians instead migrated alone. This pattern was much more pronounced among adult men than women. Still, within this latter component of the movement, unaccompanied migration was particularly frequent among single women aged fifteen to twenty-nine, who practiced it at a rate of 60 percent (for the entire female migrant population, children included, the rate was 28 percent).[32] And this pattern was typical not just of women departing from Quebec. Julia Arsenault, a twenty-one-year-old Acadian school teacher from Cocagne, New Brunswick, crossed the border at Vanceboro, Maine, in February 1919, heading for New Bedford, Massachusetts.[33] And Elizabeth Saulnier left from a Nova Scotia city, Yarmouth, for Haverhill, Massachusetts. Judging from the words "abandoned domicile" scribbled on her entry manifesto, a family crisis may have prompted this twenty-four-year-old unmarried domestic to migrate. She was one of few migrant women who did not provide the name of a family member, a relative, or a friend at her destination. But she knew her way around the Haverhill area, having spent the previous eight years in nearby Lynn.[34]

This gradual change in migration patterns—from families to individuals—is reflected in the substantial increase in the average age of French-Canadian out-migrants. If the entire sampled population is considered, four out of five migrants were aged fifteen and above, with the largest component (nearly one out of two) belonging to the prime working age, between the ages of fifteen and twenty-nine (see table 3).

Although we do not have similar statistical data for the nineteenth cen-

Table 3. *Age Groups and Sex Distribution of French-Canadian Out-Migrants by Subperiods*

	1906–18		1919–24		1925–30		Total	
	N	%	N	%	N	%	N	%
Females								
0 to 14	238	33.2	184	25.0	44	13.3	466	26.1
15 to 29	281	39.2	329	44.7	175	52.7	785	44.0
30 to 44	110	15.4	121	16.4	65	19.6	296	16.6
45 to 59	55	7.7	64	8.7	33	9.9	152	8.5
60 and over	30	4.2	33	4.5	15	4.5	78	4.4
Age unknown	2	0.3	5	0.7		0.0	7	0.4
Subtotal	716	100.0	736	100.0	332	100.0	1,784	100.0
Males								
0 to 14	230	22.5	181	17.0	47	9.3	458	17.7
15 to 29	448	43.8	585	55.1	285	56.4	1,318	50.9
30 to 44	179	17.5	198	18.6	100	19.8	477	18.4
45 to 59	114	11.2	69	6.5	49	9.7	232	9.0
60 and over	47	4.6	24	2.3	22	4.4	93	3.6
Age unknown	4	0.4	5	0.5	2	0.4	11	0.4
Subtotal	1,022	100.0	1,062	100.0	505	100.0	2,589	100.0
Sex unknown	19		3		1		23	
Total	1,757		1,801		838		4,396	

tury, a study showing the age structure of French-Canadian migrants to Rhode Island in 1880, a year when the exodus was in full swing, suggests the magnitude of this demographic shift: in that year, in fact, as much as 44.5 percent of the migrating population were children aged fifteen or under.[35]

As the twentieth century advanced, the proportion of children and consequently of family units within the migrating population kept declining; by the second half of the 1920s it had reached a low of 10.8 percent (from 26.9 percent during 1906–18). As we saw in the previous chapter, important economic and legal changes had occurred in both Canada and the United States, changes that affected the prospects that the "migration project" offered potential candidates and that produced new strategies in which age was a crucial consideration.

Of course, crossing the border alone did not in itself preclude the possibility of a family migration. A family head, for instance, could make the move alone and be followed thereafter by his wife and children. Or an adult son who had remained in Canada working on a farm or in a shop, or pursuing his studies, could later decide to join his family across the border. Rodrigue Trifili and Eugène Caron exemplify these cases. The former, a native of Saint-George, Quebec, crossed the border on December 1916 at Jackman, Maine, which was his destination; he left behind his wife and children and declared to border officials that his migration was a permanent one. It is likely that the rest of his family joined him sometime thereafter.[36] As for Eugène, a nineteen-year-old laborer living in Sudbury, Ontario, he took a train to Detroit in September 1916 and gave the name and address of his mother as a reference at his destination.[37] If the family is extendible both in time and space, these separations and subsequent reunifications provide eloquent illustrations of such extendibility.

Still, for every Eugène Caron there were many other French Canadians whose migration did not occur within the framework of family reunification. When in fact we combine two attributes of this population, age and marital status, we uncover what progressively became one of the leading migration patterns: adult unmarried migrants whose move did not entail nuclear family reunification. This segment of the migrating population (both sexes combined), already numerically significant before World War I, kept increasing until it reached a proportion of approximately one out of three during the second half of the 1920s. The progression was even more drastic within the female component of this migrating population: whereas during the pre-1919 years adult unmarried women made up 14 percent of the entire female population, by the second half of the 1920s their proportion had jumped to nearly 26 percent.[38] Alice Laliberté was representative of this growing segment of the French-Canadian migrating population. In 1919 this nineteen-year-old single daughter of a small-holder left her family and her five-dollar-a-month job as a domestic, and soon after her arrival in Lowell found a job in one of the local textile mills. Yet, leaving her family behind was not easy; as she recalls it, during the first few months she felt so sad and homesick that several times she was on the point of taking a train back to Quebec : "I wanted to go back to Quebec . . . things just were not going well!" Finally she was convinced to stay on by one of her uncles who lived in nearby New Bedford: "My uncle said: 'No. You will not go back to Quebec.' So he put an ad in the newspaper and found me a job in an American family . . . taking care of cooking. They paid me ten dollars a week and on top I learned English. It was such a nice family . . . I stayed there three years."[39]

Similarly, neither in Alice Magnan's case nor in Willy Charette's was family reunification a motivation for the move. When Alice entered the United States in 1911, she was twenty-eight years of age and unmarried. She had already migrated once before, for her family had moved from Quebec City, where she was born, to Toronto. There she must have found ample opportunity to enter the field of nursing—a trade she hoped she could put to use in the fast-growing economy of Chicago. Willy too had experienced a previous move—from his native parish of Saint-Jean de Matha, Quebec, to Montreal, where he had been working in construction. Aged twenty-three and unmarried, he set his compass toward Lowell, where the many textile mills and factories offered ample possibility for employment. Yet neither of them were traveling in unknown territory. Alice had a cousin in Chicago, whose presence had likely encouraged her move and influenced her choice of destination. Similarly, Willy probably chose Lowell because he had an uncle there who acted as a reference.[40]

Thus, although the migration of these unmarried adults falls outside the pattern of nuclear-family migration, their moves tended to occur within kinship networks, often stretching through several generations. What is important to underline, is that both patterns unveil the basic links of the migration chains that marked the population flow from French Canada to the United States and that to a large extent determined not only its geographical configuration but also its demographic makeup. Both patterns also reflect socioeconomic changes on both sides of the border.

III

The significance of socioeconomic changes in the age structure and the marriage status of French-Canadian out-migrants is also reflected in the occupational composition of migrants. In the twentieth century, as during the peak years of the exodus, the majority of French Canadians—certainly those leaving Quebec—left predominantly agrarian districts, many of which were undergoing a process of commercialization and industrialization. This is of fundamental importance for a proper understanding of the particular occupational structure the movement exhibited as the new century unfolded. Throughout the thirty-year period under study, French Canadians who left Quebec towns and cities with populations of five thousand or more (as enumerated by the 1921 census) comprised only 27 percent of the movement, and half of these were leaving from the Montreal metropolitan area.

Part of the explanation is that despite the significant rate of urbanization during that era, the move from country to city was far from uniform over the province's territory. The Montreal area grew from 346,000 in 1901 to nearly 1,000,000 in 1931, followed by the Quebec City area which doubled its population to 141,000; but aside from these two, the province could count only three small cities, each with a population a little over 20,000 (in 1921), and a handful of even smaller ones with populations between 5,000 and 10,000. Of course, natural growth played an important part in these increases, as did immigration, particularly in the Montreal area.[41]

Thus, much of the new urban population was absorbed by relatively few cities and towns, and the rest of the intraprovincial moves occurred within the vast network of smaller towns. And to a very large extent, these smaller towns along with countless rural parishes provided the socioeconomic context of out-migration. When one considers a net migration to the United States estimated at 320,000 between 1900 and 1930, one cannot but conclude that a significant number of French-Canadian Quebeckers became urbanized not in their own province but in scores of cities and towns south of the border. The same applies to French Canadians living in the Atlantic provinces, and to a lesser extent to Franco-Ontarians.

In an important sense, urbanization is intimately associated with the productive structure of a given territorial area. And although during the 1900–30 era Quebec accelerated its industrialization and modernized its commercial activities, the province did so by retaining much of its late-nineteenth-century industrial geography. Industrial/commercial centers became bigger, but within an economic space dominated by Montreal and a few other centers. Of course, as mentioned earlier, new towns mostly associated with the transformation of agricultural products did emerge; but apart from a few exceptions such as in the Saguenay-Lac-Saint-Jean region, they did not expand into large urban centers. Nor did the geography of the province's agrarian economy undergo significant change. True, farming and livestock became more efficient and commercialized, and important new sectors such as dairy production played a leading role in both the regional and provincial economy. Still, these were sectors that became less and less labor intensive. They contributed significantly to the overall economic performance of the economy without engendering major changes in the structure of the population or in the occupational composition of the parishes and small towns in which they were located.[42]

This sheds much light on why a large majority of out-migrants moving to the United States left from agrarian districts, and why they gave the movement its particular occupational configuration.

The two most important occupational categories were, in fact, farmers (including a variety of agriculture-related occupations) and laborers (see table 4). Farmers represented 9 percent of the entire male adult out-migrant population, and they left from virtually all regions of Quebec— with a minority from French-Canadian settlements in other provinces, such as Ontario, New Brunswick, and Nova Scotia. Only family histories can tell us whether they were mostly marginal producers and smallholders. This was certainly the case with the Ouellets, who migrated from Saint-Pascal-de-Kamouraska, Quebec, in 1908. As one of the Ouellet children recalls, "My father was just not able to make a living from his land . . . and he needed money to repair the house."[43] Similarly, Jacques Hamel had to migrate with the whole family to Warren, Rhode Island, because he could no longer make payments on the smallholding he had bought in Lawrenceville, Quebec. Unable to find interested tenants, some simply left their farms unattended, hoping to come back a few years later with the money needed to resume farming.[44] Others left the farm to one of their sons while seeking in the United States the means to improve their farming operations once back in Quebec. Those who sought to sell their farms were not always lucky. After spending several years in Lewiston, Maine, Anne Lagacé's father returned to his parish to sell his smallholding, but prices were so low that he gave up and returned to Lewiston.[45]

The farmers in our sample tended to be older than the average male out-migrants, and a substantial majority of them were married. Moreover, theirs was not a migration aimed at pursuing farming activities south of the border: with few exceptions, in fact, they chose large urban-industrial New England centers that held well-established Franco-American communities. A few chose districts directly across the border mostly in Vermont—such as Newport, Saint-Albans, or Winooski—and it is not unlikely that some of them may have sought to pursue agricultural activities. One

Table 4. Male French-Canadian Migrants by Major Occupations and Sectors of Activity, 1906–30 (in percentages; N = 2,062)

Businessmen, professionals, and supervisory personnel	4.2
Clerical and miscellaneous white-collar workers	4.0
Farmers	9.0
Farm laborers	8.7
Natural resource workers (mining, logging, fishing)	4.7
General laborers	34.6
Production workers (factory and independent crafts)	23.3
Students	1.3
Others	8.2
Unreadable	2.0

Note: Cases dismissed (no occupation declared): 74.

of these was forty-six-year-old Augustine Larocque, who in November 1918 left his parish of Saint-Gérard and moved permanently to Saint-Albans, Vermont. In that mostly agrarian district across the border, Larocque had a brother who may have helped him to pursue farming.[46]

But for the majority it was a farm-to-city move. Outside New England, it was the city of Detroit that attracted the largest number of French-Canadian farmers, drawing them mostly from Ontario districts and, to a smaller extent, from Quebec and Alberta.[47]

Considering the agrarian context of most out-migrants, the relatively low proportion of farm laborers is striking. Their migration rate nearly matched that of farmers (8.7 percent). Although we do not have comparable data for the nineteenth century, we know from the few existing studies and contemporary reports that at the peak of the exodus the occupational groups most prone to emigrate were farm laborers and smallholders.

Two interrelated hypotheses may explain the decline of the farm laborer group, not just within the migration flow, but also in agrarian Quebec in general. One is that the increasing commercialization and mechanization of farming activities reduced considerably the need for workers whose main source of earnings had come from selling their labor to farmers. The other is that the transformations occurring in agrarian Quebec entailed the growth of nonfarming activities, if not in all parishes, certainly in the larger ones as well as in the expanding towns: activities most often embodied in the small dairy plant, in the saw- and gristmill, in the implement repair shop, and the like. Equally important, commercialization also entailed the expansion of infrastructures such as roads and bridges, the construction of buildings, and increased activities in fluvial transportation. What this means is that the landless laborer who in nineteenth-century agrarian Quebec had to choose between turning to a nearby farmer for employment, moving to a colonization area, and seeking a wage south of the border, had in the 1910s and 1920s a much wider variety of earning options right in his parish or region. Although he might still participate in farming, much more of his labor was sold in nonfarming enterprises. Combining these two hypotheses in one formula, one could say that the farm laborer of the nineteenth century became simply a laborer as the twentieth century advanced. In his classic study of the Saint Denis parish based on fieldwork done in the 1930s, Horace Miner captured part of the transformations that increased the need of common laborers in that parish. He described how many of the activities of common parish interest (such as construction of roads and repairs to the church) that in the past had been done voluntarily through the ancient institution of corvée were now done by hired labor, preferably local.[48]

The hypothesis discussed above would find confirmation in the exceedingly large number of laborers within the migration movement. Laborers made up by far the most numerous occupation, constituting 34.6 percent of all adult male migrants. But contrary to what one may expect, most of them departed not from cities and large towns but from agrarian parishes such as the ones described above. The overwhelming majority departed from the Province of Quebec; but those leaving from large towns and cities with populations 5,000 and over (including the Montreal and Quebec City metropolitan areas) represented only 19 percent of all out-migrant laborers. Greater Montreal, the country's largest urban agglomeration and the leading center of industrial and commercial activities, sent out only 8.5 percent of laborers.[49] Clearly, the large and fast-growing Montreal district, with its highly diversified economic activities, provided ample opportunities for laborers who could shift easily from one job to another. And to a lesser extent this was also true of the other major cities and large towns in Quebec. But despite Miner's finding, the fact remains that in the majority of small towns and parishes the market for general laborers was more limited and less diversified, and sooner or later left no other possibility than to seek work elsewhere. Such places therefore supplied the largest proportion of laborers to the migration movement to the United States.

It is also likely that although "farm laborer" and "laborer" were recorded by border officials as separate occupations, in the real experience of some of these migrants the two occupations overlapped: in certain seasons one might find work in farming activities such as harvesting, and during other periods of the year work in other sectors or trades. Joseph Remi Armand Bélanger, for example, is one of several migrants who declared to border officials two occupations: farm laborer and shoemaker. This twenty-three-year-old single Quebecker native of an agrarian parish in the Eastern

Fig. 9. Bélanger brothers and friends, deliverers for the Manchester (New Hampshire) Coal and Ice Company, ca. 1900. Courtesy of the Manchester Visual History Project and *Ovo Magazine.*

Townships had moved at some point to Granby, a larger and mostly agrarian center in the same region; and the two-year sojourn he had made in the United States just prior to his permanent migration, in 1924, had been spent in a Vermont agrarian district.[50]

We do not know how Bélanger divided his time between the two activities. But his case serves to illustrate the frequent phenomenon of multiple activities, not only among unskilled laborers, but also among traditional craftsmen—a category that since the advent of industrialization and its penetration in the countryside (through small factories or through the growing arrival of cheaper manufactured products) had been among the most vulnerable to the emergence of a new capitalist order.

In fact, once we account for the three single largest occupational groups—laborers, farmers, and farm laborers—altogether representing 52.3 percent of the adult male migrating population, we are left with a wide range of occupations among which traditional-artisanal crafts were prominent: their presence in the movement was roughly equal to that of the two other most frequent sectors: petty trade and services, and factory production. Typical illustrations of these occupations included watchmaker, silversmith, and saddler, as well as butcher, storekeeper, and barber. From the early days of the exodus, fast-growing *petits Canadas* had provided opportunities for ambitious petty traders and traditional crafts- men, who could find in their neighborhoods a potential clientele who spoke their language and could be reached through village-based ties and kin networks. Of course, besides ambition, length of residence and knowl- edge of the local ethnic milieu increased the chance of success. A butcher from Saint-Gabriel-de-Brandon, Charles Marion, sold his shop in 1921 and moved with his family to Fall River. Setting up a butcher's shop in 1921 Fall River required greater means than Charles could command, however, so he had to settle for a job in a cotton mill. But soon, after find- ing he could not stand this work, he put an end to his migration experi- ence.[51] Things went better for Adrien Hamel, who was able to pursue his barber trade soon after arriving in Warren, Rhode Island. He set up a shop with only two chairs and spent several of his weekdays idle; but on weekends the lineup was so long that he had to hire a helper and keep giving haircuts till midnight. In less that two years, he managed to save $2,000. "At 10 cents a shave and 25 cents a haircut, just imagine how many I must have given," he told us with a proud smile. The savings were enough to convince him and his wife to move back to Quebec, where they bought a 150-acre farm and took up farming and husbandry.[52] On the other hand, Léon Kirouack illustrates the opportunities that the ethnic labor market offered to someone who, besides ambition, had a longer and more intimate knowledge of the local Franco-American milieu. Though born in the Rivière-du-Loup district, Léon had grown up in Nashua, New Hampshire. He was spared mill labor and was sent to school where he learned the basic writing skills that allowed him to take up the printer's trade. The several years he spent as a printer and writer for Nashua's *L'Impartiel* and for Lowell's *L'Étoile* expanded his knowledge of the community and encouraged him to exploit his entrepreneurial skills. Besides owning a printing shop, he set up and directed a baseball club for the Mouvement Catholique Canado-Américain. Moreover, he saw in his faithful assistant, Armand Gauthier, the physical and athletic qualities that could turn him into a professional wrestler. Léon became Armand's promoter, organizing matches that took the two men all over New Eng- land. In later years, Léon would cherish those intimate moments in his liv- ing room when Jack, his little son, would hang from Armand's iron arm. Léon was also able to pass on to his son both the excitement of an arm wrestling match and a passion for writing that one day would make him one of America's cult literary figures.[53]

As for the migrants holding factory-related occupations, their presence in the southward movement was limited, understandably when one con-

siders that their province—and certainly the Montreal area—was one of
the most important centers of industrial activity in Canada. Clearly, the
larger urban and manufacturing centers were able to retain much of their
industrial workforce and at the same time constantly require common laborers, few of whom, as we have seen, saw any need to migrate to the
United States.

To some extent, this demographic-occupational scenario also applies to
French Canadians out-migrating from the most industrialized province of
the country, neighboring Ontario. The age structure of out-migrating
Franco-Ontarians was identical to that of Quebeckers: four out of five migrants were aged fifteen and over, which correlates with the coexistence
of both family and individual migration patterns. A more striking similarity was the significant presence of laborers, whose frequency (34 percent)
was identical to that of Quebeckers. Owing to the different urban/indus-
trial geography of this province, however, the proportion departing from
large towns and cities was much larger (32 percent) than among their
Quebec counterparts. The geographical proximity to important U.S. industrial and commercial centers may have played a significant role, as
many of these city departures were across-the-border migrations involving
Windsor and Detroit, the two Sault Sainte Maries, and the two Niagara
Falls. Conspicuous was, in fact, the relatively small number of laborers departing from Ontario's two most important industrial centers, Toronto
and Hamilton. The majority of laborers came from smaller towns, though
to a lesser extent than in Quebec. Their diversity in terms of their economic base was, however, much greater. Moreover, some of these Ontario
towns had long been centers of French-Canadian settlement either because they were close to Quebec, such as Cornwall, or because they had
become new poles of attraction for Quebeckers on account of the development of the mining and the railroad and canal construction industries—centers such as Sudbury, a town located in the heart of north Ontario's leading mining district, and Welland, the center of one of the most
important canal constructions.[54]

Some quite noticeable differences with their Quebec counterparts,
however, emerge when one observes the remaining occupational composition among Ontario's French-Canadian out-migrants. One is immediately struck by the very insignificant presence of traditional crafts, which
leads us to believe that if these occupational groups had been pushed out
of their towns and villages by the arrival of factory-manufactured products, this had occurred at an earlier era than in Quebec; it may also mean
that few of these craftsmen had left Quebec for Ontario. On the other
hand, the most frequent blue-collar occupations were those associated

with factory production; and among them, very conspicuous was the significant proportion of out-migrants engaged in metalwork—many of them in skilled trades. They made up 14 percent of all male-held occupations, and constituted the majority of blue-collar workers if the "laborer" group is excluded.[55]

Worthy of notice is also the significant number of white-collar occupations among both women and men. As the historical literature on Franco-Ontarians has shown, working and living in a predominantly anglophone environment had rendered many of them bilingual, which opened up opportunities in the U.S. white-collar labor markets that were seldom available to out-migrants from agrarian Quebec.[56] As we shall see in the following chapter, their overall occupational profile brings them closer to English Canadians than to their Quebec counterparts.

◁◇▷

French-Canadian emigration also brought to the U.S. economy a significant number of women who had previous wage labor experience (table 5). Although the movement comprised a small proportion of professional nurses and teachers along with a comparable contingent of clerical workers, by far the most frequent occupation was "servant," representing 32.9 percent of the total. An almost equal proportion (28.6 percent) included a group of blue-collar occupations, many of them associated with factory production.

But as in the case of French-Canadian men, among women too there were significant differences between migrants originating from Quebec and those from other provinces. Ontario and Maritimes women comprised an insignificant proportion of blue-collar workers; more conspicuous were the many servants and white-collar workers among them. Servants, for instance, constituted as much as 57.7 percent of the (mostly Acadian) women out-migrating from the Maritimes, and 42.8 percent of those departing from Ontario. White-collar workers, instead, were slightly more numerous among women departing from Ontario, representing 31.4 percent as against the 29.5 percent sent by the Maritimes.[57] The corresponding rate of white-collar women out-migrating from Quebec was only 7.3 percent; yet, surprisingly, more that half of the latter were school teachers, which contrasts with the mostly clerical and office workers among their counterparts from Ontario and the Maritimes. As in the case of French-Canadian men, here too language proficiency must have played a key role in directing these women to different labor markets. Leontine Guenette exemplifies the majority of French-Canadian teachers who most likely envisaged a job in a parochial school of some *petit Canada*,

Table 5. Female French-Canadian Migrants by Major Occupations and Sectors of Activity, 1906–30 (in percentages; N = 433)

Professionals and supervisory personnel	7.8
Nuns	7.6
Clerical and miscellaneous white-collar workers	10.5
Production workers (factory and independent crafts)	28.6
Servants	32.9
Students	4.0
Others	5.1
Unreadable	3.5

Note: Uncounted are 714 adult women who declared "no occupation" and 180 who declared "housewife."

where French was the language of work. This twenty-nine-year-old single woman from Sainte-Anne des Plaines, Quebec, was headed for a school in Central Falls, Rhode Island, a city that had a large French-Canadian community.[58] But previous teaching experience in Quebec did not automatically ensure a teaching job, not even in a city that—like Woonsocket—had one of the largest concentrations of French Canadians. Josephine Dumontier, for instance, migrated to that city with her husband in 1924, after having taught school for six years in Saint-Barthélomy. Unable to find a teaching job, she had to settle for factory work in a cotton mill. It was a new experience to which Josephine was unable to adjust. "I went to work just to see what it was like to work in a factory, for all the women I knew there worked in factories; but the first day I went and entered the place I told myself, 'This is not for me, I will not last long here.'" She decided to stay home and look after her baby niece so that her sister could go to work. Not long after, Josephine and her husband put an end to their migration project and returned to Quebec.[59] Odette Guendon and Marie Hetu, on the other hand, were stenographers, an occupation they certainly learned and practiced using the English language, Odette in Sydney, Nova Scotia, and Marie in Ottawa. They migrated to two cities—Cambridge, Massachusetts, and Detroit—which offered ample opportunities to put their skills to profit.[60]

Although servants comprised the largest occupation among the French-Canadian women migrating from Quebec, blue-collar workers also made up a significant contingent, most of them in trades associated with textile production. Their presence points to the enduring link between Quebec women and the New England textile mills, a link that was strengthened by the fact that the majority of these textile workers were repeat migrants, often returning to the same U.S. location in which they had either grown up or worked.[61] Therèse Roy, for instance, a forty-year-old single woman from Warwick, Quebec, had worked earlier for two years in New Bedford, Massachusetts, no doubt in one of the city's mills as a spinner. Now, in 1910, she was returning to the same city, where she had a brother.[62] Louise Guerin was born in Biddeford, Maine, the state's main textile-producing city. Her family must have subsequently returned to Quebec, but only temporarily, for Louise declared she had also lived in Biddeford from the age of fifteen to seventeen. When she crossed the border this time, she was twenty years old and a weaver, and was once again heading for Biddeford.[63]

Obviously, as both historical studies and oral testimonies have shown, finding a job in a New England textile mill did not require having previous experience in that field of manufacturing. Since its early days, one of the marks of the textile industry had been its ability to rapidly turn domestics, farm girls, housewives, and children, into doffers, spinners, carders, and weavers. Several of the immigrants mentioned above—Alice Laliberté, Eugénie Savoie-Coté, and Josephine Dumontier—found the mill gates open to them upon their arrival despite their lack of previous experience. Much as in the nineteenth century, a substantial proportion of French-Canadian women of working age who in the years 1908–29 declared to U.S. border officials occupations such as domestics, or no occupation at all, ended up in a textile mill. Still, political and economic developments south of the border made the New England textile mill something that could hardly be taken for granted. New legislation turned the migration of French Canadians into a more selective process, as reflected in the dramatic decline of children among the migrating population. As state after state passed and enforced child labor legislation, migration became a highly risky venture for French-Canadian families. Gone were the days when a family could count on the revenue brought home by several of their children. Increasingly, French-Canadian children who had completed their years of compulsory education had to wait until they reached the prescribed age to start work in a mill, and cease to be a burden on the family economy. Elmire Boucher, still a baby when she arrived in Fall River with her family at the turn of the century, recalls the array of activities her parish organized "to keep the youth busy, so they wouldn't hang around in the street." Organizers must have had their hands full, for Elmire's parish included a French-Canadian population of 2,200 families, larger than most Quebec municipalities. By the time Elmire became a teenager, she had a large choice among the various "parish youth corps" and the many parish congregations for the young. She joined both Les Enfants de Marie and the parish guards. "I belonged to one of these corps for girls. They taught us military exercises. We did sixty-four movements with nine-pound rifles."[64] In Lewiston, Maine, and Springvale, Connecticut, the two fifteen-year-olds Anne Lagacé and Eugénie Savoie-Coté had to resort to illicit methods to be hired in the mills. Anne remembers the several times her foreman sent her to hide in the toilet so the state inspector would not see her. Eugénie, instead, borrowed a birth certificate from her sixteen-year-old cousin.[65] These were practices that had a long history in each New England mill. But by the second decade of the 1900s, French-Canadian-born teenagers who could resort to them were much fewer. And so, as we saw earlier, the New England textile economy of the early 1920s drew from French Canada mostly young adults, often from parishes and families that had a long migration tradition, and often young men and women who had grown up in Quebec perhaps contemplating the day when they would be old enough to tread the path their older siblings and cousins had already taken.

Despite the high proportion of textile workers in our sample, their number and their dates of departure reflect the gradual decline in the flow of Quebec women to textile mills. Very few of these migrations, in fact, occurred after the mid-1920s—the years during which the New England textile industry experienced major financial and organizational difficulties leading to drastic reductions in its workforce. Moreover, these were the years when U.S. visa regulations made Canadians think twice before moving across the border. Women like France Gerin, a millhand who migrated to Lawrence, Massachusetts, in 1926, and Rose Dubois, a weaver who in 1927 crossed the border on her way to Holyoke, Massachusetts, symbolized the end of an era—one that had witnessed a massive transfer of female labor from an agrarian society to the mills and factories of industrial New England.[66]

The emigration from French Canada had brought to countless American cities and towns not just agriculturalists, laborers, shopkeepers, and workers belonging to various trades, but also people like Alma Kerouac, Lorette Beaulieu, Arthemise Pion, Joseph Lachapelle, Henry Berlis, Herigault Pelletier, and Jean Gosselin. They were nuns and priests sent by various Quebec-based religious orders to look after the educational and spiritual needs of their fellow French Canadians. Arthemise Pion, for instance, was awaited at Sainte-Anne Parochial School, in Woonsocket, where as a "teacher nun" she would teach the children of French-Canadian immigrants. Alma Kerouac and Lorette Beaulieu were on their way to convents, one in Golfstown, New Hampshire, the other in Salem, Massachusetts, where very likely they spent their time not just in prayer but also in administering spiritual and material services to needy compatriots.[67] The same can be said of Jean Gosselin, whose destination was the Saint-Augustine Rectory in Manchester, New Hampshire.[68]

The constant stream of nuns and priests toward French-Canadian communities in the United States could make for an interesting chapter in the religious history of the two countries. In the context of this book, it serves to add an additional touch to the reality of a migration movement that extended through many decades—a movement that served the different economic and demographic needs of both countries and that, much more than the migration of English Canadians, produced a new sociocultural geography in North America. Although the Great Depression shrunk the movement to a hardly visible stream, it did not alter that geography. True, the majority of French Canadians were now "Franco-Americans," most of them benefiting from the material betterment that their adopted country had made possible. But Quebec, Ontario, or New Brunswick remained nearby, in imagery, in trips, and in the firmly established networks that kept the movement alive even when it had ceased.

Fig. 10. Windsor, Ontario, and Detroit, Michigan, ca. 1930.
Courtesy of the National Archives of Canada, PA 48177.

CHAPTER FOUR

◈

Emigration from English Canada, 1900–1930

I n any given day during the first three decades of the twentieth century, for every French Canadian who emigrated to the United States,
two Anglo-Canadians did likewise. By the end of the 1920s, their numbers had risen to nearly three-quarters of a million.[1] Considering the proportion of Anglo-Canadians within the Dominion's population, their rate
of emigration approximated that of French Canadians.

The "exodus"—this word continued to resound in many counties and
regions of the country—was far from being a French-Canadian phenomenon. Like their French counterparts, Anglo-Canadians crossed the border
in the hope of improving their material conditions, whether they were
leaving a stagnating Maritime town, a bustling Ontario metropolitan area,
or a newly settled community in the West. Their migrations took them to
all the states along the Canadian-American border and to others beyond,
and undeniably contributed to their economic and social transformation.
But despite the significant impact that this massive shift of the Anglo-
Canadian population had on both the sending and the receiving societies, it has left little trace in North American historiography.

Cultural and linguistic factors are the major reasons for this serious la-
cuna. For, unlike French Canadians, the Anglo-Canadian presence in the
United States did not give rise to the kind of ethnic institutions nor to the
kind of residential clusterings that historians normally associate with immigrant settlement processes. This had been largely the case in the nineteenth century; it became even truer in the twentieth. Although, as we
shall see, Anglo-Canadians entered the mainstream of urban, industrial

97

America, the historian looks in vain for prominent symbols of group identity such as the national parish, the ethnic press, or the mutual benefit society. And so the virtual invisibility of these traditions in the American sociocultural landscape has made it difficult to identify those institutional markers that provide an entry into the particular universe of an immigrant group and that open up paths of research on its composition and inner dynamics.

Nor does the historian get much help from contemporary American observers, be they newspaper reporters, social workers, or politicians. Progressive America, at least that segment most concerned with the plight of immigrants or with the political capital that their votes could represent, simply did not seem to have noticed Anglo-Canadians. If, as America opened her doors to a growing variety of nationalities, immigration often became synonymous with a "social problem," Anglo-Canadians were simply not seen as part of that problem. Perhaps the failure to be counted in the national history of the United States—except in census records and populations statistics—grows from the kind of belief expressed at the height of the exodus by an observer who claimed that Anglo-Canadians were "to a great extent Americanized before they even emigrated."[2] A flagrant reflection of the assimilative concerns of white Protestant America, this positive stance toward Anglo-Canadians should not exempt the historian from seeking to understand the processes that led this population to cross the border.

The little we know about emigration from English Canada comes from the efforts of a handful of mostly Canadian scholars. Despite the light their works have shed on a few regional contexts, the phenomenon has thus far failed to receive the place it deserves in Canadian and U.S. national narratives.[3] This neglect may also be due to the fact that, except for the Maritimes, the flow of Anglo-Canadians to the south failed to engender among contemporaries the kind of political clamor and denunciation so prominent in French-Canadian public discourse.

But besides the lack of institutional visibility in the United States and the relative public neglect by contemporary Anglo-Canadians, another factor may have discouraged historians from delving into this field of migration history. Whereas the historical research on French-Canadian outmigration focuses largely on a single province plus a few well-delineated districts outside Quebec, emigration from English Canada occurred from coast to coast in an era when Canadian regionalism was consolidating long-standing socioeconomic traits. And thus the historian of Anglo-Canadian emigration is far from confronting a culturally and religiously homogeneous population resembling French Canadians.

All that emigrants like Eli Mason, Roderick Morrison, Daisy Dean, Zoriana Neterpka, and Archibald McLane had in common was, essentially, the English language. Eli left an isolated Nova Scotian coastal village that for generations had lived off fishing and subsistence farming. Before heading south, Roderick lived in Quebec's Eastern Townships, that anglophone enclave in Quebec where Scottish, Irish, and English ancestries had long intermingled and yielded a distinct cultural universe. Daisy, a professional nurse, was a well-educated Canadian woman pursuing a career in the tertiary sector of fast-growing metropolitan Toronto. Zoriana, a Canadian-born of Ukrainian ancestry, left a small prairie town which, like many surrounding towns and districts, had been a leading destination of central and eastern Europeans brought by railroad companies to the Canadian frontier. Archibald, a Vancouver mechanic, had been born in Canada from Canadian parents, his ancestry perhaps going back to one or more Scottish counties that in the nineteenth and twentieth centuries constantly supplied new Canadians.[4]

Examples showing the great variety of regional contexts and sociocultural profiles composing the Anglo-Canadian migrating population could be multiplied. They speak eloquently to the complexity of this migration movement—it is far more complex than its French counterpart—and to the necessity of shifting the scale of analysis from the continent to regions or even more closely circumscribed locations and groups. Only then, once we have encountered Anglo-Canadian emigrants with their actual socioeconomic and cultural attributes, do we begin to understand the human dimension of migration.

One further consideration will help explain the wide historiographical gap between French- and Anglo-Canadian migration and will sharpen the comparative perspective adopted in this chapter. It has to do with both the regional and occupational distribution of Canadians in the United States. In many ways, at the origin of the historical literature on French-Canadian migration stands the New England textile mill. Much of the exodus experienced by French Canadians in the nineteenth and twentieth centuries is inseparable from the growth and expansion of that industrial sector, resulting in a unique ethnic regional concentration in the wider American urban landscape. And even if—as the previous chapter has shown—a significant number of French Canadians headed to other U.S. regions and joined the labor force of various industrial sectors, the movement's association with the New England textile mill has survived as a sort of historical a priori. One should not be surprised then if, ever since Tamara Hareven made French-Canadian immigrants part of the "new social history" through her studies of the Amoskeag Corporation in Manchester, New Hampshire, French-Canadian immigrants have been set more often than not in that specific urban-industrial context.[5]

Instead, regional dispersion and occupational diversity were the hallmarks of the Anglo-Canadian movement. Although some migration streams were more prominent than others, producing in the United States a population distribution that was far from even, only rarely did they result in regional and residential concentrations of the sort found among French Canadians. Nor did Anglo-Canadians constitute the predominant labor force of any given industry. The geography of English Canada was, of course, one main factor; another—more complex to analyze and more challenging to the historian—was the far greater variety of economic and industrial contexts that sent men, women, and children across the border in search of a more rewarding life.

I

When in 1908–11 a special commission of inquiry appointed by the U.S. Senate researched and compiled the staggering amount of data on the presence of the foreign born in the country's manufacturing apparatus, the industrial sociogeography of Anglo-Canadian immigration emerged in its basic features. One of the most wide-ranging and time-consuming initiatives in the history of public inquiries, the Immigration Commission sought to throw light on what many sectors of public opinion saw as the problem of the "inferior races" among the immigrant population and in the American economy.[6]

Owing to the racialist criteria inspiring the commission, that negative label was attached to central-eastern and southern Europeans, to such an extent that Italian immigrants were separated into two groups—northern Italians and southern Italians. More significantly for our purposes, longitudinal data gathering was implemented to distinguish an "old" immigration and a "new" one, so as to identify more effectively the presence of the latter type within the country's manufacturing economy (The distinction became canonized in the subsequent immigration literature and public discourse.) The foreign-born employees sampled in each industry were divided according to the duration of residence in the United States, as measured by a twenty-year scale subdivided in yearly and quinquennial periods. The results did corroborate the commission's hypotheses as far as the "new" immigration was concerned. In sector after sector, the data showed that the majority of central-eastern and southern European workers in the sample had resided in the country less than ten years. In clothing manufacturing, for instance, a sector of major Italian concentration, 47 percent of the sampled Italians (northern and southern combined) had resided in the United States less than five years, and 79 percent less than ten years.[7] Similarly, in the slaughtering and meat-packing industry, where Polish immigrants were the single largest ethnolinguistic group, more than half of them had resided less than five years and 80 percent less than ten years.[8]

Quite ambiguous, however, were the data meant to document the existence of an "old" immigration; for the existence of a "new" did not automatically produce an "old."[9] National groups that had been part of the earliest waves of immigration, such as the English or Germans, had continued to arrive in significant numbers during the fifteen years preceding the commission's report.[10]

The group whose immigration experience perhaps shows better than any other the artificiality of the distinction between old and new were the Canadians, both English and French—a group the commission classified as old immigration. In all, 20,165 of them, men and women, English and French, were surveyed, spread through the country's major industries. Their length of residence shows the continuity of the inflow over the previous twenty years and longer: 37 percent of them had resided in the United States twenty years and over, another 47 percent had resided for periods ranging between five and nineteen years, and 16 percent for four years and less. Of the two linguistic groups, Anglo-Canadians had a higher proportion of longtime residents: 44 percent of them had resided in their country of adoption for twenty years or more.[11] Theirs had therefore been an enduring presence, one that had accompanied the industrialization of the United States through its various stages, particularly in the northern regions of the country, while at the same time one that renewed itself through the constant arrival of newcomers.

Hidden among the hundreds of statistical tables and endless compilations contained in the commission's report is a rich snapshot of that presence, one that warrants an attentive look for what it can tell us about the migration movement in many of its spatial, demographic, and socioeconomic articulations.

The most striking aspect emerging from the data is the high position Anglo-Canadians held in the occupational hierarchy of industrial America. Although the commission's data did not provide occupational breakdowns, that position can be deduced from the data on earnings based on all industries combined. Not only did the average weekly earnings of Anglo-Canadian men aged eighteen and over ($14.15) stand well above the average for all the foreign born ($11.92), but Anglo-Canadians had a considerably higher percentage of workers in the top earning levels; 12 percent of them fell in the three highest earning brackets ($20 or more) as against 4.3 percent of the foreign born; and 5 percent were in the top bracket ($25 or more) as against the 1.6 percent of the foreign born.[12] Moreover, although the overall earning position of Anglo-Canadians was only slightly lower than that of white American workers ("native-born of white native father"), in several important industries Anglo-Canadians had higher earnings than their American counterparts. In the iron and steel industry, for instance, where the average weekly earnings of American workers was $16.54, Anglo-Canadian workers averaged weekly earnings of $18.04. Here Anglo-Canadians also had a considerably higher proportion of their workers in the top earning bracket: 15.9 percent, against 9.9 percent among Americans.[13] With very slight variations, this was true both in eastern United States, where most Anglo-Canadian iron- and steelworkers very likely originated from the Maritimes, and in the Midwest, which had traditionally drawn most Canadian immigrants from Ontario. A similar high performance emerges from the commission's data on another important industry, the manufacturing of agricultural implements and vehicles. Here Anglo-Canadian workers outscored not only American workers but also English immigrants—the group that consistently ranked among the highest in most industries.[14]

We know little about the backgrounds of these workers. But the commission included two indicators that shed important light on their socioeconomic profile. One is the broad occupational sector in which the newcomer was engaged before emigrating. Although a large proportion of the sampled Anglo-Canadian workers (31.8 percent) had been farmers or farm laborers, a significant number (27.3 percent) had been associated with industrial manufacturing, and a few (4.3 percent) had been in trade activities. General laborers represented only 6.4 percent of the sample. Moreover, a large portion of the sample, 30.3 percent, was classified into a general category ("other occupations") which most likely included the leading nonfarming sectors such as craft production, transportation, and mining.[15] The data relating to the agricultural implement and vehicle manufacturing sector were more precise and reveal a closer relation between work in that industry and occupational background in Canada. Here, indeed, the proportion of Anglo-Canadian workers who had been engaged in industrial manufacturing rose to 38.2 percent, the highest among all immigrant groups. Another sizable number of workers, 22.9 percent, had been engaged in "hand trades." Conversely, the proportion of occupations associated with farming was much lower than in the nationwide data—down to a mere 12.2 percent.[16]

Fig. 11. McGoey's wreck, Langdon, North Dakota, August 11, 1911. Born in Toronto, Thomas McGoey and his family moved to the Red River Valley of North Dakota in 1887, where he took up the electrical trade. He is credited as being the first resident of North Dakota to pilot his own plane, making the first successful flight on July 12, 1911. Photograph from the Fred Hulstrand History in Pictures Collection, NDIRS-NDSU, Fargo.

Clearly, the American industrial giant had been drawing from Anglo-Canada a working population that included significant contingents of men whose previous experience in factory and craft production had equipped them to adjust to the American industrial context and consolidate their position in the higher ranks of the occupational hierarchy.

This portrait is enriched by data on language proficiency, which may serve as an indicator, however approximate, of the degree of education among immigrant workers aged fourteen and over. Nearly 97 percent of all Anglo-Canadians could read and write, a score that placed them to the top of the hierarchy, even above English immigrants. The bottom was mostly filled by immigrants from southern and central-eastern Europe. Of the sampled southern Italians, for instance, only 50.4 percent could read and write.[17]

Anglo-Canadian women were much less present in industrial manufacturing; consequently their number in the sample is smaller and mostly concentrated in a few manufacturing sectors. Still, their performance

within the overall female workforce paralleled that of their male counterparts. With weekly earnings of $8.09, their average was above that of all
the foreign born combined, and even higher than that of Americans.
Moreover, they had one of the highest proportion of workers (19.9 percent) in the top three wage brackets.[18] Quite surprisingly, compared to
Canadian male workers, they comprised a much higher proportion (43.2
percent) who had been associated with manufacturing production at the
time of emigration. Another large group, amounting to 21 percent, had
held occupations in the needle trades. Only 16 percent had been associated with farmwork and 8.6 percent with domestic services.[19]

Finally, the commission's data allow us to assess the higher rank held by
Anglo-Canadian industrial workers vis-à-vis their French-Canadian counterparts. Nationwide, the gap in weekly earnings between men of the two
groups was considerable, with French Canadians even ranking below the
combined average of all foreign-born groups.[20] This indicator suggests
a concentration of French-Canadian men in semiskilled and unskilled
jobs—a position that may largely be explained by the sharply different occupational backgrounds and social profiles of the two groups. For a much
higher proportion of French-Canadian men, working in American factories must have entailed a drastic change of life and labor conditions, since
as many as 61.5 percent of them (as against 31.8 percent among Anglo-
Canadians) had been farmers or farm laborers at the time of their emigration. Moreover, only 13.6 percent of them had been associated with industrial manufacturing, a proportion that stood in sharp contrast with the
27.3 percent found among Anglo-Canadians.[21]

A factor contributing to the higher occupational rank of Anglo-Canadians compared to their French-Canadian counterparts was no doubt the
considerable gap between the two groups in the level of literacy at the
time of immigration. Only 78.9 percent of French Canadians could read
and write, whereas the corresponding rate among Anglo-Canadians was,
as we have seen, nearly 97 percent.[22]

This occupational scenario, however, appears somewhat reversed when
one looks at the data on female industrial workers. Although both Anglo-
and French Canadians ranked higher than all the foreign born combined, and even higher than American workers, it was French Canadians
who held the upper position, however slight.[23] This may be explained by
the fact that twice as many French-Canadian women entering the United
States had some previous experience in industrial manufacturing. But it
may also be due to the sampling procedure adopted by the commission,
which left out nationality groups whose numbers in any given industry
were too small. The more diversified presence of Anglo-Canadian women

in the American industrial apparatus, in contrast with the high concentration of French-Canadian women in textile manufacturing, resulted in an overrepresentation of the latter group in the sample. Not surprisingly, the size of the Anglo-Canadian women's sample was less than one-fifth of that of French-Canadian women, 77.9 percent of whom were concentrated in cotton manufacturing.[24]

Despite some of the limitations in the sampling procedure adopted, the commission's report provides the most detailed portrait of the presence of Canadians in the nationwide American industrial apparatus and their ranking among immigrants and native Americans alike. Yet, the commission's concern with industrial manufacturing—the sector that at the time employed the majority of the foreign born—left out a substantial proportion of Anglo-Canadians who had crossed the border to work in other sectors of the economy. Thanks to the data provided by the *Soundex Index*, we can identify the great variety of work milieus that Anglo-Canadians left behind, and we can follow these migrants across the border to specific regions and economic sectors. Equally important, we can examine the most important attributes of this population—age, sex, and married status—and reconstruct the main patterns of their migration.

II

The Anglo-Canadian flow of population to the south was a truly continental movement in that all provinces of the Dominion contributed their portion of out-migrants and nearly all the states of the American republic were chosen as destinations. This continentalism, however, emerges from the sum total of regional realities. To the overwhelming majority of Anglo-Canadians, though, migrating meant moving within the confines of their geo-economic region, and very often crossing the border into the adjacent state. People like Frank Hearst, who in 1911 left his New Brunswick county and crossed the continent to reach his Alabama destination, or the Nermiah family, who in 1913 migrated from Fernie, British Columbia, to Key West, Florida, or Joseph Gettings, who boarded a train in Montreal bound for Alaska, are exceptional cases.[25]

Despite the relativity inherent in the notion of distance, particularly when applied to the pursuit of a desired action, it is nevertheless an element one can hardly ignore in accounting for the range of destinations chosen by migrants.

A combination of physical proximity and of what one may call "proximity of opportunities" largely explains the spatial configuration of Anglo-

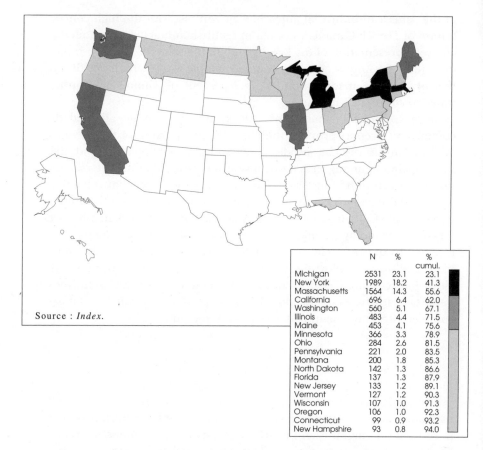

	N	%	% cumul.
Michigan	2531	23.1	23.1
New York	1989	18.2	41.3
Massachusetts	1564	14.3	55.6
California	696	6.4	62.0
Washington	560	5.1	67.1
Illinois	483	4.4	71.5
Maine	453	4.1	75.6
Minnesota	366	3.3	78.9
Ohio	284	2.6	81.5
Pennsylvania	221	2.0	83.5
Montana	200	1.8	85.3
North Dakota	142	1.3	86.6
Florida	137	1.3	87.9
New Jersey	133	1.2	89.1
Vermont	127	1.2	90.3
Wisconsin	107	1.0	91.3
Oregon	106	1.0	92.3
Connecticut	99	0.9	93.2
New Hampshire	93	0.8	94.0

Source : *Index.*

Map 2. Main U.S. destinations of Anglo-Canadians, 1906–30

Canadian migration. Because of its location within the industrial geography of the continent, Ontario was the province where those two kinds of proximity came the closest to overlapping. Although the fact of being the most important donor province (contributing 42.2 percent of the entire movement) can be explained by the large size of its population, Ontario's physical proximity and economic integration with what by the turn of the century had emerged as America's "industrial heartland" provides a more concrete explanation. Not surprisingly, two out of three out-migrating Ontarians chose as their destination either of the two adjacent states of Michigan and New York, and Michigan became the destination for 42 percent of the province's southward flow. Many of the remaining destinations were either in the midwestern states of Minnesota, Ohio, and Illinois or in western Pennsylvania. The regional dimension of emigration from Ontario becomes clearer when one looks at the movement from the perspective of the receiving states. Thus, 76 percent of the Anglo-Canadian immigrant population in Michigan originated in Ontario, and two out of three Anglo-Canadian immigrants in New York and Ohio came from that same province.[26]

A concurrence of physical proximity and availability of opportunities also shaped the spatial configuration of the movement in the Pacific region. Over half the population migrating from British Columbia chose the adjacent state of Washington as their destination, with a substantial additional portion flowing down the Pacific coast to California or to the neighboring states of Oregon and Montana. Shifting the perspective south of the border, of all the Anglo-Canadians in Washington State, 53 percent originated in British Columbia and an additional 33 percent from the neighboring prairie provinces.[27]

At the other extreme of the continent, Atlantic Canada, the pattern of spatial distribution of out-migrants was also primarily a regional one. Here again physical proximity and the range of opportunities the Atlantic states offered played an important role in directing the migration flow toward certain destinations. Although the neighboring state of Maine attracted a sizable portion of Anglo-Canadian Maritimers, by far the most important destination was farther down the Atlantic coast: the populous and highly industrialized Massachusetts, the choice of one out of two Maritimers (see table 6).

If the focus is placed on each of the three individual Maritime provinces, however, the patterns are more complex: physical proximity reemerges as a leading factor in well-circumscribed microregions. For instance, Massachusetts remained the leading destination for Anglo-Canadians departing from New Brunswick, yet it was so only for 38.1 percent of them; an almost equal number chose neighboring Maine, the majority of them originating from five border counties, which confirms the existence of what some geographers have termed a "transborder region"—in this case the only significant one east of Lake Ontario.[28] At the same time, Nova Scotian Anglo-Canadians chose Massachusetts at a much higher rate (62.6 percent) than other Maritimers. Owing to the geographical position of the province—much of its territory extends south as a sort of peninsula—one can hardly use the same spatial criteria that apply to inland regions. It had been this insularity that throughout much of the nineteenth century had turned a majority of Nova Scotians toward the "Boston state," linking the two locations by migration fields that lasted well into the twentieth century. When in 1922 the MacPhersons—a large family living in Inverness County, Nova Scotia,—were struck by tragedy, Mrs. MacPherson, now a widow, turned

Table 6. *Anglo-Canadian Migrants to the United States by Provinces of Departure and Major States of Destination, 1906–30 (in percentages)*

	Nova Scotia	New Brunswick	Prince Edward Island	Quebec	Ontario	Prairies	British Columbia	Province Unspecified	Total N	Total %
Michigan	4.1	2.8	2.6	11.3	41.6	11.4	3.3	27.3	2,531	23.1
New York	8.9	6.6	5.6	31.4	27.8	4.6	3.6	16.8	1,989	18.2
Massachusetts	62.6	38.1	59.7	12.3	1.8	1.7	1.1	25.5	1,564	14.3
California	2.8	1.1	0.9	5.2	5.2	12.2	17.4	3.5	696	6.4
Washington	0.6	1.1	0.9	0.6	0.8	9.4	53.6	3.0	560	5.1
Illinois	1.2	0.1	—	4.3	4.4	10.1	0.7	2.8	483	4.4
Maine	5.4	37.8	16.7	3.7	0.2	0.6	0.2	2.0	453	4.1
Minnesota	0.1	0.4	—	1.2	2.0	12.6	0.9	0.8	366	3.3
Ohio	0.4	0.1	—	2.3	4.2	2.5	0.5	1.7	284	2.6
Pennsylvania	1.5	0.7	0.4	3.5	2.4	1.8	0.7	1.7	221	2.0
Montana	0.5	0.1	—	0.2	0.3	7.3	4.2	1.4	200	1.8
North Dakota	0.1	—	—	0.1	0.3	5.8	0.5	1.4	142	1.3
Florida	0.7	0.4	0.4	1.0	1.7	1.4	0.7	0.9	137	1.3
New Jersey	1.5	0.7	0.4	3.2	1.0	1.2	—	0.9	133	1.2
Vermont	0.5	0.1	0.9	9.3	0.3	0.2	—	0.8	127	1.2
Wisconsin	0.1	0.7	—	0.2	0.8	2.5	0.2	1.4	107	1.0
Oregon	0.1	0.1	0.4	0.3	0.3	2.7	5.1	0.8	106	1.0
Connecticut	1.7	3.8	1.3	1.4	0.4	0.3	0.4	1.4	99	0.9
New Hampshire	1.9	1.8	3.8	3.3	0.1	0.2	0.2	0.8	93	0.8
Rhode Island	2.6	1.3	4.3	1.1	0.2	0.1	0.4	0.5	78	0.7
Other states	2.7	2.2	1.7	4.2	4.2	11.4	6.3	4.6	579	5.3
Total	100	100	100	100	100	100	100	100		100
N	1,171	741	233	1,022	4,623	1,969	552	637	10,948	

Note: Cases dismissed (last permanent place or destination in the United States unknown): 982.

to Boston because she had relatives and friends living there and was confident that several of her children could find jobs. One of them, Elizabeth, recalls how amazed she was at the number of friends and relatives that came to visit her and her family. "Half of the people that could ride came up here. Neighbors, girls and boys, they came up at that time . . . we used to set the table three times on a Sunday, we'd have so many coming. Nieces and nephews of ours would come, and cousins, and oh, half of the neighbors came up by the time we'd eat. We were never a day lonesome."[29]

To a lesser extent, a comparable pattern emerges from the tiny province of Prince Edward Island. Of its Anglo-Canadian out-migrants 59.7 percent chose Massachusetts, but Maine exerted a significant pull for 16.7 percent. Despite this range of destinations with its combination of short- and medium-distance flows, Maritimer out-migrants had one thing in common: with the exception of a small number bound for Michigan and western New York, they all chose coastal Atlantic states as their destination.

The Prairies, the largest and most sparsely populated area of Canada, was the region that exhibited the widest range of destinations. Since no major centers of industrialization lay across the border to the south, no one state predominated as a destination. Prairies out-migrants chose midwestern and western states such as Michigan, Illinois, Minnesota, Washington, and California with approximately equal frequency. When we look at the movement from the perspective of receiving locations in the United States, we see the important role of adjacent states. A majority (53 percent to 80 percent) of the Anglo-Canadian immigrants received by the four states of Minnesota, North Dakota, Montana, and Idaho came from the Prairies. Smaller but significant proportions of Prairies immigrants were also received by other far-western states such as Oregon and Washington.[30]

But it was Ontario that produced the greatest variety of patterns in the distribution of its out-migrating population; and as the province that by far contributed the most to the Anglo-Canadian movement, it deserves close scrutiny. In Ontario, short-distance migrations predominated, not merely because the overwhelming majority of its population was concentrated in the southern belt of the province, but also because its two most important neighboring states, Michigan and New York, had some leading centers of industrial and economic activity in cities near the border. Detroit and Sault Sainte Marie, Michigan, and Niagara Falls and Buffalo, New York, adjacent as they were to the Ontario cities of Windsor, Sault Sainte Marie, and Niagara Falls, produced the largest amount of short-distance migrations in all of Canada. Moreover, less than one hundred kilometers separated the two most important steelmaking centers of the entire region: Hamilton, Ontario, and Buffalo. And to these instances of

Fig. 12. John McKay's threshing outfit, Milton, North Dakota, ca. 1905. Ontario-born
John McKay moved with his wife and children to the Dakota Territory in 1882,
where they took up homesteading. Photograph from the Fred Hulstrand History
in Pictures Collection, NDIRS-NDSU, Fargo.

inland proximity, one should add that on the American shore opposite
many cities and towns fronting on Lake Ontario or Lake Huron were the
major industrial and commercial centers of upstate New York and eastern
Michigan. In his study of out-migration from one lakeside district in eastern Ontario, for instance, Randolph Widdis has shown the importance of
cities such as Watertown and Syracuse in attracting Ontarians from counties across the lake.[31]

Of all the transborder urban areas, the Windsor-Detroit one was the
most significant along the entire Canadian-U.S. border in terms of the
volume of short-distance migrations it produced. In fact, nearly four out
of five migrants leaving Windsor for U.S. destinations chose the city immediately across the border. At the same time, as one looks at towns located
further away from the province's southern industrial heartland, the rate of
across-the-border migrations decreases considerably. Thus, although Sault
Sainte Marie, Michigan, drew 69 percent of its Canadian immigrant population from her twin city across the border, only 45 percent of the migrants

Fig. 13. Railroad workers, Ontario, ca. 1920.
Courtesy of the National Archives of Canada, PA 66795.

departing from this Ontario city chose its Michigan twin as their destination. The rest spread through a variety of locations, mostly in Michigan, including of course Detroit, which attracted 14 percent of them.[32]

This combination of short- and medium-distance migrations originating from Ontario emerges with added clarity when a closer focus is placed on Detroit. As the most important magnet in the entire Canadian migration movement, Detroit's role as a continental crossroads of population and labor power calls for special attention. The city's place in the spatial configuration of migration in the Great Lakes region became a central one; for, throughout the thirty-year period covered in this book, this Michigan industrial metropolis became the chosen destination for 30 percent of all Ontario's Anglo-Canadian out-migrants, and for 15 percent of the entire Anglo-Canadian movement. Angus Crowdis, for instance, was one of many young Nova Scotians who tried their luck in the Michigan industrial metropolis. After his return from France, where he served in the armed forces, Angus held a job as carpenter in a Sydney steel plant until he grew dissatisfied and in 1922 headed for Detroit with a group of nine friends. For Angus, and perhaps for his friends, Detroit was the first choice among U.S. destinations, although it proved unsatisfactory for this young Nova Scotian, for soon after arriving he set out on a job hunt that took him to Buffalo, from there to nearby Welland, Ontario, and finally to Everett, Massachusetts, where a friend helped him find work. Eventually, he found what he wanted in the Massachusetts shipyards, where the pay was considerably higher, his career perspectives brighter, and the social life with local Maritimers richer than he might have hoped for.[33]

Moreover, Detroit and its industrial surroundings attracted Anglo-Ontarians from all corners of the province. If the majority originated from the heavily populated and industrialized southwestern section of the province and from the Toronto metropolitan area, substantial numbers left for Detroit from districts as far apart as the mostly agrarian counties of southeastern Ontario near the Quebec border, from northern mining centers such as Sudbury and Sault Sainte Marie, and, farther north, from railway towns such as Thunder Bay. Moreover, the Ontarians moving to Detroit belonged to the widest occupational spectrum, even though the occupational composition of the flow to that city changed with the progressive transformation of the local blue- and white-collar labor markets.[34]

Like their French-Canadian counterparts, Anglo-Canadians departed from metropolitan areas, large and medium-sized cities, industrial and commercial towns, and rural districts. As one may expect, however, the variety of what we could call "the geography of out-migration" was much greater than that of French Canada, and to a large extent reflected the diversity in the socioeconomic structures among the various provinces. Manitoba and New Brunswick, for instance, stood at opposite extremes with regard to the role played by urban and rural districts as sending areas. In the former, nearly two out of three out-migrants had resided in the province's largest city, Winnipeg. In New Brunswick, on the other hand, only 23 percent of out-migrants left from the province's two large urban centers, Saint John and Moncton; the majority left from small towns and villages throughout the province.[35] This is not surprising when one considers the high degree of concentration of Manitobans in the province's capital as well as the city's overwhelming role as an industrial and commercial center. New Brunswick, on the other hand, rested on a predominantly agrarian economy and its population was dispersed throughout its various counties. Consequently, the contrast in the two economic and demographic structures was reflected in the much higher number of Manitoban out-migrants associated with industrial manufacturing and the tertiary sector.

Between these two extremes stood provinces such as British Columbia and Ontario, where the urban/rural mix of the sending districts was more balanced. Thus in British Columbia, 41 percent of out-migrants originated from Vancouver, with Victoria accounting for another 12 percent. The role of smaller towns as sending areas, whether based on mining or agriculture, was roughly proportional to their demographic weight within the province.[36] A similar geography of out-migration emerged in Ontario. Here, despite its large population size, Toronto accounted for only 26 percent of the province's out-migrants. But unlike the other provinces in the Dominion, Ontario had a significant constellation of large to medium-sized cities, from Windsor in the west through London, Hamilton, and Kingston to Ottawa in the east. It was from these large urban areas, then, that more than half of Ontario's out-migrants departed. Moreover, among the frequent districts of out-migration were large towns whose urbanization had grown from a variety of economic activities ranging from manufacturing to mining, and from railway transportation to commercial agriculture. Typical among these towns of out-migration were Chatham, Sarnia, Sudbury, Port Arthur, and Guelph. This left a minority of less than 25 percent originating from small towns and rural parishes, a pattern of out-migration that sharply contrasted with Quebec's and that inevitably became reflected in the occupational composition of its U.S.-bound population.[37]

III

But who were these Anglo-Canadians who chose to work and live across the border? What kind of human and economic resources did they contribute to the United States? And how do their patterns of migration compare with those of French Canadians?

As table 7 shows, men outnumbered women in the Anglo-Canadian migrant population (by 57 percent to 43), a proportion similar to that of men in the French-Canadian group (59 percent). Moreover, out-migration appealed to the younger strata of the Anglo-Canadian population, much as it did in French Canada. By far the most important age group was that of men and women between fifteen and twenty-nine (45 percent of the migrating population), followed by persons aged thirty to forty-four (24 percent), which means that approximately two-thirds of the Anglo-Canadian migrants were in their prime working and reproductive age.

Table 7. Age Groups and Sex Distribution of Anglo-Canadian Migrants by Subperiods, 1906–30

	1906–18		1919–24		1925–30		Total	
	N	%	N	%	N	%	N	%
Females								
0 to 14	505	22.7	430	23.2	110	10.2	1,045	20.3
15 to 29	895	40.2	786	42.4	581	53.9	2,262	43.9
30 to 44	480	21.6	400	21.6	227	21.0	1,107	21.4
45 to 59	197	8.9	142	7.7	99	9.2	438	8.5
60 and over	139	6.2	93	5.0	54	5.0	286	5.5
Age unknown	9	0.4	1	0.1	8	0.7	18	0.4
Subtotal	2,225	100	1,852	100	1,079	100	5,156	100
Males								
0 to 14	506	16.9	473	18.6	125	10.4	1,104	16.4
15 to 29	1,328	44.3	1,118	43.9	658	54.7	3,104	45.9
30 to 44	776	25.9	667	26.2	272	22.6	1,715	25.4
45 to 59	255	8.5	217	8.5	104	8.7	576	8.5
60 and over	130	4.3	64	2.5	39	3.2	233	3.5
Age unknown	6	0.2	7	0.3	5	0.4	18	0.3
Subtotal	3,001	100	2,546	100	1,203	100	6,750	100
Sex unknown	14		5		5		24	
Total	5,240		4,403		2,287		11,930	

As one may expect, the movement's adult population included both married and single persons. This latter category was more numerous among men, but their overrepresentation was far from excessive (56.1 percent) and was almost identical to that of their French-Canadian counterpart (57.5 percent). Women, on the other hand, were equally divided between married and single, differing very slightly from French Canadians, among whom the proportion of married women was only a few percentage points higher than that of single women.[38]

Thus, people like Anna Gibson, Frank Cleversey, and Olive Doyle were representatives of a dominant pattern among both Anglo-Canadians and French Canadians, namely, the migration of single young adults. A twenty-three-year-old schoolteacher from the small town of Campbellford, Ontario, Anna Gibson entered the United States at Port Huron, Michigan, in July 1911 and from there traveled to a Kansas town where an uncle of hers lived. Frank Cleversey was twenty when he crossed the border in October 1923; he had left the Nova Scotia coastal village of Pleasant Bay, where he had worked as a fisherman, and was heading for Marlboro, Massachusetts. An accountant from Chatham, Ontario, Olive Doyle chose Detroit as her destination, most likely because a cousin of hers lived there.[39]

Some women, like Olive Doyle, crossed the border accompanied by a family member—in her case, by her twenty-four-year-old sister. But they were a minority. The majority made the trip alone.[40] Although most French-Canadian single women did likewise, this practice was much more widespread among Anglo-Canadian women.

But as table 7 shows, Anglo-Canadians also had a significant proportion of children aged fourteen and under, representing 18 percent of the total and comparable in size to that of their French counterpart (21 percent). The presence of this sizable proportion of children, coupled with the substantial proportion of married adults, clearly indicates the existence of family migration as another important pattern.

A closer look at these demographic indicators reveals that family migration was predominant among one specific component of the Anglo-Canadian population, namely, Canadians whose origins were other than British (or French). Though a minority, one out of five Anglo-Canadian out-migrants belonged to this group. Most of them had been born in Canada of parents belonging to a wide variety of ethnolinguistic origins. The largest contingent was of German background, followed in importance by eastern Europeans, Scandinavians, and Italians, who together constituted more than two-thirds of all the Anglo-Canadian migrants of non-British origin. A striking demographic characteristic of this group was, in fact, the presence of nearly twice as many children compared to Canadians of British origin, and a significantly higher proportion of married adults among both males and females.[41]

The demographic profile outlined above remained fairly constant during much of the period under study; during the second half of the twenties, however, it underwent a rapid change as the proportion of children declined sharply—a drop that was offset by an increase in the number of migrants belonging to the 15–29 age bracket and resulting in a much greater participation in the movement by unmarried men and women.[42] Once again, it was a trend that had an almost identical parallel among French Canadians.

IV

If the demographic profile of Anglo-Canadians and the migration patterns it engendered were strikingly similar to those of French Canadians, the same was far from being the case when the focus is switched to the migrants' occupations. Anglo-Canada, in fact, sent out a working population that was considerably more skilled and diversified and reflected a more developed and heterogeneous economic universe. Looking at the Anglo-Canadian movement as a whole, one is immediately struck by the consid-

Fig. 14. Honey Brothers roller mills, Park River, North Dakota, ca. 1905. The Honey brothers left Canada and settled in Park River during the late nineteenth century. Photograph from the Fred Hulstrand History in Pictures Collection, NDIRS-NDSU, Fargo.

erable presence of men belonging to the highest occupational echelons of an industrial society. Prominent among them were businessmen mostly operating in the trade sector, along with professionals, and supervisory personnel. This group constituted 14.4 percent of all male occupations, a proportion nearly four times higher than that of French Canadians (table 8).

The four most frequent occupations in this group were merchants, contractors, physicians, and engineers, followed by managers and supervisors associated with a variety of industrial and commercial sectors. This group hardly matches the occupational profile that immigration historians ordinarily encounter in their studies. A closer focus on the profile of one of the most numerous out-migrants belonging to this elite group, physicians, reveals that nearly half of them migrated from Ontario. Judging from the average age of the group—the majority were in their twenties and thirties—most of these physicians were at an early stage of their career.[43] The information provided by the Index suggests, moreover, a variety of career trajectories. Some of them, for instance, moved to the United States to get additional training. This was the case of thirty-eight-year-old Ontario-born Herbert Drury, who in September 1916 crossed the border at Saint Alban,

Table 8. *Male Anglo-Canadian Migrants by Major Occupations and Sectors of Activity, 1906–30 (in percentage;* N = 5,462)

Businessmen, professionals, and supervisory personnel	14.4
Clerical and miscellaneous white-collar workers	5.6
Farmers	11.8
Farm laborers	6.1
Natural resource workers (logging, mining, fishing)	3.5
General laborers	15.1
Production workers (factory and independent crafts)	33.8
Students	3.0
Others	3.8
Unreadable cases	2.9

Note: Uncounted are 166 migrants who declared "no occupation."

Vermont, on his way to Harvard College; his reason for migrating, he declared to border officials, was "to study."[44] More frequent, however, was the case of Canadian physicians who moved to practice their profession in U.S. hospitals and other health institutions. Thus, thirty-four-year-old Roy Smith left his natal city of Hamilton, Ontario, in January 1922 and gave Highland Park Hospital in Detroit as his destination.[45] Similarly, John Alfred O'Regan, a twenty-five-year-old native of Saint John, New Brunswick, went to begin work at Bellevue Hospital in New York City.[46] Although the majority of these physicians migrated from major Canadian cities where they might have trained, a significant minority departed from small towns, where the possibilities for career advancement were certainly more limited.

When one adds other departing professionals (bacteriologists, surgeons, dentists, and lawyers) who had spent many costly years receiving training, one cannot but view such emigration as an example of brain drain, evidence of both the advanced state of Canadian educational institutions and the desire of these men to seek professional advancement beyond the borders of their nation-state.[47]

The degree of industrialization the Dominion experienced during the first three decades of the century was also reflected in the considerable growth of the tertiary sector and the concomitant expansion of the clerical labor market. A sizable number of male Anglo-Canadians employed in white-collar jobs joined the out-migration movement to the United States. They came from virtually all branches of the tertiary economy: from communications, insurance and finance, health, education, and manufacturing enterprises.

Equally significant was the proportion of out-migrants registered by immigration officials as "students"—young men who were not yet in the active workforce but who were most likely destined to enter white-collar employ-

ment or join a profession. It was a pattern barely perceptible in the movement originating from French Canada. The majority of these Anglo-Canadian students migrated simply because they were taken along by their parents, who must have seen no problem in the adjustment of their children to
the American educational system. Others, however, moved south of the border while their professional education (in law, medicine, or engineering)
was in progress, and one may safely speculate that their desire to pursue
their studies in an American professional school or to seek employment in
their fields must have played a considerable role in their decision to emigrate.[48] Arthur Goulding, for instance, a twenty-eight-year-old Toronto medical student, entered the United States in January 1917, headed for the
Harvard Medical School.[49] Another medical student, twenty-four-year-old
William Little, left Barrie, Ontario, in July 1920 for a hospital in Scranton,
Pennsylvania, perhaps to pursue practical training. Harry Scales was a
thirty-two-year-old law student from Moose Jaw, Saskatchewan, who in November 1916 moved to San Diego with his wife. As a reference, he gave a law
firm in Moose Jaw where very likely he had been employed.[50]

    Where the occupational composition of the Anglo- and French-Canadian
movements resembled each other was in the proportion of farmers and
farm laborers. Anglo-Canadian farmers accounted for 11.8 percent of all
male occupations, a slightly higher percentage than the 9 percent migrating from French Canada. Anglo-Canadian farm laborers, on the other
hand, made up a smaller proportion than their French-Canadian counterparts, but the two percentages (6.1 and 8.7) suggest a parallel trend.
The constant shortage of farm laborers, particularly in the prairie
provinces, no doubt had an impact on the southward flow of this group of
Anglo-Canadians. Moreover, farm laborers were one of the main targets
of the Canadian government's recruiting campaigns in Great Britain. The
government, moreover, was the prime mover in organizing "harvest excursions" that brought thousands of Canadian farm laborers to the grain-
fields of Manitoba, Saskatchewan, and Alberta.[51] But for many of them,
the earnings they netted from one or more harvest seasons were far from
meeting their long-term life prospects. Owen Caldwell and Louis Bannister were among them. A farm laborer from Kings County, Nova Scotia,
Owen experienced one such excursion when in 1921, at the age of fifteen, he and his three brothers took advantage of the free fare and spent
the summer in the fields of Manitoba. Louis had left his New Brunswick
village to join a harvest excursion in Alberta one year earlier. Both young
men returned east, and though motivated by different circumstances,
they both turned to the United States to find the future they sought.
Owen waited until the following spring when, at sixteen, he moved to

Fig. 15. Field crops, Alberta, ca. 1915.
Courtesy of the National Archives of Canada, PA 11752.

Philadelphia, where he had some brothers and sisters. Louis spent few more years in the western Canada in lumber camps. Back in New Brunswick, he worked for a while as longshoreman. His decision to move south was prompted by his failure to get a job he felt he deserved. "So I was pretty disgusted then. I was mad. Real mad. So I said, 'All right, I'm leavin' this country. This is not for me.' I came out and went to the United States Immigration Office and applied for a visa to come up here [Boston]."[52]

Agrarian Anglo-Canada's contribution to the out-migrating movement was far from uniform throughout the Dominion. When the scale of analysis is lowered at the regional level, striking differences emerge in the rates of contribution. Thus, the three prairie provinces, whose total population was considerably smaller than that of Ontario, accounted for more than half of the out-migrating farmers; the rest were almost equally divided between Ontario and the Maritimes. This sharp regional variation may be largely explained by the predominantly agrarian economy of the Prairies—especially Saskatchewan and Alberta. Although our sources do not allow us to establish what proportion of Anglo-Canadian farmers moved to the United States to pursue the same activity, they do throw light on the significant number for whom migration entailed abandoning farming and entering an urban and industrial economy. There is no doubt that this was the case for the 44 percent of Maritime farmers who chose as their destinations large urban centers such as Boston and Lynn,

Massachusetts; Portland and Waterville, Maine, and Detroit. Even higher was the proportion of Ontario farmers who moved to large or medium-sized cities—Detroit alone became the destination for 36 percent of them. The likelihood that the pursuit of farming in the United States was part of one's migration strategy was higher among farmers out-migrating from the prairie provinces, a larger proportion of whom moved to rural counties in Michigan, Minnesota, North Dakota, and Montana. Even in this case, however, important cities such as Detroit, Minneapolis, Chicago, and Great Falls, took a large number of men from the Prairies. For them migration meant turning their back on rural life and starting anew as urban workers.[53]

Blue-collar workers completed the occupational scenario of Anglo-Canadian male migrants. As one may expect, they constituted the most numerous group, accounting for slightly over 50 percent of all occupations. Though a majority, their proportion was considerably smaller than that of their French-Canadian counterparts. One reason for this sharp contrast between the two movements was, as we have seen, the significantly higher presence among Anglo-Canadians of elite occupations and white-collar workers. The other was the much smaller proportion of general laborers within Anglo-Canadian blue-collar out-migrants. Although they constituted the single most important occupation, they accounted for only 15.1 percent, which was less than half the proportion of French-Canadian laborers (34.6 percent) and in all probability the smallest proportion of any international migration into the United States during that era.

If laborers are excluded, we are left with a blue-collar population amounting to only 37 percent. But what is striking is not merely its relatively low representation within the movement but their rank within the occupational hierarchy of Canada—or of any early-twentieth-century industrial society. The trend that the U.S. Immigration Commission had found in its extensive inquiry is confirmed by our data, so it seems to have endured until the end of the 1920s. The large majority of blue-collar Anglo-Canadian out-migrants, in fact, belonged to skilled trades, mostly in industrial and independent production, in building construction, and in transportation. Nearly half of them were engaged in the ten following trades, in order of frequency: carpenters, machinists, mechanics, painters, bricklayers, electricians, blacksmiths, molders, plasterers, plumbers, and tailors. Given the degree of organization among these trades on both sides of the border, one may safely assume that a number of the tradesmen were members of their respective unions or likely to join one once in the United States. William A. Calvin, for instance, had joined the International Brotherhood of Boilermakers, Iron Shipbuilders, and Helpers of America (IBB) in 1914, in his city of Saint John, New Brunswick, while in the employ of the Canadian Pacific Railroad. After serving in World War I with the Canadian Army, Calvin carried his work experience and his union membership to the United States, where after two years as boiler-maker for the Florida Seabord Railroad, he was elected chairman of his local shop committee. His activism in the IBB took him to the presidency of District Lodge 40 and, in 1929, he became vice-president of his inter-national union.[54] Vancouver-born Scott Milne, on the other hand, joined Local 125 of the International Brotherhood of Electrical Workers when he got a job as an electrical lineman in Portland, Oregon, where he had migrated soon after the war. Milne may be taken as representative of many young migrants who learned their trade in Canada and, once in the United States, entered the mostly unionized skilled crafts.[55] Prominent among these skilled trades were also a wide range of occupations mostly associated with industrial production, from toolmakers and ship builders to crane operators. Equally prominent were occupations typical of the transportation industry, such as railway and streetcar conductors and team-sters. The movement did have its mill workers, factory hands, and furnace men—semiskilled or unskilled occupations—but they were a minority; and even if this group is added to the larger contingent of laborers, we are still left with an overall blue-collar workforce, one that was more qualified to enter the American industrial and urban economy than most interna-tional migration movements of that era.

Of course, regional variations were very much part of this occupational landscape. And much as in the case of migrating farmers, some of these variations were due to regional specialization. Thus although fishermen made up a very small portion of the movement, it should not come as a surprise that the overwhelming majority (88 percent) came from a re-gion—the Maritimes—where fishing had long been a widely practiced oc-cupation. Similarly, three out of four out-migrating miners came from two regions whose economy relied considerably on that resource industry, British Columbia and the Maritimes.[56]

The impact of the regional context on the occupational composition of the movement was reflected in a more complex manner in Ontario. As the most populated and industrialized province, and the closest to the fast-growing labor markets of the American Midwest, Ontario sent the largest and most diversified blue-collar workforce. Moreover, compared to the other provinces, Ontario sent a significantly higher proportion of workers belonging to the ten most frequent trades mentioned above: 57 percent of them were from Ontario, as against 15.3 percent from the

Prairies, 12.4 percent from the Maritimes, 9.1 percent (Anglo-Canadians) from Quebec, and 6 percent from British Columbia.[57]

The proportion of Ontarians was even greater, as high as 62.6 percent, in the skilled trade most associated with industrial production, machinists. And here, as in several other trades tied to machine production, the presence of Detroit in the region must have played a considerable role. "Motown" became the destination for 70 percent of all out-migrating Canadian machinists; but of these, nearly two out of three came from Ontario. They had lived and worked mostly in large and medium-sized cities, though a number of them had experienced at least one previous move after being born in a town or city other than the one from which they out-migrated.[58] Representative of this pattern was John Sweeney, a forty-four-year-old widower of Irish ancestry who was born in Caledonia, a small Ontario town, and who, when he migrated in May 1923, was working and living in Toronto. Twenty-two-year-old Harold Walker, on the other hand, was one of the few machinists who moved to Detroit from Brantford, the same relatively small city in which he had been born. For John Sweeney, his move was his first migration to the United States, but Harold Walker, like many other machinists, had moved previously to the United States, in his case as a child brought to Buffalo by his parents.[59]

But Ontario was also the leading sender of unskilled workers. The province in fact accounted for 46 percent of all out-migrating laborers—a percentage, however, that is not overly excessive when one considers that 42 percent of the entire Anglo-Canadian migrating population left from that province.[60]

Nowhere else in Canada did the contrast between the occupational composition of out-migrating Anglo- and French Canadians emerge more starkly than in Montreal. The Dominion's leading metropolis held a place of its own as the urban universe in which coexisted the largest number of French and Anglo-Canadians, along with a sizable population of European immigrants—a distinctiveness that has inspired considerable scholarly literature and endless political analyses.[61] Although Anglo-Canadians constituted a minority (24 percent, in 1921, as against 63 percent French Canadians), they were the dominant group in industry, finance, commerce, and many professional and blue-collar sectors. The various production and maintenance shops, passenger stations, and rail yards of the Canadian Pacific Railway, the city's largest employer, provide a compelling illustration of the occupational positions held by the two groups. Canadians of British origin, along with a minority of British immigrants, made up much of the managerial and supervisory personnel and held the majority of white-collar jobs. The fact that, certainly in the private sector, English was the language of business helps explain the differing career opportunities open to the two groups. In a largely francophone city, French Canadians were understandably the largest component of the company's blue-collar workers; still, Anglo-Canadians were significantly overrepresented in most of the skilled trades, particularly in the production and maintenance of locomotives.

This pattern of occupational segmentation marking some of the leading sectors of the Montreal economy became reflected in the composition of its out-migrating population. The Anglo-Canadian contingent comprised a strikingly large proportion of elite professions, supervisory personnel, and various types of white-collar occupations (salesmen, agents, and clerks); altogether, they made up a staggering 40.5 percent of all Anglo-Canadian male occupations, and stood in sharp contrast with the 15 percent of their French-Canadian counterparts. Consequently, the proportions of blue-collar out-migrants in the two groups diverged significantly; they constituted 54 percent of the Anglo-Canadian contingent—a proportion slightly higher than the national average within that ethnolinguistic group, but much lower than the 79 percent French-Canadian blue-collar workers out-migrating from Montreal. The national trend, however, was only partially reflected in the composition of the two blue-collar contingents. Thus, Anglo-Canadians did send out a much smaller proportion of unskilled workers; its laborer component, for instance, made up only 18 percent of blue-collar workers, a sharp contrast with the 33 percent among French-Canadian blue-collars. Still, the proportion of skilled trades within each one of the two groups was quite comparable, which should not come as a surprise when one considers the important place of Montreal in the industrialization of the province and the wide range of opportunities offered to French Canadians who were willing and able to enter skilled trades.[62]

◆

This analysis of the Anglo-Canadian occupational contribution to the United States—as well as the loss it entailed for the Canadian economy— would of course remain partial without including in it the place held by women in the movement. As mentioned previously, women made up 43 percent of the out-migrating population, the large majority of them of working age. True, as many as 62 percent of them declared "no occupation" or simply "housewife," a status which, however, should not be interpreted as precluding waged employment once in the United States. Still, over one-third of them were women active in the Canadian labor force, and an analysis of their occupational affiliations will shed essential light on the character of the movement and also enrich the comparative analysis of the Anglo- and French-Canadian components of the movement.

Owing to their large number and to the wide range of regional and local contexts of out-migration, virtually all occupations associated at the time with "women's work" were represented. "Servant," the leading female occupation in the Dominion, was also the most important one among out-migrants; it accounted for 26 percent of all female occupations—a rate somewhat lower than the 32.9 percent sent by French Canadians (table 9). The most striking feature of the movement, however, was the strong presence of professional and white-collar occupations. Altogether, they made up over 40 percent, and most prominent among them were those denoting basic—if not advanced—training and education in fields such as nursing, teaching, and administration. They also included a wide variety of clerical occupations, mostly associated with office work and sales, along with a small number of cooks and waitresses. Moreover, as in the case of their male counterparts, female out-migrants included a significant proportion of students—13.3 percent—more than half of them in the field of nursing.

The overrepresentation of nurses, both professionals and students, which may undoubtedly be viewed as a distinctive feature of the movement, largely resulted from the ongoing demand coming from American hospitals and other types of health institutions. In her survey of newly accessible U.S. Immigration and Naturalization Service files pertaining to Canada, the historian Marian L. Smith refers to the "never-ending list of hospitals applying to import Canadian nurses" and to the many special permissions granted by U.S. immigration authorities to exempt recruiting institutions from the provisions of the contract-labor law.[63] Women like W. Blampin and Cynthia Kelley may serve as illustrations of the numerous cases in which nurses or student nurses provided U.S. border officials with the names of the health institutions they were headed for. In the case of twenty-six-year-old W. Blampin, a nurse who in 1922 departed from Grandby, Quebec, the destination was Women's Hospital in Philadelphia. As for Cynthia Kelley, she was going to City Hospital in New York. A twenty-year-old student nurse from Sudbury, Ontario, she declared to U.S. border officials that her move was "permanent"; most likely she was envisioning a career in a city that offered ample opportunities in her field.[64]

The other distinctive feature of the movement, clearly related to the weight of the above-mentioned occupations, was the strikingly small presence of production workers, whose proportion amounted to a mere 15 percent. Moreover, only a portion of these workers could be associated with factory production; the leading occupations in this group—dressmaker, seamstress, and tailor—could in fact be pursued as independent crafts as well as in factories.

Thus, in a very important way, the female component of the Anglo-Cana-

Table 9. *Female Anglo-Canadian Migrants by Major Occupations and Sectors of Activity, 1906–30 (in percentages;* N = *1,553)*

Professionals and supervisory personnel	6.3
Nurses	13.2
Clerical and miscellaneous white-collar workers	23.2
Production workers (factory and independent crafts)	15.0
Servants	26.0
Students	13.3
Others	1.1
Unreadable cases	1.9

Note: Uncounted are 2,183 adult women who declared "no occupation" and 357 who declared "housewife."

dian movement paralleled its male counterpart. Far from evoking images of an industrial proletariat flowing across the border toward unskilled or semi-skilled factory jobs, most of these women embodied the transformations occurring during that era in both the Canadian and the United States economy—a progressive growth of the service sector and the opportunities it provided in a variety of professions and white-collar occupations. It was clearly a context most conducive to a rapid integration into the mainstream of American economic life, whether in a metropolis or in a small town. Here too, this movement stood in sharp contrast to most of the movements originating at the time from Europe, and certainly to the French-Canadian one.

Compared to the latter movement, in fact, Anglo-Canada sent a significantly higher proportion of women in professional, supervisory, and white-collar occupations, as well as a much higher proportion of students. The smaller presence of these occupations in the French-Canadian movement may be attributed only in part to obstacles in the Quebec economy and educational institutions. Linguistic and cultural factors may have played a more important role by limiting job possibilities in English-speaking America and restricting most of them to the institutional networks in the *petits Canadas,* where a teacher, a nurse, or a clerk could still work in French. This hypothesis is corroborated by the fact that the only occupational group whose representation in the two movements were comparable was "servant"—hardly the kind of job requiring advanced language skills.

The other striking difference between the two movements is represented by the wide gap in the proportions of blue-collar workers. Not only was the French-Canadian proportion nearly twice as high that of its Anglo-Canadian counterpart, but the majority of the occupations were in industrial production, with a large concentration in textile manufacturing. Clearly French-Canadian migration traditions had survived well into the twentieth century. Though at a lesser rate than in previous generations, French-Canadian women continued to seek economic and social betterment in New England textile mills.

Although all regions of Canada contributed to this occupational profile, the component originating from the Maritimes stands out from the rest of Anglo-Canada, both for the large number of wage-working women relative to the region's population and for the degree of overrepresentation of certain occupations. This was in fact the region that sent the highest number of teachers and of students, most of them in nursing and other health sectors. Moreover, in comparison with the largest sending province, Ontario, the number of nurses departing from the Maritimes was decidedly overrepresented. Yet, it was also the region that sent, in absolute numbers, the largest contingent of domestics.[65] The strong presence of these two groups on opposite sides of the occupational spectrum defies easy explanation and calls for microstructural studies of the region. Our data, however, confirm a trend that had characterized the out-migration movement from the Maritimes during much of the nineteenth century, namely, the presence of single young women flowing in large numbers to the "Boston state"; the migration traditions established by those women entering largely domestic service and shoe- and textile-manufacturing survived well into the twentieth century. But now work in factories and mills had largely given way to employment in health and educational institutions and in commercial organizations.

This occupational characteristic of the Maritimes movement could not but be reflected in its demographic profile. Unlike the overall Anglo-Canadian movement, the Maritimes in fact sent more women than men; and among them the proportion of the young adults (age fifteen to twenty-nine) was 60.3 percent, considerably higher than the proportion nationwide (44 percent). Within this latter age group, Maritimer out-migrants stood even more apart from the rest of the movement, since the proportion of single young adults, 71 percent, contrasts significantly to the 49.8 percent of the national movement.[66]

Clearly, out-migration from the Maritimes stands as one of the leading illustrations of the importance of regional diversity in assessing the significance of Anglo-Canadian migration to the United States, and of the central place held by women in that movement.

V

The wide variety in local economic contexts within both English and French Canada had undoubtedly a determining effect in shaping the occupational physiognomy of the two movements. Besides the possibility it opens for innumerable microhistorical studies, it allows us to differentiate between those who migrated to escape poverty and the fear of an uncertain economic future from those who drew from their local universe the skills and education enabling them to seek further advancement south of the border. But between the extremes of a hard-pressed farm laborer and an ambitious professional nurse, between the two types of motivations that prompted them to move on, there is a wide spectrum of local, family, and personal circumstances that bring us closer to the role of human agency in the migration process. As conceived here, human agency manifests itself not merely in the assessment an emigrant makes concerning wage rates, working conditions, and the potential for career advancement, but also in the extent to which the emigrant relies upon social relations to make the migration project possible and successful. Viewed from this perspective, the experiences of Anglo- and French-Canadian out-migrants converge substantially.

Much like French Canadians, a significant number of Anglo-Canadians traveled within migration fields whose spatial and cultural contours had been shaped by the moves of previous generations of migrants. And as in the case of their French-Canadian counterparts, the presence of kin and friends played a considerable role in the choice of a new place in which to work, live, and raise a family. A migrant like George Beattie who, as he told federal researchers in 1912, had "no relatives, no friends in the world" was a rare occurrence, yet one that in its different variants was much a part of the migration experience. He had migrated to the United States in 1900 at the age of thirty-seven, attracted by the higher wages he was certain to find south of the border. When in 1912 federal researchers interviewed him, he had lost his wife and children—he did not explain how. Moreover, respiratory problems had forced him to quit his trade—he was a carriage painter—and his work record had become a long succession of outdoor laboring jobs that had taken him to various parts of the lower Great Lakes region: "loading and unloading cars" for the Adams Express Company in Chicago; "placing cakes of ice into the ice-house" in southern Wisconsin, a job he left after two days because of the unsanitary conditions in the fifty-men-per-room bunkhouse provided by the company; and "loading cars with cakes of ice" for the Condensed Milk Company in Juneau Junction, Wisconsin, a job that lasted two weeks because of the arrival of warm weather. Back in Chicago, he moved from one job to another while living in rooming houses and cheap hotels. Between jobs he shoveled coal for a steamer and helped in the kitchen of a restaurant. Then he was back again in southern Wisconsin for more of the same.

While recounting his long job history, George reminded his interviewers that "the life of a carriage painter lasts ten years once tuberculosis or blood poisoning hits you." He opened his notebook and showed the ten jobs he had held during the summer prior to the interview: from a one-month job as a farmhand to a two-day job at a rescue mission "preparing the auditorium for a charity ball." While in Chicago, George had sought companionship by attending the meetings organized by the Brotherhood Association, a local workers' welfare organization headed by one J. E. Howe. But although he liked the speakers, he was disappointed by the attitude he saw in most of the attendants: "[those] people come only to get free coffee and rolls and do not pay any attention to what is being said." Still, George had not given up his dream: saving "enough money to start a carriage painting shop and oversee the work."[67]

The identification of migration fields extending southward from English Canada is a much more arduous task because of the much wider range of destinations among Anglo-Canadians even within regions, a diversity that contrasts significantly to the high degree of spatial concentration marking French-Canadian emigration. Moreover, very seldom did Anglo-Canadians create those visible signs of ethnicity that the historian finds in most districts of immigrant settlement, and certainly among French Canadians. This was as true of a metropolis like Detroit, which comprised a large number of Anglo-Canadians, as it was of smaller industrial cities like Syracuse and Watertown, New York, or Lynn, Massachusetts, in which Anglo-Canadians made up a significant portion of the population.[68]

Despite the lack of these ethnic institutional markers, the data on border crossings allow us to identify some important migration fields in Anglo-Canadian migration.

Conventional wisdom has long stressed the ongoing back-and-forth traveling of Canadian migrants across the border. But this was practiced only by a minority of Canadians working and living in well-circumscribed transborder districts. Such traveling was certainly typical for people living in cities such as Windsor or Sault Sainte Marie, Ontario, who commuted daily to work in the adjacent U.S. city. But they were not migrants, and when U.S. border control was intensified through stricter regulations, Canadians considered eligible were provided with special "commuter" permits.[69]

For the majority of Canadians—English and French alike—who moved to the United States, migration was undertaken to maximize their earning potential, either to finance a future resettlement back in Canada or to consolidate their economic situation in their new society. The only public source that enlightens us on this phenomenon, the Immigration Commission's report, documents the number of trips that a sample of Canadian-born industrial workers made back to the Dominion. It found that nearly half of them (47.8 percent) had not left the United States since their immigration, and 23.9 percent had made only one trip. Those who made two or more trips were 28.6 percent, most of them longtime residents.[70]

The *Index* data provide us with a rare longitudinal view on the migration experience of U.S.-bound Canadians by allowing us to identify those migrants who had experienced one or more previous sojourns in the United States. Among them were David Watkins, William Bailey, and Sadie Karlofsky. A fifty-three-year-old fisherman from Atwoods Brook, Nova Scotia, David's migration to Massachusetts in 1917 was his second one; he had previously worked and lived in that state from 1914 to 1915. William had lived in the United States longer, from 1905 to 1909, in Lowell, Massachusetts; and now in 1911 this young and unmarried machinist from Kingston, Ontario, was heading to Detroit where a friend of his worked. Sadie had previously been in the United States; she was one of a small but significant number of Canadian out-migrants who had been born in the United States. A twenty-year-old bookkeeper, she had subsequently moved with her family to Winnipeg and likely became part of the growing Jewish community in that city. When in 1923 she recrossed the border heading for Brooklyn, New York, she declared to immigration officials that she had lived in New York in 1912 and 1919.[71]

Experiences such as these were common among a large portion of the Anglo-Canadian out-migrating population, much as they were among French Canadians. If children aged fourteen and under are excluded, as much as 42.7 percent of the remaining population had previously lived in the United States.[72] This means that people like David Watkins and William Bailey had been "return migrants" before moving again to the United States and, as such, would constitute essential data for a separate study on return migration.[73] Moreover, this pattern occurred in all provinces and regions of the Dominion. It was most frequent in British Columbia, where two out of three out-migrants had previously lived in the United States. In the three Maritime provinces, on the other hand, only one out-migrant in three had had a similar experience. Such variations may also be detected at the city level; Hamilton, Ontario, with a rate of repeat migration of only 28.4 percent, contrasts significantly with Winnipeg, whose corresponding rate was 50.2 percent.

But as frequent as this pattern appears to have been, it only hints at the existence of migration fields. The Index data, however, open a rare window into the extent of these fields by indicating whether the places of the previous residence in the United States were the same as the destinations now chosen by our repeat border crossers. Edward Bulstrode, for instance, a twenty-four-year-old machinist from Walkerton, Ontario, migrated in June 1911 to Detroit, the same city in which he had lived from 1900 to 1903 and where he had an uncle.[74] Like him, 57.5 percent of all repeat migrants chose the same state in which they had previously sojourned. In the case of British Columbia, for instance, 66.1 percent of repeat migrants returned to Washington State, where they had already lived. Similarly, 59.5 percent of Maritime repeat migrants chose locations in Massachusetts, to which they had previously migrated.[75]

In some respects, these data can be read as simply confirming the pattern of intraregional migration discussed earlier in this and the previous chapter. But they also allow us to look beyond the mere geographical dimension of that pattern; for the act of returning also indicated familiarity with the chosen destination—with its labor markets, its local institutions, and often the people one had contacted. This must have certainly been the case among the Maritimers who returned to Massachusetts, and in particular among the large proportion (50.4 percent) for whom migration meant going back to Boston and its immediate surroundings; or among the majority of Winnipeg repeat migrants returning to Minnesota, 75 percent of whom went to Minneapolis; or yet again among Toronto repeat migrants who moved to Michigan, 91.1 percent of whom returned to Detroit.[76]

The many Canadian and American locations linked by ongoing migration help us see this southward population flow as endowed with a degree of spatial rationality that resulted from the migrants' knowledge of their destinations, a knowledge derived from their actual experience. This knowledge, however, could also result from information reaching prospective Canadian migrants from siblings, relatives, and friends working and living in the envisaged destination. Mary McDonald, for instance, was part of the majority of Anglo-Canadians who were migrating to the United States for the first time. Yet when in 1923 she decided to leave her Nova Scotia town and migrate south of the border, her destination acquired a larger meaning than merely a place to work. For in Brockton, Massachusetts, this twenty-year-old store clerk had an aunt who had most likely been in contact with her and made her transition to the new environment easier and less risky. For twenty-one-year-old Stanley Murdock, migrating to the United States was also a new experience. This meat cutter from Wallaceburg, Ontario, had a friend in Detroit, his chosen destination, who most likely had provided information on job opportunities and helped him in his search for work and housing.[77]

As table 10 shows, a majority of Anglo-Canadians, whether repeat or first-time migrants, made the move under the auspices of family members and various types of kin (about 55 percent). For another small but signifi-

Table 10. *Anglo-Canadian and French-Canadian Migrants by Type of Relationship with the Reference Person(s) at Destination (in percentages)*

	Anglo-Canadians	French-Canadians
Spouse/son/daughter	11.1	11.0
Parents/brother/sister	24.7	27.2
Other kin (uncle, aunt, cousin, in-laws)	18.8	26.7
Friend	12.1	8.3
Board/hotel	1.2	0.4
Institutions (including companies)	4.8	3.2
Other	7.6	10.6
Undetermined	19.7	12.6
N	11,930	4,396

cant minority of 12.1 percent, the contact person at the destination was a friend. Even when well-delineated migration fields had not emerged—or are not visible through the available data—nearly four out of five Anglo-Canadians relied on close social relations when undertaking their migration. However important jobs and career opportunities may have been for prospective migrants, these data invite us to look beyond the mere economic dynamics of migration and appreciate its social character: personal loyalty, solidarity, and a willingness to share a positive experience with less fortunate townspeople, be they siblings, relatives, or friends.

If approached from this perspective, the similarity between the Anglo- and French-Canadian movements should not appear surprising. Despite the significant differences in their occupational backgrounds and in the types of labor markets they sought out in the United States, both movements received a comparable support from the network of social relations that had been built by generations of migrants. The only noticeable difference between the two groups was the larger proportion among French Canadians of more distant types of kin (uncles, cousins, in-laws), a factor that no doubt would find its explanation in the demographic history of French Canada and in the higher degree of spatial concentration of its migrants.

VI

For Canadian migrants headed for the United States, the border was not a mere point of transit concretized by a routine interview with an immigration official. It was also a legal entity, a prescribed stop in the course of which they were subjected to a variety of controls and their admissibility was formally declared or denied.

For the majority of our migrants, this first encounter with the American state was soon put behind, as they resumed their journey of hope to the envisaged destinations. But for a significant minority, both Anglo- and French Canadians, the border turned out to be an insurmountable barrier, one that put an end to their migration project and forced them back to their towns or villages. For J. M., the journey that would have taken him from his New Brunswick town of Saint John to an unspecified location in the United States came to an end on 24 February 1923 at Calais, Maine. There this nineteen-year-old unmarried laundry worker of English ancestry was declared a criminal and classified as "debarred"—the official term used for those whose entry was denied. We do not know what his alleged crime was or the evidence that immigration officials used against him. Unless he was detained and turned over to Canadian authorities, he most likely returned home to his mother, whose name he had given as reference.[78]

During the era under study, aborted migration projects such as J. M.'s were a minority, but frequent enough as to make up 6.7 percent of all attempted entries. Prospective migrants who got caught in the nets set by immigration authorities were only slightly more numerous among French Canadians (8 percent) than among their Anglo-Canadian counterparts (6.1 percent), another point of convergence between the two movements. Apart from the conspicuous absence of people belonging to elite occupations in both the white- and blue-collar sectors, the debarred included children and adults, men and women, single and married, and came from a variety of regional and occupational backgrounds.[79] In fact, all the social ethnolinguistic and demographic attributes that have been the focus of the above analysis, including the distinction between English and French Canadians, recede into the background, leaving only one essential attribute: the migrant's status as a physical and juridical persona, and his or her qualifications for being allowed to cross the border and become an asset to American society.

The variety of debarred cases emerging from our sample sheds some rare light on the kind of obstacles prospective Canadian migrants could face, and the extent to which the border acted as an economic, moral, judicial, and health filter.

One of the major considerations was whether the migrant's economic conditions were precarious and whether he or she would become a public charge in the United States. This was, for instance, the assessment that immigration officials made when J. E. stood before them on 19 July 1924. A twenty-seven-year-old Montreal riveter, J. E. was accompanied by his wife and their three children. He must have certainly argued that once in Holyoke he would earn enough to support himself and his family; but his argument was of no avail, for immigration officials declared him "liable to public charge" and stamped "debarred" on the border manifest, thus putting an end to this family's plans.[80] Economic concerns also led immigration officials to screen Canadians who sought to move to a given location after having contracted a job with a U.S. employer, a flagrant violation of the contract-labor law. We don't know whether R. E. M., a twenty-five-year-old man of Scottish ancestry from Peterborough, Ontario, was unaware of the existence of that law or whether border officials tricked him into admitting that a job had been set aside for him by a Buffalo employer. Perhaps the name and the Buffalo address that this painter gave border officials was the clue that led them to terminate his journey at Niagara Falls.[81] Still, the possibility that some debarred migrants were unaware of the contract-labor provisions must have been real, judging from the several cases in our sample in which the name of a U.S. employer appears in the manifest. One of these was W. P., a twenty-four-year-old Nova Scotian farm laborer who had previously moved to Alberta and from there sought, in November 1916, to cross the border at Sweet Grass, Montana. We don't know whether he volunteered the information or not, but the name of his Montana employer is clearly spelled out, followed by the reason for his debarring.[82]

Canadians, like all immigrants allowed into the United States, had to be healthy human beings, physically, mentally, and morally, if the gates were to be opened—a condition not all of them met, at least not in the judgment of immigration officials. Physical fitness tests carried out by medical personnel could of course detect those physiological problems that disqualified a migrant from crossing the border. Frequent causes for debarring migrants could be generic, such as "physically defective." Others might be more precise and include diagnoses such as tuberculosis, deafness, dumbness, epilepsy, arteriosclerosis, or valvular heart disease. Quite significantly, the classification "liable to public charge" was often associated with one of these health conditions.

Much more complex and less objective must have been the procedure followed to declare someone insane. The scene during which, one spring day in 1914, C. H. was barred from entering the United States for being judged insane may only be left to one's imagination. This forty-year-old upholsterer from Oakville, Ontario, on his way to Detroit, a city where he had previously lived from 1911 to 1913, may very well have become insane during his American stay or after his return, back in Ontario.[83] The barring of another Ontario man gives reason for puzzlement. A twenty-three-year-old single man from Stratford, he too had previously been in the United States; and now, a few years later, border officials were declaring insane this man whose occupation, a barber, forced him to spend most of his working days with a razor in his hand.[84]

Insanity was the most severe case of mental disorder in our sample.

A milder form, also resulting in the debarring of migrants, was "feeble mindedness."

Equally stringent was the control exerted on the moral character of migrants, though in these cases one is left to wonder about the source of the information that immigration inspectors used to justify their debarring. One doubts whether women like Hatty L. or Anna R. would have declared at the border that they were prostitutes. But this was the official reason immigration agents wrote down to deny them entry. Unless the agents relied on informants' reports (whether true or false), their personal, subjective assessment of the woman standing in front of them must have played a key role. Was it because Hatty, a waitress from London, Ontario, was only eighteen years old, single, and traveling alone? Or was it that she gave no reference person in Detroit, the city for which she was headed that hot July day of 1910? Or was it the way she dressed, talked, and gestured that aroused suspicion among the Detroit border agents, who might have been familiar with the red-light subculture of that city?[85] Similar questions come to mind in the case of Anna, a forty-two-year-old French-Canadian widow. Anna had been in the United States several times before, and recently she had moved to Saskatchewan. From there she sought to reach the city of Omaha, Nebraska, in April 1911, but was stopped at the Winnipeg border crossing and declared a prostitute. Unlike Hatty, she supplied a name and address of a reference in the United States, but she did not provide any specific occupation.[86]

Women stopped at the border and charged with prostitution were few compared to those whose entry in the United States was prevented on the ground that they were criminals. And what is equally surprising is the fact that women fell into this latter category as frequently as men. Once again, we do not know on what kind of evidence these charges were based, nor whether the crime label was used with such a latitude as to include prostitution. Thus, for instance, our source leaves us in the dark as to the kind of crimes A. R. was found guilty of. Her profile was typical of the thousands of Maritime women who for generations had migrated to New England mill towns. Single and twenty-eight years of age, this Nova Scotian cotton weaver had been in the United States several times. But on December 1917 she was stopped at the border while on her way to Bridgeport, Connecticut, and debarred as a criminal.[87] Still, some cases of debarring lead us to suspect that the crime must have often been associated with moral behavior. In the case of M. M., for instance, who was stopped on her way to New York, where her sister awaited her, border officials were more precise in specifying the reason for debarring her: next to "criminal" they wrote "adultery."[88] Perhaps this Ontario-born thirty-two-year-old woman, who also had previously lived in the United States and had subsequently moved to Montreal, aroused the agents' suspicion. For, although she declared herself to be married, she made no reference to her husband and, besides, stated that she had no occupation.

The border officials debarring M. M. and other persons accused of crime may have acted so on the basis of hard evidence. Yet we know that suspicion was sometimes sufficient ground to reach a conclusion that precluded a migrant's entry. This was how the officials at Rouses Point, one of the border posts between Quebec and New York, proceeded when B. R. sought to reach Plattsburg. A thirty-two-year-old widow from Montreal with no stated occupation, she was debarred because, as the officials wrote in the manifest, she was a "suspected criminal."[89]

This is not to say that the migration flow to the south did not include in its midst some real criminals, however few in number. The Canadian/U.S. case was far from being the only one in which migrating was synonymous with escaping to another country in the hope of reducing the chances of being caught.

But the border performed most often its role as filter with men and women who were guilty only of being illiterate. Illiteracy became one of the most frequent grounds for debarring immigrants after the enactment by Congress of the literacy law in February 1917. Enforcement of the literacy regulation interrupted the migration of Anglo-Canadians, French Canadians, and foreign-born Canadian citizens. By far, however, the majority of migrants declared illiterate were French Canadians, at a frequency four times higher than that of the other two groups. The majority were middle-aged and older men, often of a rural background. M. D., for instance, was fifty-eight years old and a farmer from Saint Michel, Quebec. He had been in New Hampshire several times before, but now, in 1923, the literacy law turned him into an "undesirable," and his attempt to reach his daughter in Trasburg, Vermont, came to an end at a border crossing.[90] But the literacy requirement could also stop young Anglo-Canadians, men like C. D., a nineteen-year-old teamster from Halifax, Nova Scotia, who in May 1922 sought to reach Salem, Massachusetts, where his father lived. C. D.'s debarring, however, must have produced a family drama, for he was traveling with his mother, and one may safely speculate that the purpose of their journey was to reunite the family.[91]

J. L. was among the first Canadians to fall victim to the new regulation when in June 1917 immigration officials debarred him for being illiterate. A retired sixty-nine-year-old man from Sainte-Flavie, Quebec, J. L. was a carrier of migration traditions that for generations had linked rural Quebec to New England mill towns. He had been in Fall River, Massachusetts, several times, as early as 1882 and as late as 1914. When the gate to the United States closed in front of him, he was once again on his way to Fall River, possibly to spend the last years of his life with one of his sons.[92] He probably did not even bother to take the test. He probably never managed to make sense out of a law that declared undesirable a man who in his modest way had contributed so much to the American economy.

VII

That same economy that had helped fulfill the hope for a better life for hundreds of thousands of Canadians was also responsible for bringing the migration movement to a virtual stop. The October 1929 crash and the rapid worsening of the American economy had an immediate impact on the flow of population from Canada. With unemployment rising stubbornly and fearfully month after month, the U.S. Immigration and Naturalization Service moved to close the door to Canadians wishing to enter the United States in search of work.[93]

Yet, the movement of Canadians southward had already started to decline before the Great Depression hit North America. The year 1927 marked a sharp decline that became irreversible in the ensuing few years. By 1928, the rate of migration had in fact become a little over half what it had been the previous year, and 1929 witnessed an even smaller number of border crossings. As the twenties drew to a close, the migration flow southward had shrunk to a trickle of mostly single young men and women determined to have their share of the opportunities their forerunners had enjoyed. They were the last remnants of a long and rich migration tradition.

The turning point, however, came after 1929. By 1930 Canadian entries to the United States amounted to a few thousand—only 24 percent of what they had been the previous year and a mere 17 percent of the 1928 flow. Beyond their individual and human significance, these moves stand as historical reminders that a long era had come to an end.[94]

The closing of the border to job seekers limited entries largely to cases of family reunification. Kathleen Boyd and Rose Blanche Charbonneau exemplify these moves. An eighteen-year-old housewife from New Brunswick, Kathleen crossed the border in December 1930 at Houlton, Maine, and traveled to Mars Hill, Maine, where she joined her husband. The purpose of Rose Blanche's move was similar: to join her husband in Stowe, Vermont. In her case, however, her husband came to Roxton Pond, Quebec, to pick her up, and the two made the journey together, crossing the border at North Troy, Vermont, in June 1930.[95]

Wives moving to join their husbands had become by 1930 the most frequent pattern of family reunification, though not the only one; siblings and children were also among those who crossed the border to rejoin their families. Anna Howlett, for instance, a twenty-five-year-old schoolteacher from Andover, New Brunswick, had a brother living in the Maine town to which she moved in September 1930. Lydia Aubut, a two-year-old toddler born in Kenogami, Quebec, was brought by her aunt to her foster father, who lived in Millinocket, Maine.[96]

Family and kin ties were also at the base of the other frequent pattern of cross-border mobility in 1930. It involved Canadian immigrants who were returning to their homes in the United States after a brief sojourn in Canada. Vera Allen, a twenty-eight-year-old married woman from New Brunswick, had resided in the United States for the past thirteen years. Her short visit to Canada was likely motivated by a desire to visit her mother, who lived in Lawrence Station, New Brunswick. She then re-crossed the border at Calais, Maine, in April 1930 on her way to Rumford Falls, Maine, where her husband and perhaps her children were awaiting her. And Marie Jeanne Chamberland, another New Brunswick married woman, reentered the United States in April 1930 to rejoin her husband in Van Buren, Maine; her brief trip to Canada had taken her to her native town of Saint Leonard, where her father lived.[97] By 1930, Canadians were crossing the border for much the same reason that they crossed provincial borders or that Americans traveled across state lines: primarily to keep family and kin relations alive.

And then occasionally there were people like D. B., M. W., or Q. Q., who, either out of ignorance or stubbornness, tried their luck only to see themselves debarred by immigration officers. The latter, a nineteen-year-old laborer from Megantic, Quebec, told border officials that he wanted "to work in the woods" and even provided the name of the Maine company where he intended to seek work. Probably he was not even given a literacy test, for the officials wrote "suspected illiterate" in the manifest and declared him "liable to public charge."[98]

Throughout 1930, while Canadians and Americans alike struggled to make ends meet in the hope that the economic scourge that had descended upon their countries would soon come to an end, life along the Canadian-U.S. border had become quiet. Gone were the trains filled with people carrying trunks and suitcases; gone were the long lineups in front of U.S. border officials. The "line" had ceased to be the compulsory stop it had been for tens of thousands of Canadians on their way to a new life. Few Canadians now cared to look beyond it except when thinking of their dear ones, who most likely shared the same fear and insecurity.

Fig. 16. Canada-bound immigrants playing leapfrog on the SS *Empress* of Britain, ca. 1910. Courtesy of the National Archives of Canada, C 9661.

CHAPTER FIVE

❖

The Remigration Movement from Canada

In February 1924 Abraham Bellow boarded a train in Montreal bound for Chicago. His wife Elisabeth and their children followed him shortly thereafter. The Bellows had lived in Montreal for about ten years and were part of a significant stream of Jews who had escaped czarist Russia and had found a new home in Canada. Some of the most vivid images of the Montreal neighborhood in which they first settled would later become part of the American literary heritage in the works of one of the Bellow children, nine-year-old Saul.[1] But they were also part of a wider population for whom Canada became a temporary home.

From the turn of the twentieth century to the onset of the Great Depression, in fact, one out of five persons who joined the migration flow from Canada to the United States was someone who had first immigrated to Canada and had resided there for a certain length of time.

In the historical literature on migration to North America only passing references to this phenomenon are made. The focus has largely been placed on the massive movement of nineteenth-century Britons who could benefit from the cheaper fares provided by imperial transatlantic transportation, and who, once in British North America, moved quickly to their final destination: the United States.[2] But Britons were not the only ones to pursue this trajectory. The lack of effective controls along the Canadian-U.S. border throughout much of the nineteenth century—coupled with the fact that, before 1891, states and not the federal government had jurisdiction over matters pertaining to immigration control—made Canada an important gate through which men and women of all nationalities sought to enter the United States legally or illegally. As shown in chapter 2, even the creation of a system of inspection along the entire boundary line did not prevent overseas immigrants from transiting through Canada, many of them sneaking through the border.

Historians will never know how many immigrants entered the United States illegally through the Canadian border. This fact, which may be seen as one limitation of this book, itself points to one role Canada unwillingly played in international and transatlantic migrations. Yet in this book we are not concerned with those migrants who used Canada as a legal and economic subterfuge. Rather, we are concerned with those who chose the Dominion as their country of immigration and who saw in it an opportunity for a better life. And their number kept increasing to such an extent that by the early decades of the twentieth century the rate of immigration to Canada relative to the country's population was higher than that of the world's leading migrant destination: the United States.[3] Yet, like the Bellows, many of these immigrants who had come to Canada to start a new life decided for economic or other reasons to migrate again, this time south of the border.

The biographical information provided by the *Soundex Index to Canadian Border Entries* makes it possible to identify this component of the population that crossed the Canada-U.S. border, allowing us to analyze a dimension of this migration movement that has long remained outside the concerns of historical scholarship: the extent to which Canada served as a country of intermediate migration for hundreds of thousands of immigrants, mostly Europeans, whose ultimate destination became the United States.

In some respects this phenomenon could be viewed as a form of step migration, but at a transcontinental level and involving at least three countries. Just as migration, whether internal or international, frequently entailed more than one move before a final destination could be found, so these Europeans who had first chosen Canada as their country of immigration found it convenient later on to move again, this time by crossing the border and seeking a better life in the United States.

Of course, this is an ex post facto consideration, valid mainly for analytical purposes, as we cannot know if these migrants consciously pursued this trajectory from the moment they set their compass toward North America, or if their decision to remigrate to the United States was one that matured only during their stay in Canada. But these two courses were by no means mutually exclusive, and as this chapter will attempt to show, both happened. The decision to emigrate and remigrate is an issue that defies quantification. Yet, the analysis of some key structural, conjunctural, and political factors surrounding the remigration movement will help provide some answers; at the same time, it will help us to define with greater precision the particular place that Canada held in the international flows of populations and labor, and thus will situate the Dominion more firmly in the workings of an Atlantic socioeconomic structure.

I

Who were these remigrants? What regions or districts of Canada did they leave and what were their preferred destinations in the United States? Do their demographic and occupational profiles shed additional light on the dynamics of local and continental labor markets? Are there distinctive patterns that set these remigrants apart from the millions of Canadians who crossed the U.S. border?

Given the wide range of nationalities and countries of birth in our sample, we have classified them into four major groups, adopting a geographical criterion that is commonly used in migration historical literature and that also takes into account Canada's particular relationship with European immigration. The single most important regional group among remigrants was the one originating from *Great Britain*—representing nearly 30 percent of our sample. Remigrants originating from *western European* countries constituted the smallest proportion of the movement (8 percent). More highly represented were remigrants originating from *Scandinavia and Finland* (12 percent). The largest group (50 percent), however, consisted of people originating from *central-eastern and southern Europe* (see table 11). The majority had come from Russia and the various countries belonging to the Austro-Hungarian empire. As to the portion originating from southern Europe, it was made up overwhelmingly of Italians. Although population statistics of these multiple movements are nonexistent, the picture that emerges from our sample suggests strongly a direct relationship between influxes of immigration to Canada and remigration. In fact British and central-eastern Europeans were the largest components of immigrants to Canada, and they had come from the regions on which recruiting efforts had been concentrated. Hence, there were more of them "on the move" throughout the North-American economy than was the case with other European groups.[4]

All Canadian provinces produced their share of remigrants, although the major contributors were those that had the largest immigrant populations. Thus, Ontario ranked first as a province of departure, followed by the ensemble of the western provinces. In Quebec the remigration

Table 11. *European-Born Remigrants by Major Groups and Country of Origin, 1906–30
(in percentages;* N = *4.638)*

British Isles	29.4
England	51.2
Scotland	27.3
Ireland	16.8
Others	4.7
Western Europe	8.4
Germany	34.5
Belgium	25.4
France	15.8
Netherlands	12.6
Others	11.7
Central-eastern and southern Europe	50.1
Russia	34.9
Italy	26.8
Austria	16.3
Greece	4.2
Hungary	3.9
Poland	3.6
Romania	3.2
Others	7.1
Scandinavia and Finland	12.1
Sweden	38.6
Norway	26.5
Denmark	9.5
Finland	25.4

phenomenon originated almost exclusively from Montreal, which should not be surprising since it was the leading destination for immigrants to Quebec.

This correlation between immigrant spatial concentrations and remigration is confirmed by the extremely low performance of the Atlantic provinces—the Canadian region that received the smallest volume of immigrants on account of the chronic crisis marking its economy throughout much of the era.

Enlarging this spatial analysis by including the destinations brings out the regional character of the movement (see table 12). Preferred destinations are shared in common by both remigrants and Canadian out-migrants, which reinforces one of the main theses of this book, namely, that migration from Canada to the United States occurred largely within the parameters of continental regions.

In the choice of destination, physical distance seems to have played a significant role, since nearly two-thirds of all destinations were in U.S. border states. Of these, the states of New York, Michigan, and Washington

Table 12. Remigrants to the United States by Canadian Regions/Provinces of Departure and Major States of Destination, 1906–30 (in percentages; N = 4.638)

	Maritimes	Quebec	Ontario	Prairies	British Columbia	Province Unspecified	Total
New York	12.2	40.4	32.1	5.7	1.8	19.0	23.3
Michigan	4.8	7.7	27.5	7.7	0.5	28.8	15.7
Washington	3.2	1.1	1.5	10.4	73.0	13.1	13.3
Minnesota	—	1.0	6.0	20.9	1.8	4.2	6.8
Massachusetts	33.0	11.7	4.1	2.8	1.1	2.6	6.0
Illinois	3.7	7.4	5.3	9.3	2.0	3.6	5.8
Pennsylvania	72.2	8.5	6.2	3.7	0.3	6.5	5.7
Ohio	1.6	3.5	5.2	3.0	0.8	3.3	3.6
California	0.5	1.1	1.8	4.0	7.7	2.6	2.8
North Dakota	1.1	0.4	0.4	9.1	0.3	2.9	2.2
New Jersey	2.7	3.3	2.0	0.8	0.3	0.7	1.7
Montana	—	0.3	0.2	6.3	2.1	1.6	1.6
Maine	11.2	2.0	0.2	0.4	—	1.0	1.1
Wisconsin	—	0.4	1.2	2.9	—	2.0	1.2
Connecticut	1.6	2.3	0.8	0.6	—	0.7	1.0
Indiana	1.6	1.0	1.0	0.8	—	1.0	0.9
Oregon	—	—	0.1	1.9	3.1	—	0.8
Other states	10.6	7.8	4.3	9.5	5.2	6.5	6.4
Total	100	100	100	100	100	100	100

were by far the most frequent choices; taken together they received more than half of the remigrants. They were followed, in order of importance, by Minnesota, Massachusetts, Illinois, and Pennsylvania.

One striking aspect of this spatial configuration is the near absence of the New England region from the list of preferred destinations. Although Massachusetts did attract a sizable flow of remigrants, the low performance of the other New England states confirms the role of distance as well as the correlation between immigration to Canada and remigration to the United States. The Canadian provinces that normally supplied New England with large contingents of Canadian out-migrants, namely, the Maritimes and Quebec, had few remigrants to send out simply because—with the exception of Montreal—immigration had been extremely limited.

Remigrants moving to the United States departed from various socioeconomic settings: metropolitan areas, middle-sized cities, and small frontier towns. Of course significant variations occurred among the different nationalities, as will become clear when the demographic and occupational dimensions of the movement are discussed. For instance, remigrants from Scandinavia as well as from some central and eastern European countries had a greater propensity to depart from agrarian districts and small

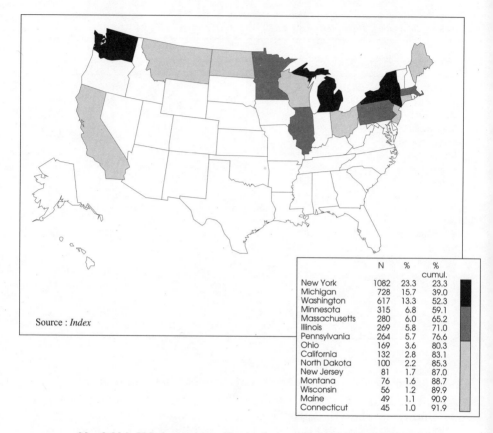

	N	%	% cumul.
New York	1082	23.3	23.3
Michigan	728	15.7	39.0
Washington	617	13.3	52.3
Minnesota	315	6.8	59.1
Massachusetts	280	6.0	65.2
Illinois	269	5.8	71.0
Pennsylvania	264	5.7	76.6
Ohio	169	3.6	80.3
California	132	2.8	83.1
North Dakota	100	2.2	85.3
New Jersey	81	1.7	87.0
Montana	76	1.6	88.7
Wisconsin	56	1.2	89.9
Maine	49	1.1	90.9
Connecticut	45	1.0	91.9

Source : *Index*

Map 3. Main U.S. destinations of foreign-born residents of Canada, 1906–30

towns associated with natural resource industries than did British remigrants. Yet, in all the groups that made up the remigration movement, cities figured preeminently as their last residence before heading south.

Some remigrants had lived and worked in cities ever since their arrival to Canada. Others, particularly those involved in some of the highly seasonal resource industries, had moved to the city in search of steadier employment. Among the central and eastern European remigrants residing in Ontario, for instance, 37 percent departed from the two most important industrial centers, namely, Toronto and Hamilton. Cities with populations of ten thousand and over were the preferred places of departure for another 33 percent of the group, and the remaining 30 percent had resided in small towns and districts spread throughout the province.[5]

Increasingly, moreover, the city became a logical destination for the many immigrants who had tried, without much luck, to become independent homesteaders and had to join the army of wage labor, often permanently. As for immigrants who had found work in resource industries, the prevailing labor market in this sector—with its seasonality, harsh working conditions, often substandard wages, and consequent high labor turnover—led them to make a number of moves that sooner or later brought them to the city. But for these men on the move, the Canadian city was not simply a place to seek steadier employment; it was also a center of information on job opportunities existing in nearby U.S. cities and districts, as well as a good place to join one of the ethnic networks that were bridging the two countries. So the city became a springboard for yet another move.

Like most migration movements, this one too experienced fluctuations engendered by economic conjunctures and international events. Although remigration to the United States continued until the coming of the Great Depression (thereafter it subsided to a trickle), it was by far most intensive during the years prior to the end of World War I.

This pattern constitutes yet another clear indication of the direct relationship between immigrant influx to Canada and remigration to the United States. As is well known, the Great War brought transatlantic migration to a near halt; and even though European emigration to Canada resumed at the end of the war, its volume was much more limited because of the rise of restrictionist sentiment and the unstable condition of the postwar Canadian economy. The decline of newcomers to Canada meant that there were fewer candidates for remigration.

It should not be surprising then if over 80 percent of the remigration movement among central-eastern and southern Europeans occurred before 1919. The imbalance was even more pronounced among Italians, 91 percent of whom remigrated to the United States before that date.

At the same time, to the extent that antiforeigner sentiment and restrictionist policies enhanced the preferential status of immigrants from Great Britain, the remigration movement within this group was little affected by those events. The outbreak of the war did, of course, interrupt temporarily their flow into Canada, but the resumption of immigration enlarged the population of potential remigrants; and many of them took the road to the south, as attested by the fact that throughout the first three decades of the century, more than 40 percent of the entire British remigration occurred after 1918.[6]

People who remigrated to the United States belonged to specific sectors of the immigrant population, and observing some of their key demo-

Table 13. European Remigrants by Sex and Age Groups, 1906–30 (N = 4.638)

	Western Europe		British Isles		Central-Eastern and Southern Europe		Scandinavia and Finland	
	N	%	N	%	N	%	N	%
Females								
0 to 14	15	13.4	37	9.3	38	11.8	5	6.1
15 to 29	50	44.6	193	48.5	176	54.5	51	62.2
30 to 44	33	29.5	130	32.7	80	24.8	20	24.4
45 to 59	9	8.0	25	6.3	15	4.6	4	4.9
60 and over	5	4.5	13	3.3	14	4.3	2	2.4
Subtotal	112	100	398	100	323	100	82	100
Males								
0 to 14	10	3.6	39	4.0	45	2.3	4	0.8
15 to 29	125	44.8	574	59.6	1,192	59.7	312	65.0
30 to 44	115	41.2	293	30.4	621	31.1	144	30.0
45 to 59	26	9.3	50	5.2	125	6.3	16	3.3
60 and over	3	1.1	7	0.7	12	0.6	4	0.8
Subtotal	279	100	963	100	1,995	100	480	100
Sex unknown	1		1		4		—	
Total	392		1,362		2,322		562	

graphic characteristics will shed further light on the movement.

The first important characteristic concerns its age structure. As table 13 shows, the majority of remigrants were fifteen to twenty-nine years old, at their prime working age; this group made up 58 percent of the entire movement. They were followed in importance by people aged thirty to forty-four, amounting to 31 percent. People aged forty-five and older constituted a very small portion (7 percent), and even smaller was the presence of children under fifteen (4 percent).

Of course, within this general demographic picture, some notable differences existed among the various European groups. Among remigrants from Scandinavia and Finland, for instance, children were virtually nonexistent, and this group had the largest proportion of people in the 15–29 age bracket (nearly two out of three). This was in sharp contrast with remigrants from western European countries, who had the smallest proportion of young adults belonging to that age group, and whose age structure was the most balanced compared to the other three groups.

Equally significant was the gender composition of the movement. To a

Table 14. *European-Born Remigrants by Major Groups, Marital Status, and Sex, 1906–30 (in percentages; N = 4.638)*

	Single M/F	Married M/F	Widowed M/F	Undetermined
British Isles	69.3/53.5	28.8/39.7	1.3/6.3	1.1
Western Europe	63.3/40.4	32.6/52.6	3.1/6.1	1.9
Central-eastern and southern Europe	55.9/35.5	42.3/55.5	1.3/7.8	1.7
Scandinavia and Finland	76.3/53.7	21.5/40.2	0.8/6.1	1.4

very large extent, remigration to the United States was overwhelmingly a male phenomenon, as four out of five persons who made up the movement were men. Here again, important differences may be observed among the various European groups, with the British group and the Scandinavian and Finnish group standing at opposite extremes. The latter group had, in fact, the smallest proportion of women (15 percent), while the British had the largest (29 percent).

This demographic characterization of the remigration movement would not be complete without taking into account the marital status of its members. The most striking feature of the movement, though one that should not come as a surprise at this point, was the numerical importance of unmarried men; one out of two remigrants was a single man, most likely a young adult (table 14).

But the demographic scenario was more complex than it might appear on the surface. The movement in fact included single and married persons both within the male and the female components of the population. And as one might expect, single men greatly outnumbered married men (by 63 to 35 percent; 2 percent were widowers). In the case of women the figures were virtually balanced (47 and 45 percent), but the number of widows was much higher (8 percent). Moreover, as with the other demographic aspects discussed above, significant differences existed within the various European groups. Thus, Scandinavians and Finns had by far the highest proportion of single men: three men out of four belonged to that category. This was in sharp contrast with men from central-eastern and southern Europe, who had the lowest proportion of singles (56 percent) and consequently the highest proportion of married men. Sharp variations can also be found among female remigrants. Central-eastern and southern Europeans had the highest rate of married women (55.5 percent) and consequently the lowest rate of singles (35.5 percent).

At the other extreme were women from Great Britain and from the Scandinavian and Finnish group, who had comparable rates of married women (39 and 40 percent) and the highest rates of single women (53 percent in both cases).

Thus, married men and women, although less numerous than their single counterparts, constituted an important component of the remigration movement. The fact, however, that children were a numerically insignificant portion of the movement points to two major patterns: one is that married remigrants were frequently childless couples or made up very small family units; the other pattern—involving primarily men—was that despite their married status, these remigrants were crossing the border alone simply because their children and wives had remained in Europe. Nearly 70 percent of all married remigrants entered the United States unaccompanied, and of these a very small minority declared the names of their partners as the contact person at destination.[7] One of them was Sarah Rubenstein, a twenty-one-year-old Russian-born married woman. She had left her parents in Russia, but on a December day in 1917 she traveled alone from Toronto to New York City to join her husband.[8] Although some of them were leaving their partners or families behind in Canada, perhaps in view of a subsequent reunion, again they were a small minority, judging from the fact that when asked to provide the name and location of a reference, such a person was most frequently a family member living in the home country. John Baritokis and Saverio Varteo are representative of this pattern. The former had migrated to Canada, leaving his wife in Crete and naming her as a reference. A thirty-year-old laborer, he resided in Montreal when he remigrated in October 1913 to Cleveland, Ohio, where his brother-in-law lived. Saverio Varteo also gave as a reference the name of his wife back in his home country. This thirty-four-year old laborer from Calabria, Italy, had reached Canada via New York in April 1906. Three years later he was in Edmonton, Alberta, from where he remigrated, choosing Boston as his destination.[9]

◆

In addition to indicating their high mobility, the demographic attributes of remigrants shed light on another important feature: their occupational composition and the relationship between remigration and labor market dynamics. An analysis of the occupations of this population reveals that virtually all categories of labor, including white-collar and professional employment, were represented and that, consequently, the remigration movement fed virtually all sectors of the U.S. economy. Obviously there were major differences in the degree of representativity of various skill levels and economic sectors. Equally important, significant differences existed among the various European groups that comprised the remigration movement.

One of the most striking aspects was the nearly insignificant presence of agriculturalists. Farmers were virtually absent from the movement. The rare cases were primarily western Europeans, but they made up only 5.7 percent of that group. The proportion of farm laborers was slightly higher; still, they were a small minority, representing less than 5 percent of all male remigrants.

This extremely low presence of agriculturalists is very revealing of the complexity of labor dynamics that underlay the remigration movement. When one considers that European agriculturalists had been the prime targets in the recruitment efforts pursued by both the Canadian government and private employers, and that a large volume of those newcomers had been directed to agrarian districts, one may find it puzzling that so few of them joined the remigration movement. While acknowledging that a substantial number of immigrant agriculturalists persisted in their attempt to settle permanently on the land and became independent farmers, it is very likely that many others failed in that endeavor and turned to other activities, whether in the resources sector or in the urban economy. Even more likely is the hypothesis that among the very many farm laborers brought to Canada, large numbers switched occupations and became general laborers.[10]

This no doubt explains the overwhelming presence of laborers in the movement: nearly one out of two male remigrants declared themselves laborers. The largest proportion was found among remigrants from central-eastern and southern Europe, where they made up two-thirds of all occupations. Laborer was the most important occupation in all our four European groups, although the proportion declined considerably within the British group, where they represented 20.6 percent of all occupations. In many other cases, immigrants arrived to Canada as laborers and remigrated to the United States still as general laborers, even if they had been engaged in specific sectors of the extractive industries. Working in lumber camps, for instance, as many recruited immigrants did, did not make them loggers. There were plenty of jobs in and around logging sites which did not require the skills of a logger but simply general laboring abilities. Hence, the proportion of remigrants who declared themselves loggers was even smaller than that of farm laborers.[11]

Clearly, remigration was not a movement growing out of the Canadian

Fig. 17. Railroad construction crews in the West, ca. 1900. Courtesy of the National Archives of Canada, C 46151.

countryside, though for many remigrants an agrarian district may have been the initial point of departure in a series of moves that ultimately brought them to the Canadian-U.S. border.

The variety of occupations involved—and the generic labels used in the *Soundex Index*, which often make it difficult to judge the skill level an occupation required or to identify the economic sector it belonged to—defy attempts to draw up a detailed classification. Nonetheless, the data allow us to observe some distinct trends that shed further light on the economic significance of the remigration movement.

Leaving aside the two occupational groups mentioned earlier, agriculturalist and laborer, the most frequent occupations can be grouped into three categories: white-collar occupations, small independent producers, and factory-related work. Whereas the latter two categories were found, in varying degrees, in all four European groups, white-collar remigrants were largely concentrated among the British and, to a lesser extent, the western European group. The white-collar category as used here is large enough to include the variety of occupations reflecting the growing tertiary sector of the economy. These ranged from a few highly specialized professions, such as architects, to the more frequent office clerks. No doubt, language proficiency and forms of training comparable to those practiced in North America are the key factors explaining the stronger white-collar presence among these two European groups.

Factory-related occupations, though clearly identifiable, were not as represented as one might expect of a society undergoing a rapid process of industrialization. Their relatively limited presence within the overall remigration movement was clearly a consequence of the overwhelming place taken by laborers. Once the laborer category is excluded, factory-related occupations were about equally divided between skilled and semi-skilled work. And here the general tendency was that the skilled occupations were found concentrated within the British group and the rest scattered among the other European groups.

Within this broad scenario, one can observe some specific tendencies that yield insight into the relation between occupations and cultural traditions.

For instance, Scandinavians and Finns, though representing the second smallest population within our groups of European remigrants, had by far the highest number of carpenters. Coming from societies in which wood had a prominent place in architecture, they gravitated to trades that made ample use of that natural resource. Although carpentry was a trade that could be practiced both in rural and urban contexts, the majority of these carpenters opted for the city. Prominent among the places in which they resided before remigration were major western cities such as Vancouver and Winnipeg. Likewise, their U.S. destinations overwhelmingly included urban centers west of the Great Lakes in cities ranging from small mining towns like Butte, Montana, to large centers like Minneapolis.[12]

Equally significant was a tendency that lay hidden within the overall occupational configuration of remigrants from central and eastern Europe, a group that, as mentioned above, was overwhelmingly composed of laborers. The *Index* makes it possible to identify the Jewish component of that population and focus on their occupations and remigration patterns. The great majority of them (70 percent) originated from Russia, the remaining portion from a variety of central-eastern European countries. Their occupational structure clearly sets them apart from the other remigrant groups.

Striking, indeed, is the extremely low presence of laborers in their midst (a mere 6.7 percent). The majority were skilled industrial workers and men practicing artisanal trades.[13] The single most important occupation among men was tailor, involving 23 percent of all Jewish remigrants. At the time of their departure for the United States, virtually all these tailors worked and lived in Canada's leading centers of clothing production, namely, Montreal, Toronto, and Winnipeg. These were also the cities that had the largest Jewish communities, in particular Montreal, where half of these tailors resided. In remigrating to the United States they chose destinations known for the significant presence of the clothing industry—New York City, Chicago, and Philadelphia—as well as smaller cities large enough to harbor a Jewish community, such as Buffalo, Cleveland, or Paterson, New Jersey.[14]

Some of the other skilled occupations declared by Jewish remigrants, such as machinist, were clearly associated with factory production. Others, such as blacksmith or bookbinder, could have very well been pursued independently. Independence, in fact, seems to be the element that most characterizes the occupational range of these Jewish remigrants, considering the significant number of artisans, merchants, and peddlers. The other significant element is the fact that many of these occupations were community oriented (bakers, butchers, and to some extent tailors). Undoubtedly, more than in any other European group, religious and cultural traditions affected the occupational composition of Jews and may in turn have played a central role both in the decision to remigrate and in the choice of destination. By the eve of World War I the network of Jewish communities extended throughout much of North America, making it easier for these remigrants to adjust to their newly chosen cities.

Although remigration was primarily practiced by men, a small but significant minority of women were part of the movement. Even if the majority of them (53 percent) declared no occupation or simply "housewife," several others brought to the U.S. economy their experience as wage earners. Given the relatively small number of wage-earning women, their occupational range was considerably narrower than that of men. Still, some clear tendencies emerge from the data.

The most conspicuous one is the significant presence of domestics. In fact, nearly half of the women who stated any occupation declared they were domestics; by far the largest concentration was to be found within the British and the Scandinavian and Finnish groups. As far as the British group is concerned, the high percentage reconfirms the close relationship between immigration to Canada and remigration, since during this era domestics figured preeminently in the recruiting efforts of Canadian immigration authorities—efforts directed primarily to the British Isles. By

Fig. 18. Immigrants for domestic service, Quebec, ca. 1911. Courtesy of the National Archives of Canada, PA 126101.

1911 immigrants represented 36 percent of all domestics in Canada, a large number of them brought over from Britain through special programs.[15] But considering their much smaller population, Scandinavian domestics were even more overrepresented than their British counterparts. In effect, a large proportion of Scandinavian women immigrating to Canada worked as domestics; they had earned a reputation as reliable, warm, and polite workers, and consequently some efforts were made to recruit them, primarily from Sweden.[16]

Also quite visible as a general tendency was the significant minority (17 percent) of remigrant women involved in white-collar occupations. Their presence was quite pronounced within the British and western European groups, with nursing work being the most frequent type of occupation.

The other important tendency among female remigrants was a concentration in occupations associated with the clothing and dress-making sectors, though it is difficult to assess the extent to which these occupations were practiced in factories or as independent trades. Occupations such as garment worker or mill-hand, for instance, clearly denoted a factory setting, whereas occupations such as embroiderer or seamstress were more likely to entail self-employment.[17]

One final observation should be made concerning the majority of women who declared no occupation or who defined themselves as housewives. Obviously they cannot be included in an occupational analysis. Still, we know from the immigration literature that lack of an officially designed occupation was far from keeping them away from labor markets or waged self-employment once their new destination had been reached and their life situation permitted it.

The various duties associated with a household economy—some of them entailing specific skills—could out of necessity be easily turned into waged occupations or into independent earning activities. Thus, the significant presence of housewives within the remigration movement must be viewed as a major input of labor power into the U.S. economy, as well as an important contribution to the history of trades, neighborhoods, and ethnic groups in the United States.

◆

During the first three decades of the twentieth century, Canada emerged as a leading player in the international movement of population and labor. Its unprecedented economic and territorial expansion led it to resort massively to foreign labor, engendering rates of immigration superior to those of the United States. Adjusting immigration policy to both structural and conjunctural economic needs, Canadian authorities and pro-immigration forces put into effect a variety of recruiting and advertising methods that brought millions of immigrants from the major regions of Europe.

Although Canada sought as best as it could to satisfy this population need, a substantial minority of newcomers found it more convenient—economically, socially, and culturally—to remigrate to the United States. Judging from their demographic and occupational attributes, they represented the most mobile sector of the immigrant population, and for many of them, heading south of the border was just one further step in a series of international migrations that had originated in their native villages or towns.

A closer focus on Italian and British remigrants will capture additional aspects concerning the complexity of the remigration phenomenon and its significance for Canada, the United States, and the two European countries concerned.

II

Within the European immigrant population of Canada at the beginning of the twentieth century, few groups stood at such opposite extremes as did the Italians and the British, both for their numbers and position within the Dominion's socioeconomic and cultural landscape and in terms of their reception by Canadian society. British immigrants, the leading targets of Canadian immigration policy and of important industrial and agrarian employers, were welcomed by most sectors of public opinion, and by the turn of the century they were well entrenched in Canadian labor and politics, and were often found in the higher echelons of industrial and service enterprises. Italians, on the other hand, constituted a tiny group—barely 10,000 in 1901, or .2 percent of the Canadian population—and with few exceptions worked as laborers and lived in the poorest sections of major cities or in scores of railroad and resource towns. Moreover, as they became increasingly visible in the Canadian urban landscape, Italians faced an often hostile public opinion that depicted them through negative stereotypes of an undesirable group.[18] But despite these differences and the fact that most newcomers from both groups made Canada their new homeland, significant numbers of Italians and Britons left the Dominion to work and live in the United States, thus giving rise to two distinct but parallel remigration movements.

When during the last third of the nineteenth century Italian transatlantic migration became a mass movement, the most frequent choices were South American countries such as Argentina and Brazil, with the United States gradually moving to first place and maintaining that position until the gate was virtually shut by the restrictionist laws of 1921 and 1924.[19]

Compared to those vast transatlantic population flows, emigration to Canada was the proverbial drop in the bucket. According to Italian official statistics, for every forty thousand individuals who on a yearly average left for North America during the last two decades of the nineteenth century, only about five hundred declared Canada as their destination. On this side of the Atlantic, few of them appear in Canadian census records. Those who do were mostly small merchants and traditional craftsmen. By the end of the century they had become the nuclei around which Italian enclaves had formed, mostly in Canada's largest cities, Montreal and Toronto.[20] There is no way of knowing how the nearly six hundred Italian laborers working in 1886 on the Hereford rail line—in a southeastern region of Quebec not far from the U.S. border—got into Canada. In fact, historians might have never known of their existence had it not been for a bitter strike they engaged in and the violence that accompanied it.[21] But it is quite likely that a significant portion of them had been recruited in the United States, a practice that became increasingly frequent in the ensuing years.

In fact, until chain migration linked Italy to Canada, geographical proximity to the United States was the main factor turning the Dominion into a country of immigration for growing numbers of Italians. Another factor was the mostly temporary pattern of migration, in which Italian villages and small towns sent their men to sojourn in the New World only long enough to save the cash needed to settle accounts with a landlord or to buy a small plot of land back home.[22] While reformers and government officials in Italy fiercely debated the virtues and sins of the various countries receiving Italian emigrants (Canada was either neglected or referred to as an inhospitable land) many Italian migrants were discovering the Dominion on their own. Pushed by their desire to fulfill the goals of their *campagna americana*, they moved from one workplace to another in a search for jobs that often made the U.S.-Canadian border a mere line to be crossed, much like a bridge or a mountain range.

Thus, for many of the tens of thousands of Italians, mostly agriculturalists, who in the latter decades of the nineteenth century were drawn to the U.S. economy by cheaper and faster transportation and by an unprecedented need for general laborers, it was not uncommon to find themselves north of the border soon after knowledge of available work in Canada had reached them. Some of them managed to find steady work in mines and railroad towns and remain there long enough to decide to stay and even bring over their families from Italy. Migratory processes such as these were at the origins of the first Italian enclaves in hinterland towns such as Copper Cliff and Thunder Bay, Ontario. For others, what had been a temporary stay associated with a specific seasonal job led them toward a major Canadian center where an enclave of compatriots provided them with a wider range of ethnic services.[23]

Moreover, as Canada entered a vigorous cycle of industrial growth necessitating massive quantities of common laborers for internal improvement projects, railway construction and repair, and the exploitation of its mineral resources, the recruitment of Italian workers increasingly benefited from labor agents operating directly from Canadian cities. Thanks to the Royal Inquiry set up in 1905 by the Canadian government to investigate labor agents' practices, we know in detail the scale of recruitment of the leading Montreal *padrone*, one Antonio Cordasco. To make sure that he filled the labor needs of the Canadian employers who sought his services—the most important of which was the Canadian Pacific Railway—he not only sent agents to Italian villages but also tapped the Italian labor re-

sources of U.S. cities such as New York, Philadelphia, and Buffalo, form-
ing work gangs for railway projects and mining districts as far apart as
Nova Scotia and British Columbia.[24]

But increasingly Italian laborers developed their own networks of information, as an Italian government official inspecting a northern Quebec
mining camp observed: "No sooner does a letter from some relative or
friend reach a work camp saying that in another location daily wages are
ten cents higher, or that working conditions are better, or that overtime is
slightly better paid, than all the Italians are seized by a sort of mania to
move to that location."[25] And "that location" could be in Canada as well as
south of the border.

The previous existence of small enclaves, and the knowledge of these
cities and towns that was circulated in Italian villages and towns by these
sojourners, was the main factor leading to the development of the first migration chains. By the early twentieth century, these chains were in full
swing, channeling to Canadian cities and resource towns not only sons of
peasants and smallholders but also women and children. Among the immigrants from the Italian region of Molise living in Montreal between
1906 and 1920, more than half originated from three villages.[26]

As destination points in the migrants' itineraries, such communities
could attract people not only directly from Italian villages but also from
various Canadian locales and from the United States. Raffaele Tarasco's
case may have been a rare one, but it expresses the pull that a network of
relatives and friends could exert. A young peasant from the southern region of Molise, he arrived in the United States in 1910 and spent several
years working for a railway company until he was able to realize his dream
of moving to Montreal to be with his step-father and some of his fellow
townsmen.[27] Another young peasant who had spent several years working
in West Virginia mines, Nicola Manzo returned to his village of Fredonia,
a village already linked to the Canadian economy by the back-and-forth
travel of sojourners. There he got married and in 1911 remigrated to
North America, this time to Canada. After working in several provinces as
a laborer and sometimes a harvester in the Prairies, he finally chose to settle in Montreal because of the presence of fellow townspeople.[28]

The fifteen years preceding World War I saw the growth—alongside the
stable and permanent Italian communities in Montreal, Toronto, Vancouver, and several railroad and resource towns—of a more mobile population of immigrant Italian men: some of them, still single, were compet-
ing among themselves in the small local ethnic marriage market; others
were waiting the most opportune moment to take the boat back to their
villages; still others kept feeding the hinterland labor markets, moving

from one location to another, crossing and recrossing provincial boundaries and national borders, perhaps in the hope of finding somewhere in North America the right place and the right conditions to settle down.

It is this component of the Italian immigrant population that provided the persons most apt to move on in search of better opportunities, in this case by crossing the border and making the United States their new destination. And it is not surprising that potential Italian remigrants could be found both in large cities and throughout the vast Canadian hinterland.

◆

The variety of patterns of mobility that turned Canada into a country of immigration for growing numbers of Italians sheds much light on the geographical configuration of the remigration movement to the United States, as well as on its demographic and occupational composition. Italian remigration to the United States occurred largely within the confines of the three major continental regions. Those departing from the Maritimes provinces and part of Quebec tended to choose as their destinations localities in the North Atlantic states. For this regional component of the population, two metropolitan areas attracted the largest number, New York City and Boston. Similarly, those departing from central Canada moved largely to the American Midwest, and in particular to upstate New York and Michigan, where Buffalo and Sault Sainte Marie became two of the most frequent destinations. Italians remigrating to the United States from the western Canadian provinces most often chose two cities in the Northwest: Seattle and Spokane.[29]

Looking at the movement from its Canadian side, the province that sent out the largest number of Italian remigrants by far was Ontario (table 15), which should not come as a surprise, for not only was Ontario the most industrialized and most populated province but it was also there that most Italian immigrants were concentrated. Next in importance was Quebec, largely because of the significant sending role of the Montreal metropolitan area. Though sending out a slightly lower number of Italian remigrants than Quebec, British Columbia was significant for the important role played by smaller centers, mostly mining towns. Last in importance were the prairie and Atlantic provinces, the latter resembling British Columbia in sending remigrants from mining towns.

This overview of the spatial dimension of the phenomenon brings out two important points. One is that in pursuing their itineraries, Italian remigrants conformed to the regional imperative that characterized the continent-wide population movement from Canada to the United States. The other is that with the exception of destinations such as New York City

Table 15. *Italian Remigrants to the United States by Province/Region of Departure and Major States of Destination, 1906–30 (in percentages; N = 620)*

	Maritimes	Quebec	Ontario	Prairies	British Columbia	Province Unspecified	Total
New York	14.3	39.4	50.0	15.0	1.9	25.5	32.4
Washington	—	2.3	2.1	10.0	70.8	21.6	15.8
Pennsylvania	4.1	15.2	9.5	5.0	0.9	15.7	9.0
Massachusetts	51.0	7.6	2.1	10.0	3.8	9.8	8.5
Michigan	2.0	6.1	13.6	—	—	7.8	7.4
California	—	1.5	3.7	7.5	8.5	3.9	4.0
Minnesota	—	1.5	6.2	12.5	0.9	—	3.7
Illinois	—	4.5	3.3	2.5	1.9	2.0	2.9
Ohio	—	4.5	2.1	—	1.9	—	2.1
Maine	18.4	1.5	—	—	—	2.0	1.9
Connecticut	—	5.3	0.8	2.5	—	2.0	1.8
Other states	10.2	10.6	6.6	35.0	9.4	9.8	10.3
Total	100	100	100	100	100	100	100
N	49	132	242	40	106	51	620

and Boston, a significant portion of these moves occurred within trans-border regions. In this, Italian migrants were again conforming to the general continent-wide pattern of out-migration from Canada largely into the northern margin of the United States.

Of course, exceptions to this general pattern were not infrequent. In 1907 Enzo Mondolfo, a forty-six-year-old married man residing in Toronto, crossed half the continent to remigrate to Seattle, where his brother was awaiting him. And in 1919 Filippo Battista, a twenty-nine-year-old married man residing in Vancouver, traveled from one coast to the other to join his brother in Boston.[30]

But who were these men and women who crossed the border in search of more advantageous working conditions and a more satisfying personal life? And to what extent did this movement have a distinctive character? Probably its most striking feature was the fact that the movement involved overwhelmingly men. The presence of women amounted to only 5.5 percent, and that of children under the age of fourteen barely reached 2 percent. But however few in number, the presence of women throws an important light on the rare cases in which remigration involved family units. The majority of these women, in fact, crossed the border to the United States accompanied either by their husbands or by one or more family members. In 1910 Sicilian-born Vincenza Trivalli, for instance, traveled with her husband to Buffalo, where one of their cousins lived. Aged twenty-eight and thirty-three, the Trivallis were in all likelihood childless, as were most family remigrants.[31] The case of twenty-one-year-old Rosina Tognetto, on the other hand, was clearly one of family reunification. She crossed the border in 1914 with her baby daughter on her way to San Francisco, where her husband had preceded her.[32] Hilda Baldini's move also involved family reunification; single and thirty years old, Hilda remigrated with her mother to join her father, who worked in Springfield, Massachusetts.[33] Married women crossing the border alone were a tiny minority, and in almost all cases they had their husbands waiting for them in their cities of destination.[34] An even smaller minority were single women remigrating alone. Thus, a woman like nineteen-year-old Annie M. stands as an exception within the Italian remigration movement, not only because she traveled alone from Port Huron to Globe, Michigan, but also because she was one of the very few Italian women who declared an occupation (seamstress) other than housewife and, furthermore, provided a reference at her destination who was neither a family member nor a relative. But unfortunately, her journey stopped at the border; immigration officials declared her debarred due to pending criminal offenses.[35]

Worthy of notice within the female component of Italian remigrants was the significant contingent of widows, who made up 17 percent of the entire adult female group. Our records do not tell us whether they first left Italy as widows or whether tragedy struck while living in North America. But they were the ones who most frequently remigrated alone, though in most cases to U.S. cities where a son or an in-law lived.

Once the small presence of Italian women is accounted for, one is left with a remigration population of men mostly in their prime working age (fifteen to thirty-nine) but comprising a small contingent of men in their forties. Although the majority of them were single, married men constituted a significant minority, amounting to 40 percent (1.5 percent were widowers or divorcés; see table 16).

Thanks to information recorded by U.S. border officials, we are in a position to observe the extent to which underneath the strategy of remigration was more often than not a reality of truncated families. It should not come as a surprise that the majority of those who provided a reference gave the name of a family member. What is, however, significant is that in the overwhelming majority of cases, this reference was someone living in Italy: a father, a mother, a wife. Calabrian-born Antonio Barbori was a typical case among the majority of single young men who named a parent or sometimes a sibling as a reference. He had left Calgary for Spokane in 1910 giving the name of his father, who lived in the Calabrian city of Reggio. This was not his first experience with the United States, for he had

Table 16. *Italian Remigrants by Age Groups, Sex, and Marital Status, 1906–30 (in percentages;* N = 616)

	Italian Remigrants			Total	
	Single	Married	Widowed or Divorced	N	%
Females					
0 to 14	33.3	—	—	2	5.9
15 to 29	66.7	54.5	—	16	47.1
30 to 44	—	45.5	33.3	12	35.3
45 to 59	—	—	16.7	1	2.9
60 and over	—	—	50.0	3	8.8
Subtotal	100	100	100		100
N	6	22	6	34	
Males					
0 to 14	3.0	—	—	10	1.7
15 to 29	84.7	31.9	11.1	360	61.9
30 to 44	11.4	51.1	44.4	164	28.2
45 to 59	0.6	15.3	33.3	42	7.2
60 and over	0.3	1.7	11.1	6	1.0
Subtotal	100	100	100		100
N	338	235	9	582	

Note: Cases dismissed: 4.

been there twice before.[36] The fact that he chose for a reference his father, across the Atlantic, even though he had a cousin waiting for him in Spokane, raises the issue of culture and traditional attitudes. If the reference was meant to be someone to be contacted in case of emergency or accident (which is probably how the border officials intended it), it would have made more sense to provide the name of a person residing in North America. It is likely, however, that for most of these Italian migrants, the reference person was endowed with a different meaning, one of deference and respect, making pragmatic considerations secondary.

But the reality of truncated families emerges more starkly when one observes the large contingent of married remigrants. The majority gave as references the names of their wives, and in virtually all these cases their wives lived in Italy. Thirty-eight-year-old Liborio Rotolo exemplifies this widespread reality. A native of Alfano (central Italy), he left Winnipeg in 1913 for Boston and named his wife, who lived in the province of Aquila, as a reference. Like Barbori, he had a contact person at his destination, in this case a brother-in-law, and had also been in the United States twice before.[37]

Cultural and social reasons may also help to explain why a number of these married men, however small, named as references not their wives but their fathers or mothers. Is it because in their minds and in their value systems a parent was worthier of respect and public acknowledgment than a wife? Or was it because, as sometimes happened following the departure of her husband, the wife went to live in his parents' household and had to submit to their authority? The answer probably lies in a mixture of both hypotheses.

More difficult to interpret is the sizable number of married men (thirty-nine laborers) who gave no reference at all. Was it a mere neglect of the migrant or of the border official to write down the information? Possibly. Still, behind negative answers of this sort there could have been hidden stories of broken marriages, of acts of abandonment, that sometimes make migration so much more than a mere search for economic betterment.

Clearly many characteristics of these border crossers fit a pattern that historians have associated with the phenomenon of sojourning. And we know that sojourning could last a single work season or several years—sufficient time either to confirm in the sojourner's mind his original plan of returning to his hometown or to convince him that he had found the place to settle, one that promised a better future for himself and perhaps soon for his wife and children.[38] Only individual longitudinal or biographical studies can determine why and when a sojourner ended his wandering life either by returning permanently to his hometown or by settling in North America.

Part of the answer to this issue may be found in the occupational composition of the movement. Whether departing from a large urban center or from a railroad or mining town, their working experience in Canada had been primarily that of laborers, and in fact 80 percent of them entered the United States declaring that occupation. The rest belonged to a small variety of occupations associated mostly with construction (such as bricklayer or stonecutter) or with services and small businesses (barber, waiter, peddler, shoemaker). Rare were the occupations implying factory work, whether skilled, semiskilled or unskilled.[39]

Although spatial mobility is not exclusively a function of one's occupation, the structural context in which most of these Italian laborers worked did have an impact on their mobility. Seasonal work, whether in railroad or canal construction or in lumber camps, was of course known for propelling a laborer in search of a new job to replace the one just terminated, wherever it could be gotten. But even in more stable work settings, such as mines or even factories, Italian laborers displayed high levels of mobility. In her study of the mining town of Copper Cliff, in northern Ontario, Karey Reilly has documented the volatility of a significant portion of Italian laborers who found work at the Canadian Copper Company.[40] And while in the majority of cases the separation resulted from termination of their mostly seasonal jobs, in nearly one third of the cases these migrants left of their own initiative, often without collecting their last paycheck. These dynamics were hardly different in a metropolitan area such as Montreal. In the giant Angus Shops of the Canadian Pacific Railway—the country's largest producer of locomotives and the city's largest employers of Italian immigrants—a large contingent of Italian laborers disappeared from the payroll after a few months, in many cases of their own initiative, often without even notifying their foremen.[41]

Costanzo D'Amico moved from one seasonal job to another within the Montreal urban economy, often spending periods of time in the mining region of Cobalt, in northern Quebec. And Michele Marcogliese, when asked to recount to us his work experience, answered, "I worked at fifty thousand jobs—foundries, canals, railroads, construction."[42] His simple answer evoked the description that historian Donald Avery gave of immigrant laborers in that era of Canadian economic expansion: "In one year an immigrant worker might find himself in many roles: in February a lumber worker in northern Ontario; in June a railroad navvy along the Canadian Pacific mainline in British Columbia; in August a harvester in Saskatchewan; in November, a miner in northern Quebec."[43]

D'Amico left Italy as a sojourner, and most likely because he found a wife in Montreal changed his plans and settled there. Marcogliese was brought over to Montreal as a youngster by his parents, who were part of a well-established migration chain linking the town of Casacalenda to the Quebec metropolis.[44] Among our remigrants crossing the border, no doubt some found their "Montreal" in some U.S. city or town, whereas others put an end to their labor transiency after returning to their home villages.

◆

Most of our Italian remigrants crossed the border alone and had families back in their villages—two common features of a sojourner's experience. Yet, they were not alone in North America. When asked to provide a reference at their U.S. destination, two-thirds of them gave the names of siblings, other relatives, and friends. Of course, the city of destination could make a significant difference in the type of relationship. Thus, among those going to New York one can observe a clear prevalence of siblings and other relatives. New York was, of course, the U.S. city with the largest Italian population and, hence, the one that had developed the largest number of kinship and hometown-based networks. On the other hand, among those going to the mining city of Spokane, the reference was more frequently a friend, probably a fellow sojourner or a hometown acquaintance.[45]

True, about one-third of them provided no reference and it is difficult to know whether this resulted from failure of the border official to record the information, or whether the remigrant had no name to supply. There were, however, a number of cases in which a negative answer was recorded as "none." In these few cases we are certain that the remigrant had no contact person. Calabrian-born Domenico Scolli, for instance, a twenty-four-year-old single man, moved in 1910 from Nelson, British Columbia, to Spokane. He probably had no living parents, since he gave as a reference the name of his sister in his hometown of Mammola. He was now moving to a town where he had no personal contact, as shown by the entry "none." But at least he was not alone, for he brought along his fifteen-year-old brother.[46]

Still, a large majority of these men were moving within kin and hometown networks. And this brings out what probably was the most peculiar character of this remigration movement. Although most of them were— to use Robert Harney's expression—"men without women" and paid the high emotional cost of a truncated family, they were also moving through a continent that in their eyes held more than abundant labor markets and better working conditions: North America was also a space punctuated by meaningful relations they could rely on, where they could either settle down and become a link in their own migration chain or put an end to their *campagna americana.*

Giuseppe De Luchi was one of the many Italians we retrieved in our sample who crossed the border not to remigrate to the United States but to return home—a group of border crossers this book has not analyzed. He was heading for New York to embark on a last trip across the Atlantic and on to his village in northeastern Italy.[47] In Carnuda and other villages around Treviso Province, sojourning in Argentina, Brazil, and North America had long been a way of life for the young and the not-so-young. De Luchi was thirty-eight when, having left behind his wife and probably his children, he set foot in Canada. Now, eight years older and still a laborer, he was going home. Perhaps his children were going to replace him as migrant bread providers, crossing the Atlantic and going to the same mining town his father had left: Sault Saint-Marie, Ontario. In those deep pits they had heard so much about, perhaps they would look for familiar and comforting signs.

Luigi Ferri, another Italian laborer, was fifty-two when he crossed the border into the United States, but he was traveling with an even older man, his father. Luigi was not a sojourner, at least not on this trip; he had only been one month in Canada, in the mining town of Copper Cliff, Ontario, and now he was taking his seventy-year-old father back to Pesaro, in central Italy.[48] It is likely that the older Ferri had become a widower and that he, or someone in the family, had decided that he should spend his last days in his hometown.

The experience of these migrants and remigrants unveils the extent to which their stories—many of them at least—belong as much to family histories as they do to the history of transnational migrations and multinational labor markets, or to the history of "workers of the world, unite!"

III

If the relation of Italian mass emigration with Canada was a recent occurrence, that of the British was inextricably linked with the history of Canada through the critical role it played in the peopling of the country, in the expansion of its agrarian economy, and subsequently in the process of industrialization.

After 1815 and throughout the remainder of the century, the British Isles constituted by far the leading source of immigration. Between 1825 and 1846 alone, some six hundred thousand immigrants from the United Kingdom arrived in British North America, bringing the population of British origin to nearly one-half the total population of the colonies. The majority were Irish, followed in equal importance by English and Scottish immigrants.[49]

During much of this first phase of immigration and settlement, British North America was able to attract from the British Isles a population comparable to that which headed for the United States. But by the 1840s the United States had emerged as the leading destination, and for the remainder of the century Canada was a losing competitor. As Charlotte Erickson and others have shown, the greater possibility of becoming independent farmers in the American West and, later, the vigorous expansion of the American industrial economy, with its unprecedented need for both skilled workers and common laborers, were the essential factors explaining the powerful pull exerted by the American republic.[50]

Canada continued, however, to attract from the British Isles a flow of immigrants which, although small compared to the U.S.-bound one, proved essential to the country's demographic and economic growth. By 1891, when the population movement from Europe to North America began to shift to central-eastern and southern European countries, British-born immigrants in Canada had reached 77 percent of the total foreign-born population. Their presence in Canada's economy and society had no equivalent in the United States. The massive flow into Canada of southern and eastern Europeans during the following three decades could not but alter the ratio between British and other immigrant nationalities. Still, in 1921 one out of every two foreign-born residents was a Briton.[51]

This changing composition of immigration to Canada was far from reflecting a decline in the flow from Britain. On the contrary, during the first decade of the twentieth century, a shift of historic proportions occurred. The number of British emigrants entering Canada made a spectacular jump, reaching levels comparable to those absorbed by the United States. And in the ensuing decades Canada surpassed her southern neighbor as the favored destination.[52]

Various factors converged making Canada the leading destination. Some of them have to do with the unprecedented agricultural and industrial expansion the country experienced. One cannot overemphasize the fact that the Dominion's manpower needs touched all sectors of the economy, and strictly from an occupational point of view, Great Britain was one of the few industrial countries able to meet those needs. More important, cultural affinity and imperial allegiance dictated that the Canadian authorities make Great Britain the preferred source to tap; but it is also true that many Britons, from farm laborers to highly skilled workers, saw the advantage of migrating under publicly or privately sponsored programs that not only facilitated their traveling but also provided ready employment upon arrival.

On the British side, both the government and a wide array of charitable organizations not only encouraged emigration to Canada and to other dominions but took concrete steps to sponsor the move of tens of thousands of men, women, and children. The swelling ranks of the urban poor and the growing social problems they engendered supplied the prime motivation. Emigration would help alleviate those problems, and the healthy Canadian environment would transform the often sickly and malnourished urban poor into "bricks for empire-building."[53] In the field of welfare for poor children alone, no less than sixty agencies sponsored the migration of tens of thousands of children and placed them in Canadian homes under various types of arrangements (apprenticeship, farm help, domestic help).[54] Associations operating in the field of women's welfare also saw in emigration the means to rescue hard-pressed women from the health and moral dangers of urban life. The most important of them, the

Fig. 19. Advertising Canada in London, England, ca. 1910. Courtesy of the National Archives of Canada, C 9671.

British Women's Emigration Association, targeted unemployed women especially. Working hand in hand with its Canadian associates—the Local Councils of Women and the YWCA, as well as with Canadian employers—it was able to place thousands of British women, thus becoming one of the prime movers in the recruiting of domestics. Here too imperial considerations were paramount, as one of the association's main concerns was to help reduce the surplus of women in Britain by sending them to areas in the Dominion known for their supply of single males.[55]

In the renewed imperial vision emerging in the era of Queen Victoria's Diamond Jubilee, the Boer War, and Joseph Chamberlain's rule in colonial affairs, emigration and empire settlement could no longer be left to the haphazard interplay of transcontinental economic forces; it had to become part and parcel of an enlightened imperial policy. Thus in 1905 the problem of the urban poor led the British government to pass the Unemployed Workmen Act, one of whose provisions was to provide financial assistance in the migration of qualifying adults and their dependents to the dominions. And the ensuing Imperial Conferences of 1907 and 1911 stressed the importance of emigration and settlement for the consolida-

Fig. 20. British children from Dr. Barnardo's Homes landing at Saint John, New Brunswick, ca. 1910. Courtesy of the National Archives of Canada, PA 41785.

tion of the empire. British men, women, and children, whether pushed by economic distress or motivated by ambition, would find in the Dominion's virgin lands and in their fast-growing cities a fertile soil to nurture their life goals while strengthening the empire. Far from being an ordinary migration, their move overseas would be an "imperialism of peace."[56]

It is difficult if not impossible to measure the impact of the imperial discourse on the rise of out-migration from Britain to Canada. The fact remains that the ideology of empire building found expression in the many assisted plans and recruiting schemes supported on both sides of the Atlantic. And there is no question about their success in redirecting the out-migration flow. In the last decade of the nineteenth century, dominion countries received only 28 percent of the total share from the British Isles; but from 1901 to 1912 their share jumped to 63 percent, and in 1913 reached 78 percent. Among these countries, Canada became the leading beneficiary.[57]

Canada's performance in attracting such a high volume of British immigrants, however, should not be associated exclusively with assisted migration programs. According to some estimates the majority of Britons migrated to Canada independently, basing their decision on their evaluation of the opportunities Canada afforded them.[58] The intense promotional campaigns carried out in Britain by Canadian public and private interests may no doubt have had an impact; but so did informal migration networks spanning the Atlantic. In his study of Winnipeg, one of the largest Canadian cities with a substantial presence of British immigrants, A. R. McCormack demonstrated convincingly the pervasiveness of such networks among Britons and their role in the informal sponsorship of migration. The significant presence of family units within the city's British population, the high level of intermarriage among them, the formation of a British neighborhood in the city's west end, and the presence of a rich institutional network (mutual aid societies and religious, recreational, and charitable organizations)—these were the basic constitutive elements of what one might call "a community." Furthermore, McCormack found a significant flow of remittances from Winnipeg to England whose purpose was both to provide economic sustenance to family members left behind and to help finance the migration of newcomers. From 1900 to 1914, for instance, the value of Canadian remittances to Britain grew from $929,000 to $15,430,000, which led McCormack to conclude that "because individuals tended to travel within available personal networks, the location of family and friends was clearly influential in the spatial distribution of the British."[59]

A final significant change in the migration patterns of Britons directed to Canada was the sharp decline in the Irish component of the movement. Of the nearly one and a half million immigrants from the British Isles entering Canada during 1901–14, only 6 percent came from Ireland. The overwhelming majority, 74 percent, originated from England (including a minority from Wales). The second major group, representing 20 percent, were Scots.[60] It is on this population, then, that the following discussion of remigration will be based. (The immigrant's place of birth as recorded in the Index has permitted us to exclude the Irish-born from our sample.)

Like many migration movements linking various regions of the North Atlantic economy during this era, this one too comprised people who moved permanently and others who returned to Britain after a temporary stay in Canada.

Return migration among Britons has been studied primarily with reference to the United States.[61] Yet it was a common occurrence also among those having migrated to Canada. In the case of Winnipeg, McCormack found that in 1901–11 the rate of departures back to Great Britain was almost as high as that of newcomers.[62] In the absence of comparable studies in Canada, the Winnipeg experience cannot be generalized. Still, the return phenomenon must have been considerable, especially among the many laborers working in highly seasonal sectors of the economy.[63] The propensity to return to one's home country must also be viewed as a reflection of the practice of sojourning, so widespread among several other nationalities; Britons were far from being an exception, and they too resorted to migration as a temporary strategy to gain access to earnings that would improve their conditions back home. George Peaks, Douglas Ford, and Ruby Arnold are three of the many English migrants that the Index documented as they returned home after a sojourn in Canada. A native of Riddley, England, George had landed in Quebec in June 1913 on the SS *Virginian*, having left his wife behind. But after a six-month stay he was on his way back to Earthstone, England, to join his wife. Perhaps the fact that he worked at a highly seasonal trade—he was a bricklayer—explains the short length of his stay. Douglas's sojourn in Canada was longer; he went back to England almost two years after he had arrived one July day in 1920 on the SS *Empress* of France. Moreover, Douglas was making the trip not alone but with his wife; both were going to a district in Surrey where Douglas's father lived. It is likely that Douglas, a thirty-year-old farmer, tried his luck in that field of work while in Canada, since he was leaving from a prairie district. But in the English migration movement, sojourning could also be practiced by women, whether as a family strategy or as a search for experience and career advancement. Twenty-six years old and single, Ruby was a graduate nurse from London who in all likelihood went to Canada alone. Like Douglas, she sojourned in Canada for only six months before departing from Calgary and heading back to London, where one of her brothers lived.

But for the majority of Britons, their emigration to Canada must have been viewed as a permanent move and this North American dominion their new "land of opportunity." From a demographic point of view, the significant presence of family units among British immigrants is a compelling indicator of a permanent move. Moreover, next to Jews and communal religious groups, British immigrants had the highest proportion of women. Although many of them had migrated as single women, their presence facilitated the formation of family units and thus strengthened local communities. From an occupational point of view, Canada's rapidly expanding industrial economy afforded British workers career opportunities that had become less accessible in the rigid and overcrowded labor markets of their home countries. It is true that, according to Lloyd Reynolds's estimates, nearly half of the entrants to Canada declaring occupations during 1904–14 were farm laborers and general laborers. Still, there was another half who declared occupations in industrial manufacturing and in various service sectors (from domestics to administrators) and who thus brought to the Canadian economy skills and experience that were in great demand.[64] Studies that have analyzed the ethnic stratification in Canadian resource sectors and in industrial enterprises have clearly shown the predominance of English and Scottish workers in the higher occupational echelons.[65] Which explains why the majority of the newcomers chose urban centers, the greatest proportion of them in Ontario's cities. Outside Ontario, they concentrated in fast-growing metropolitan areas such as Montreal, Winnipeg, and Vancouver, with only a small minority settling in the Maritime provinces. For many of them, the choice followed from their largely urban background, which facilitated the adaptation to their new working environment and afforded a greater hope for occupational advancement. True, as previously mentioned, British immigration to Canada comprised a constant flow of farm laborers most often recruited through government programs to meet harvesting needs. Once the harvesting season was over, most of those who did not head back home had no choice but to move on to the city and become part of an urban labor force. Not surprisingly, the most vocal critic of the sponsored harvesters' programs was organized labor; it denounced repeatedly the importation of harvesters who, as some of its leaders pointed out, were needed only for three months and who, by subsequently moving to the cities, lowered the level of urban wages.[66]

The 1921 Canadian census, the first that provides detailed breakdowns of the sectors employing foreign-born active workers, shows the extent to which the advancement that British immigrants hoped for had become a reality. The British-born were overrepresented in the major branches of manufacturing, in the various construction trades, as well as in the tertiary sectors (transportation, trade and finance, services). Only 10 percent of Canadian farmers were British born.[67]

Thus, as the first three decades of what was hailed as "Canada's Century" unfolded, British immigrants entered a country that had long been linked to their former homeland by imperial ties, by close trade relations, and by a steady flow of population that had left an indelible mark on

Canadian society and institutions. There is no doubt that as British subjects and as carriers of British traditions, they brought with them cultural and political resources that fitted them to their new environment and helped them rise to the higher echelons of Canadian industrial society.[68] Yet, this did not prevent a significant number of them from looking south of the border and seeking more rewarding opportunities there.

◆

The work of the historians Charlotte Erickson and Dudley Baines has thrown important new light on the massive migration movement from England to the United States. Their writings on the late-nineteenth-century phase of the movement have yielded a critical understanding of the economic and social context of British migration.[69] Yet a portion of this population—comparatively small but significant enough to deserve being considered a movement on its own—did not disembark at an American port but crossed from the Canadian border after having immigrated to Canada. Who were these migrants arriving from the north, and what did they bring to the American economy and society?

Half of them had resided in Ontario before remigrating to the United States. Quebec was the second most important donor province (19 percent). Western Canada furnished the remainder, and only a tiny proportion departed from the Atlantic provinces. It was a movement that largely reflected the regional distribution of the British-born population throughout the Dominion during this era (table 17).

But within this broad configuration, urban Canada was the dominant donor—both the metropolitan areas and the medium-sized and smaller cities. Although all three major donor provinces show the importance of metropolitan areas, it was most marked in Quebec, where more than two-thirds of the out-migrants had resided in Montreal. In Ontario and British Columbia, nearly half of the out-migrants had resided in the two largest cities, Toronto and Vancouver.

British remigrants who had resided in towns with fewer than ten thousand inhabitants were a minority, but they came from every province.[70] These towns were often small industrial centers in Ontario or mining towns in British Columbia, Nova Scotia, and northern Ontario. Most of the remigrants departing from agrarian areas came from the prairie provinces; a third of these remigrants had been residing in small towns mostly associated with agriculture.

In choosing their destinations, they conformed to the regional configuration exhibited by the general flow of population from Canada to the United States (see table 17). With some exceptions, the movement oc-

Table 17. *British-Born Remigrants to the United States by Province/Region of Departure and Major States of Destination, 1906–30 (in percentages; N = 1060)*

	Maritimes	Quebec	Ontario	Prairies	British Columbia	Province Unspecified	Total
New York	10.0	38.1	28.8	10.9	2.0	13.2	24.3
Michigan	10.0	7.4	27.1	14.5	1.0	30.2	18.9
Washington	—	0.5	1.9	13.0	63.7	5.7	9.2
Massachusetts	26.7	16.3	4.9	6.5	2.0	3.8	7.5
Illinois	10.0	5.4	6.0	7.2	2.9	7.5	5.9
Pennsylvania	13.3	7.4	7.1	2.2	—	5.7	5.9
Ohio	3.3	3.0	6.0	4.3	1.0	5.7	4.6
California	—	1.5	2.6	5.1	13.7	3.8	3.8
Minnesota	—	—	1.3	15.2	—	—	2.6
New Jersey	3.3	1.5	2.8	2.9	—	—	2.2
Montana	—	1.0	0.6	6.5	5.9	—	1.9
Other states	23.3	17.8	11.0	11.6	7.8	24.5	13.1
Total	100	100	100	100	100	100	100
N	30	202	535	138	102	53	1,060

curred within three broad continental regions. Taking the largest share were Michigan and western New York State, which received migrants mainly from the central provinces, with Ontario being by far the leading donor. Residents of Atlantic Canada and of a portion of Quebec migrated largely to the northeastern states. And western states, primarily Washington and California, were the main destinations for residents of the prairie provinces and particularly British Columbia.

Within this general pattern, a closer look shows that the most pronounced tendency among British remigrants, much as among the Italians, was to move within transborder areas, that is, to U.S. localities close to the border. Thus the cities of Buffalo and Detroit were the leading destinations for people departing from southern Ontario, whereas Seattle became the choice for more than half of the remigrants from British Columbia.

The major exceptions to this spatial pattern were transborder areas lacking important industrial or urban centers on the U.S. side. Thus, for instance, the overwhelming majority of those departing from Quebec (primarily Montreal) chose New York City as their destination, with Boston as the second most important choice. The other exception was constituted by some of the major U.S. metropolitan centers, in particular New York and Chicago. No doubt the opportunities these cities offered in a variety of economic sectors, coupled with the significant presence of Britons, explain the strong pull they exerted.

These patterns of spatial mobility in many ways resemble those charac-
terizing Italian remigrants. In both cases, urban-to-urban moves were
predominant, and they occurred largely within each of the three broad
continental regions. Both movements, moreover, were marked by the predominance of transborder cities as U.S. destinations, as well as by the
strong pull exerted by large metropolitan areas.

Where significant differences between these two groups emerge is in
their demographic and occupational characteristics. An analysis unveils
important patterns that shed much light on the character and significance of the British movement.

As with the Italians, the overwhelming majority of Britons were adults
and more than half of them were in their prime working age (fifteen to
twenty-nine). Unlike the Italians, however, they comprised a significant
proportion of women, and the patterns of family and single-woman migration gave the British movement much of its distinctive character (table
18). Women represented 30 percent of the total British remigrant population, and they were almost equally divided between married (45 percent) and single (48 percent), the remaining portion (6.6 percent) being
widows. The proportion of married migrants within the male population
was somewhat smaller (33 percent), but sufficient to attest to the importance of family migration within the movement. Whether entering the
United States jointly or individually, many of them were doing so as members of a family seeking a new life south of the border.

The Swains and the Kennys exemplify this pattern. London-born Ada
Swain entered the United States in 1921, accompanied by her husband
and her mother-in-law; the three had left Montreal and were going to
Chicago. John Kenny, on the other hand, made the trip alone; a Liverpool-
born elevator mechanic, he left Halifax in 1919 and crossed the border
on his way to New York City, where his wife was waiting for him.[71] It is significant that family migration occurred also among laborers, a group usually identified with the practice of sojourning and work instability. Among
the British remigrants who were laborers and married, over one-third
were accompanied by their wives, or by their wives and children.

This pattern of family migration is further corroborated by the presence of children among Britons, another rare occurrence among Italian
migrants. But the small proportion of children (only 6.2 percent aged
fourteen or under) in a total population comprising a significant proportion of married individuals is puzzling at first. It may reflect a key selection mechanism among the British, namely, that family remigration was
practiced mostly by childless couples or small families. But for some of
them it also reflected a reality that was widespread among Italians, in

Table 18. British and Italian Remigrants by Age Group, Sex, and Marital Status, 1906–30 (in percentages)

	British Remigrants			Total		Italians Remigrants			Total	
	Single	Married	Widowed or Divorced	N	%	Single	Married	Widowed or Divorced	N	%
Females										
0 to 14	20.8	—	—	32	10.1	33.3	—	—	2	5.9
15 to 29	49.4	44.1	4.8	140	44.0	66.7	54.5	—	16	47.1
30 to 44	25.3	46.9	38.1	114	35.8	—	45.5	33.3	12	35.3
45 to 59	3.9	7.7	28.6	23	7.2	—	—	16.7	1	2.9
60 and over	0.6	1.4	28.6	9	2.8	—	—	50.0	3	8.8
Subtotal	100	100	100		100	100	100	100		100
N	154	143	21	318		6	22	6	34	
Males										
0 to 14	6.8	—	—	33	4.5	3.0	—	—	10	1.7
15 to 29	72.0	30.2	9.1	422	57.2	84.7	31.9	11.1	360	61.9
30 to 44	20.3	51.4	54.5	230	31.2	11.4	51.1	44.4	164	28.2
45 to 59	0.8	17.1	27.3	49	6.6	0.6	15.3	33.3	42	7.2
60 and over	—	1.2	9.1	4	0.5	0.3	1.7	11.1	6	1.0
Subtotal	100	100	100		100	100	100	100		100
N	482	245	11	738		334	235	9	582	

Note: Cases dismissed: British = 5; Italian = 4.

which the migrant had left his wife and children on the other side of the Atlantic. In fact, a closer focus on the married male component of this remigration movement shows the extent to which family separation was part of the British experience as well. Of all cases in which the location of the wife is known, 52 percent of these men had left their wives and possibly their children in Canada, a step that most likely entailed a subsequent reunification. But in as much as 46 percent of the cases, their wives and possibly their children had remained in the United Kingdom.[72] And this contingent included men belonging to a variety of occupations, not only laborers. Scottish-born Robert Adams, for instance, left Windsor for nearby Detroit, declaring to border officials that his was a permanent emigration. The reference he named was his wife, who lived in Greenoch, Scotland, likely with her children, for Robert was thirty-eight years old.[73] We cannot know how many of these men at a later date brought their families over to the United States. For a number of them, however, their stay in North America was a sojourn that terminated with family reunification on the other side of the Atlantic.

But perhaps the most striking characteristic of the British remigration movement was the significant proportion of single, female wage earners who migrated alone or sometimes with a friend[74]—two clear indicators of a degree of economic and personal autonomy that was inconceivable among Italian remigrants. The occupations they most frequently declared were in the service sector (domestic, nurse, clerical worker) as well as in the industrial and craft-production sector. Domestics, however, were by far the most numerous group, representing about a half of all occupations,[75] which should not come as a surprise since, we already know, British-born domestics had been particularly targeted in the recruiting efforts of Canadian immigration authorities and constituted the largest component of the female British wageworkers in the Dominion. Among those who remigrated, the overwhelming majority (89 percent) were single, mostly in their twenties, with a significant minority belonging to the 30–45 age bracket. Although their occupation could be practiced in both a rural and an urban context, it was the city that afforded the greater opportunity. And in fact virtually all of them resided in the largest Canadian cities at the time of their remigration—more than half of them in Toronto and Montreal.[76]

There is no way of knowing (short of biographical analyses) whether these domestics remigrated to the United States with the intention of pursuing the same occupation. We can safely argue, however, that a significant portion of them chose their destination because a contact with a prospective employer had been made, or more often because of the presence of friends, family members, or relatives. And these destinations were not necessarily large U.S. cities. Edith Davis, for instance, moved from Toronto to Kearney, New York. Born in Nottingham, she was single and thirty-six years old when she crossed the border in 1922, traveling alone and carrying $280 in her purse (one of the largest amounts in our sample). Like many other remigrants, Edith was moving within her own network: she was leaving behind a brother, and a friend was waiting for her in Kearney.[77] Beatrice Pritchard's case is of particular interest because her permanent entry in the United States in October 1914 was preceded by a sojourn, that same year, in the town that she would then choose as her destination. A native of Wellington, England, Beatrice had landed in Quebec in June 1912 at the age of nineteen, leaving behind her father and perhaps her mother and siblings as well. At the time of her remigration she lived in Winnipeg; she was single and traveling alone, headed toward Lancaster, Minnesota—the town where she had previously sojourned and where a friend lived.[78]

A similar pattern or profile can be observed among women practicing nursing, one of the most skilled female occupations. Here too the majority of these women were single, undoubtedly a condition that had something to do with the nature of the employment. Their average age, however, was higher than that of domestics; the majority were in their thirties. Moreover, they comprised an unusually high proportion of widows, for as many as 28 percent of them had lost their husbands, some at a relatively early age.[79] Hilda Harris, for instance, was a twenty-nine-year-old widow when she entered the United States in 1907 on her way to Seattle. We do not know whether these widows—who included the forty-five-year-old Elizabeth Fincham and the sixty-year-old Louisa Roberts—had taken up nursing before or after the death of their husbands.[80] Their strong overrepresentation within the occupation, coupled with the often stringent working conditions required by nursing, make the latter hypothesis look more realistic.

Apart from these variants, nurses displayed the same personal autonomy in their remigration as did the domestics, as virtually all of them made the journey alone—whether to a border city such as Detroit or as far south as Washington, D.C.[81] And much like the domestics, their choice of destination was not strictly based on labor market considerations. Except for the few who gave as reference the name of a medical institution or an employer, the majority had siblings, relatives, or friends waiting for them.

◈

Although women gave British remigration its perhaps most distinctive character, the other 70 percent of the remigrants were men, and their demographic and occupational profiles will throw further light on the movement. When one observes their age structure and their marital status, one is struck by the close resemblance to their Italian counterparts. The predominance of single men was only slightly higher than that of the Italians, and the proportion of men in the 15–29 age bracket was quite comparable in the two groups: 61 percent for the British and 57 percent for the Italians (see table 18).

Unlike the Italians remigrants, who were overwhelmingly laborers, however, the British belonged to a wide spectrum of occupations associated with all sectors of the North American economy. One in five was a laborer, but the occupational ladder broadened upward to include semiskilled, skilled, and white-collar occupations, as well as a small proportion of professionals such as engineers and architects. If one translates these occupations into sectors of activity, the major concentration was in industrial production, transportation, and services such as trade and administration. Within the industrial production sector, particularly conspicuous were migrants whose occupations were associated with machinery and metalwork, most of whom declared "machinist" as their trade.[82] A closer focus on this subgroup will shed further light on the contribution that skilled British remigrants made to the U.S. economy.[83]

As one might expect, the majority departed from the major centers of machine production in Canada—primarily Toronto, Hamilton, Montreal, and Winnipeg, but also smaller industrial cities such as Sarnia and Saint Catherines and border cities such as Windsor and Sault Sainte Marie. For most of them, their destinations were also major U.S. industrial centers where machine production was a leading activity. Hence, Detroit was the single most important destination, and Buffalo the third most important. Here too, distance may have played a key role, as most of these machinists were out-migrating from Ontario. And in fact most destinations were industrial towns in the Great Lakes region and in northwestern New York State. It was not unusual for some of these migrants to travel longer distances, however. George Hope, for instance, a nineteen-year-old unmarried machinist living in Toronto, chose the city of Duluth, Minnesota—his decision was very likely motivated both by labor market considerations and by the fact that he had an aunt living in that city.[84]

British machinists, moreover, were men in their prime working age, the overwhelming majority of them in their twenties and thirties. Of course, this age range is wide enough to suggest varying degrees of expertise in their trade and work experience, acquired either in the United Kingdom or in Canada. Frederick Dawe, for instance, had surely learned his trade in England before he arrived in Canada at the age of thirty-two. Moreover, when in 1921 he left Hamilton, Ontario, for Buffalo he must have been confident that his trade would assure him a job there, for he provided no contact person at his destination.[85] Thomas Mayor, who arrived in Canada at the age of twenty, had likely taken up his trade in his home country. But the three years he spent in Canada before remigrating to the United States must have been important ones for accumulating work experience. Moreover, he was leaving behind a city, Montreal, which provided ample opportunity to practice the machinist trade.[86]

British machinists shared with the majority of male remigrants the fact of being—two out of three of them—unmarried men, a factor that undoubtedly enhanced their mobility. A closer scrutiny shows actually that they were among the most mobile persons in the entire British remigrant population, as nearly two-thirds of them had previously lived and worked in the United States. Their propensity to move must also be assessed in the light of two other important factors: their kinship networks, as evidenced by the significant number who gave names of family members and in-laws at their destinations; and the cross-border links that grew out of the particular nature of their trade. Many of the friends who machinists named as contacts were, quite likely, work-related friends, part of a "trade network" that facilitated the communication of information on labor market conditions, helping migrants to assess the opportunities awaiting them as well as the timing of their move.[87] Machinists who, like Frederick Dawe, moved to a place where they had no apparent personal contacts, were a very small minority.

Whether men or women, single or married, sojourning or moving permanently, Britons moved to the very center of the American industrial and urban economy bringing with them occupational skills and cultural resources that, as the historical literature has shown, permitted a rapid adjustment to their new environment. For a significant minority of them, a factor playing no small role in their rapid adjustment was the wide network of friends, relatives, and family members on both sides of the border. Whereas an Italian remigrant would only exceptionally be able to provide as a reference someone residing in Canada, a sizable number of remigrating Britons were able to do so. And now they were moving to a U.S. city where many of them had a sibling, a relative, or a friend.

In her collection of essays on British emigration, Charlotte Erickson has stressed the importance of migration networks in understanding the choice of a destination. At the same time she has acknowledged the difficulty historians have had in studying the migration networks and chains extending from British villages and cities to overseas destinations. Her investigation of this issue has even led her to doubt the relevance of such patterns as far as emigration from England is concerned. As she puts it, "We simply do not know how relevant the now conventional concept of chain migration is to English emigration."[88]

As far as the remigration movement to the United States is concerned, the random character of our sampling does not permit us to establish the extent to which having reference persons at points of departure and destination entailed the existence of migration *chains*. Only in-depth studies of particular migration fields, complimented by sufficient qualitative and biographical sources, could tell us whether such patterns occurred between given locations in Canada and given destinations in the United States. The evidence provided by the Index, however, does show quite conclusively that a substantial majority of Britons who moved through North America did so as part of kin and friend networks; and if the presence of a sister, a cousin, or a friend was not the only determining factor in the choice of their destination, it certainly played a major role.[89]

Besides the differences and similarities between British and Italian remigrants noted above, two further aspects differentiate the two movements. The first has to do with the encounter of these remigrants with the U.S. economy and society. For an important majority of Britons (nearly two-thirds) their remigration was the initial contact they were making with industrial and urban America, since only a third of them declared having previously been in the United States. For a majority of Italian remigrants, on the other hand, working and living in the United States was far from being an initial experience. Two out of three had, in fact, previously sojourned there, some of them more than once.[90] Filippo Battista's case illustrates this pattern. A twenty-nine-year-old laborer native of Città Nova, a southern Italian town, he crossed the American border from British Columbia in May 1919, heading for Boston, where his brother-in-law lived. Battista had arrived to Boston on the SS *Parisien* in March 1913 and had proceeded to Canada. But that had not been his first trip across the Atlantic, for he declared having resided in the United States in 1908.[91]

This pattern of repeat migration among the Italians certainly denotes a high degree of transatlantic and intracontinental mobility, which may best be explained by the common strategy of sojourning practiced by a population of mainly male laborers. In comparison, the overall spatial trajectory of British remigrants appears more stable and linear. The different circumstances that had brought them to Canada, coupled with their richer occupational backgrounds, translated into a wider range of opportunities and more realistic employment expectations in a country whose anglophone inhabitants took pride in their British traditions. It is thus not surprising that many of them took up Canadian citizenship, a clear indication that they saw Canada as their permanent residence. What may be surprising is the significant number of these British-turned-Canadian citizens who joined the remigration movement.

This trajectory by no means denotes a lower level of mobility through Canadian cities and labor markets. In fact the occupational mobility of British blue- or white-collar workers was incomparably greater than that of Italian laborers, and many of them took advantage of it. Still, it is safe to argue that the occupational opportunities Canada offered made the remigration strategy of the British more selective, more pondered, and possibly more definitive.

The other feature differentiating the British and Italian remigration movements is the time frame within which they occurred. Much of the Italian remigration was concentrated in the decade preceding World War I, whereas the southward flow of Britons was constant throughout the period under study, with more than one-third occurring during the 1920s. The explanation rests on the impact of the war on population movements across the Atlantic and on the different ways in which the U.S. restrictionist legislation of 1921 and 1924 affected the two groups.

The outbreak of the war did not reduce the pool of Italians residing in Canada, although we know that a number of young sojourners responded to their country's call to arms and returned to Italy.[92] It did, however, put a virtual stop to the arrival of newcomers and to the practice of sojourning, the strategy chosen by most Italian remigrants. Italians remigrating in the 1920s therefore were mostly prewar immigrants to Canada. And among those who did try to remigrate, many were debarred for not qualifying under the new restrictionist laws. Giovanni Politta, for instance, was refused admission on account of his illiteracy;[93] and when Luigi Finaro tried to enter the United States on his way to New York on 8 July 1924, he was stopped at the Newport, Vermont, border crossing, where immigration officials debarred him in compliance with the new quota law that had gone into effect just a week earlier.[94]

Young British males, very likely at a much higher rate than their Italian counterparts, also crossed the Atlantic to join their homeland's war effort.

But the population pool that produced remigrants to the United States was incommensurably higher than the Italian one. More important, the resumption of the migration flow from Britain following the war replenished the population pool in Canada, thus keeping the remigration process going throughout the twenties. And because they were British subjects or Canadian citizens, their reception at border crossings was quite different from the one reserved for Italians.

◆

Labor market requirements had long rendered the Canadian–U.S. border a permeable entity for tens of thousands of Italians and Britons in search of cash and social betterment. Their moves were not merely transfers of labor power from one side of the border to the other, but often served also to feed the socioeconomic system of Italian villages and British towns and cities. And they did so largely relying on networks of kin and friends extending across the Atlantic and throughout much of North America. But unforeseen developments in world politics led to a radical reassessment of ethnocultural attributes, and when the American state coded them into law, the 49th parallel turned into a closed wall for some, and a welcoming gate for others.

Conclusion

Throughout much of the nineteenth century and until the onset of the Great Depression, Canada was one of the leading contributors of population and labor to the United States, to such an extent that the socioeconomic and cultural history of most states and regions along the northern border of the United States may never be fully appreciated unless the presence of Canadian settlers and migrants is taken into account. Similarly, Canadian history, whether national or regional, will remain partial so long as the processes that led millions of migrants to move to the other side of the border remain hidden.

Yet, despite the revival of migration history in the historiography of the two neighboring countries during the last thirty years, very little attention has been paid to this massive intracontinental shift of population—except for the portion comprising French Canadians of Quebec. Given the complexity of the movement and the variety of local contexts it entailed, only a sustained research effort will fill this historical void.

Crossing the 49th Parallel is part of this effort. Building on the small amount of literature that treats English Canada and on the larger quantity dealing with Quebec, and drawing from a previously ignored archival source, this book has focused on the variety of socioeconomic spaces from which migration originated across the entire continent; and it has done so in such a way as to provide a basic understanding of the leading features of that movement while laying the basis for further in-depth inquiries.

Although our empirical analysis has dealt with the twentieth-century portion of the movement, it has revealed the extent to which this movement grew out of nineteenth-century migration experiences, which leads to the first major conclusion of this book: a basic continuity marked the spatial and social configuration of the movement as both the United States and Canada underwent their transition from agrarian to industrial societies. Much as they had done in the previous century, twentieth-century migrants moved within their own continental regions. Ontarians, more than any other provincial group, chose adjacent states such as Michigan and New York, whereas most Quebec French Canadians and Maritimers moved farther away from home but stayed largely within a region, New England, that had been the preferred destination since the movement originated, one brought even closer by the subsequent advances in railway transportation. In both cases, geographical proximity was an important factor; but just as important, if not more so, was the role played by migration traditions and networks developed in the nineteenth century, which linked Canadian districts to American ones and defined, in the minds of prospective migrants, the social and geographic parameters of their region.

As long as our knowledge of migration from English Canada rested on aggregate census data and on a few regional studies, one could only venture broad hypotheses on the social and economic characteristics of that movement and its articulations across the continent. Similarly, this gap in our knowledge has made it impossible to answer a question that has long been asked by historians and other social scientists: how similar were the migration experiences of French Canadians and English Canadians?

Addressing this question has been a primary concern of this book. The comparative approach we have adopted has brought to the fore more similarities than differences in the profiles of the migrant populations and in the patterns they engendered. Taken as a whole, Anglo-Canadians migrated at rates that were similar to, or at times were higher than, those of French Canadians. Moreover, the mechanisms of selection that migration entails operated in similar ways within the two movements. Hence the prominent presence of young migrants in both, the comparable rates of males and females, and the limited number of children. These demographic characteristics translated into a wide variety of patterns that are strikingly similar. In both the English and French components of the movement, the most frequent pattern was the migration of young unmarrieds, both males and females, often traveling alone. Moreover, family migration, as reflected in the small but significant presence of children, was practiced by the two groups at comparable rates.

Even more significant was the crucial role that social networks (kin and friends) played among both French and Anglo-Canadians, very likely influencing their decision to migrate and directing them to certain localities. These networks shed light on another common pattern: repeat migration. The propensity among repeat migrants to return to the same state and often the same district to which they had previously migrated has allowed us to identify those social and physical spaces that geographers have called migration fields. Such fields radiating southward from Quebec are highly visible on account of the wide array of ethnic institutions that French Canadians created in their districts of settlement; but our research has shown that migration fields were also operative among Anglo-Canadians, whose visibility as migrants receded once they entered American civil society.

◆

It was in the analysis of the overall occupational structure that the major difference between the two movements emerged. On the whole, Anglo-Canadian male migrants comprised a larger proportion of businessmen, professionals, and supervisory personnel, as well as a larger proportion of white-collar workers and skilled tradesmen—to such an extent that we saw this as one of the unique features of Anglo-Canadian migration in that era. A similar trend emerged among female migrants, though in this case the proportion of factory-related and craft occupations was significantly higher among French Canadians. This sharp contrast in the occupational profile of the two groups was due essentially to the different socioeconomic contexts from which migrants departed. Much as in the nineteenth century, twentieth-century migration from Quebec originated largely from agrarian districts and small towns that industrialization had touched only marginally. Anglo-Canadians, on the other hand, tended to leave cities and urban districts driven by industrial economies that had produced a much wider range of skills and occupations in manufacturing as well as in several service sectors.

◆

Yet when we sought to go beyond these broad features of the two movements, we saw the limitations of a comparative approach when applied to two populations that historically have been differentiated mainly by language. As this book has shown, French Canada was not synonymous with francophone Quebeckers. It included small but significant numbers of Franco-Ontarians, Acadians mostly from the Maritimes, and smaller groups who had moved to the prairie provinces—populations that have remained absent from the historical literature on French-Canadian migration to the United States. Likewise, Anglo-Canada did not only comprise a population whose ancestry was British or American; as the twentieth century advanced, an increasing proportion of Anglo-Canadians consisted of persons born in the Dominion from parents who had immigrated from a variety of mostly European countries. We sought to take into account the presence of these subgroups by adopting whenever possible a comparative framework that threw new light onto the sociocultural composition of the migrating population.

Perhaps even more important than language and ethnic background was the variety of regional contexts marking the socioeconomic landscape of English Canada in particular. Such a variety—best expressed in the contrast between a rapidly developing Ontario and a chronically depressed Maritime region—poses severe limitations to a comparative approach applied to "the two Canadas." For when due consideration was given to the structural and conjunctural contexts engendering migration, we were faced not with *one* Anglo-Canadian movement but with several. Likewise, postulating *one* French-Canadian movement would have prevented us from accounting for the different structural and cultural contexts of a Quebec rural parish, a fishing village in the Bay of Fundy, or a northern Ontario mining district.

Although the adoption of a continental scale did serve some initial analytical purposes, it was only when the scale was lowered to a regional level that the migration of Canadians acquired a fuller historical significance. If they moved predominantly within the confines of their region, this is because the interaction of physical distance, economic opportunities, and social relations turned those regions into the primary terrain through which they assessed their present situation and sought a better future. Continental regions have their topographical, historical, and geo-economic rationales; yet Canadian migrants created their own regions within those natural-historical divides—regions marked by their ongoing presence and endowed with a meaning growing out of years of accumulated collective knowledge and experience. It was within their regional context that most Canadian migrants interpreted their opportunities, mobilized their human and material resources, wove and strengthened social relations, and passed a future on to their children. In the collective imagery of many Quebeckers and Maritimers, *les États* and the "Boston state" were much closer than southern Ontario or the prairie farmlands—and not just for those who left but also for many who stayed behind. Their stakes were much more bound to what happened in those "appropriated" districts south of the border than to what happened in a provincial capital or in Ottawa. And "what happened" could mean the opening of a new factory, the rise of wage scales, or the recruitment of nurses by American hospitals; but it could also mean working and living among relatives, friends, and fellow villagers or starting a family in an environment considered more rewarding.

The implications for the history of the Canadian and the American nation-states are compelling. For it is not merely the loss or gain of population and labor power that needs to be accounted for, but the fact that the most immediate and relevant universe of real and potential migrants was not wholly contained within either one of the two nation-states.

Although the issue of national identity is outside the confines of this book, the patterns of migration we observed, the spatial links that were created across the border, and the meaning with which those spaces were invested constitute in our view essential elements in a historical reassessment of Canadian identity. They are also essential in assessing the specificity of Canadian migration in the context of the transatlantic movements of that era.

Unlike the millions of Europeans who contributed to what Walter Nugent has called "the great transatlantic migration," Canadians did not have to look very far. True, like many of their European counterparts on the move, Canadians had plenty of opportunities to exploit milieus within their own national boundaries, whether these were virgin lands awaiting settlers or boomtowns and industrial cities offering jobs and services. And most of them did try to take advantage of those opportunities, thus giving rise to some of the most sweeping socioeconomic changes in Canadian history. But their moves could as easily take them to a nearby district south of the border. In this, they were not different from the many Americans who did not have to travel very far to pursue on Canadian soil a more promising farming future.

Moreover, like most Europeans, Canadians lived in locations whose regional parameters had been shaped by nature and history. Imperially imposed patterns of trade could hardly prevent Maritimers from seeing coastal New Englanders as their natural neighbors; and from a strictly physical point of view, much of southwestern Ontario was an integral part of the Great Lakes region. At the same time, no European country shared with another a 5,500-mile boundary or had as its neighbor a nation that underwent the kind of territorial and economic expansion experienced by the United States. Thus for many Canadians the territory that lay south of the border was a natural extension of their own territory. Marcus Hansen and John Brebner have used the term "mingling" to describe the interaction occurring among Canadians and American along border regions; and other scholars have gone as far as talking of a "symbiosis" when referring to the socioeconomic processes marking those regions that were adjacent to the border.[1]

Our own findings have shown that the mobility set off by socioeconomic transformation took Canadians to places they knew best, in most cases places within their own region either north or south of the border. Unlike their European counterparts, the overwhelming majority of Canadians moved within the continent, and for most of them their regional territories offered the opportunity they sought to improve their lot. It was the presence of a nearby legal border that turned mobile Canadians into "migrants."

◆

These were not the only unique features of Canadian emigration. By switching the scale of analysis from a regional to a transoceanic one, *Crossing the 49th Parallel* has unveiled a dimension of international migration that conferred on Canada a unique place in the Atlantic socioeconomic system. One out of five migrants who crossed the border to work and live in the United States was not a Canadian but a European who had first migrated to Canada and subsequently remigrated. The occasional references to this phenomenon one finds in the historical literature indicate that this trajectory had been a frequent one in the history of transatlantic migrations. By identifying this remigrant population as precisely as the available sources allow, we could understand its full ethnocultural heterogeneity. Migrants originating from continental Europe, from the British Isles, and from Scandinavia—whether brought to Canada by recruiting agents, by sponsored programs, or by independent migration—saw the Dominion as the land where they could improve their lot; and they invested their human and social resources to make their migration project work. But a number of them, much like their Canadian counterparts, searched farther and saw in the United States an opportunity to improve their material conditions or to live a richer social life among kin and friends.

The study of the remigration movement has thus helped concretize the double role that Canada played in the transatlantic circuits of population and labor: drawing millions of Europeans to its vast territory and economic resources while at the same time contributing to the demographic and economic growth of the United States by sending a portion of this population south of the border. However significant were the occupational experiences of British-born machinists and Italian-born laborers, their remigration occurred largely within a regional context and relied to a large extent upon the support of kin and friends. For both groups over many decades, the United States and Canada were extensions of each other—until cultural and political imperatives turned the border into a insurmountable wall for some and a welcoming gate for others.

Appendix

The main archival source utilized in this book, in particular in chapters 3–5, is the *Soundex Index to Canadian Border Entries through the Saint Albans, Vermont, District*, which is part of the records of the U.S. Immigration and Naturalization Services, Record Group 85. The largest portion of this collection has been subdivided into two parts, RG M1461, covering the period 1895 to June 1924 (400 microfilm reels), and RG M1463 (98 microfilm reels), covering the period July 1924 to 1952.

The *Index* reproduces on individual cards the information recorded by U.S. immigration officials on manifests of alien passengers entering the United States from Canada ("List or Manifest of Alien Passengers for the United States Immigration Officer at Port of Arrival") at the various points of entry along the Canadian-U.S. border from Maine to Washington.

The recording of manifests was instituted in 1895 by the U.S. Bureau of Immigration (later the Immigration and Naturalization Service) as a way to control the flow of overseas immigrants entering the country through Canada. Housed for many years at the INS station in Saint Albans, Vermont, the original collection of manifests was subsequently transcribed into cards and arranged alphabetically through the system of surname coding known as "Soundex." It thus became an indispensable administrative tool allowing INS officials to retrieve and verify the date of entry of each foreign-born resident applying for U.S. naturalization, as proof of entry became mandatory for all applicants entering U.S. territory after 1905.

The *Soundex Index* collection subsequently became part of the National Archives in Washington and, after being transferred to microfilm, has been made available to researchers. Copies of the collection have also been deposited at the various National Archives regional centers. The acquisition of a copy of the *Index* by the Bibliothèque Municipale de Montréal made this study conceivable and feasible in logistic and financial terms. (For a more detailed history of this source, see Constance Potter, "St. Albans Passenger Arrival Records," *Prologue*, spring 1990, pp. 90–93.)

Besides providing basic demographic, geographic, ethnolinguistic, and occupational information, an entrant was asked if he or she was accompanied, and if so, the age of the accompanying person(s) and their relationship to the entrant. Also worthy of mention is information that makes possible a longitudinal perspective on each recorded border crossing: whether the entrant had previously resided in the United States, and if so, when and where; the place of destination, along with the name of a reference at that location and his or her relationship to the entrant; and the place of birth as distinct from the place of last residence (making it possible to identify European-born migrants and create the data bank on which chapter 5 of this book is largely based). Information of a medical and administrative nature was recorded by immigration officials on the verso of the card.

For the purposes of this study, we created a random sample of the two-part *Index* collection by selecting every eighteenth card, starting with the first reel and continuing through the following 597 reels. In doing so, we accounted for the frequent frames that were duplicated because of faulty reproduction (the INS identified such cases through the insertion of special cards). We have also excluded from our count those cards that had been inserted for purely administrative reasons—in most cases an attachment to an individual passenger card. The result was a sample comprising 42,599 individual cases, spanning 1895 to 1952.

Our study, however, has dealt with the portion of the sample covering the years 1906–30. Preliminary analyses of this sample led us to conclude that the pre-1906 portion of the collection was not entirely reliable. The fact that U.S. naturalization laws did not require a proof of entry for applicants having immigrated before 1906 may explain why the transcription of pre-1906 manifests onto *Soundex Index* cards was not done as effectively as it was later. As to the terminal date of our study, we chose the year

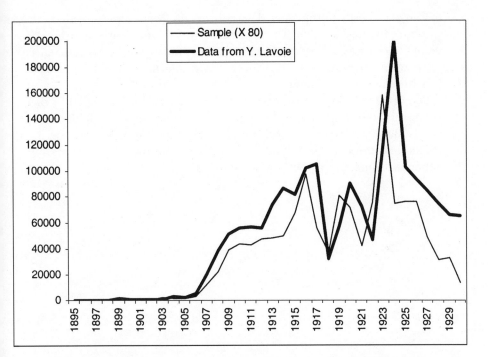

Chart A.1. Yearly fluctuations of Canadian immigration to the United States, 1895–1930. *Index* data compared to U.S. Bureau of Census data. From Yolande Lavoie, *L'émigration des Québécois aux États-Unis*, p. 10 (taken from U.S. Bureau of Census, *Historical Statistics of the United States*, Series C-88-114).

1930 because by then the emigration movement from Canada to the United States had come to an end, as explained at the end of chapter 4 and as shown in chart A.1.

A significant number of cases recorded in the *Index* (and obviously included in our sample) concern people who were not migrating to the United States but were only crossing the border in order to reach a U.S. port on their way to an overseas destination. Similarly, a sizable portion of Canadians transited simply because they saw it more convenient to make a portion of their trip through U.S. territory on their way to a Canadian destination. As these crossings did not involve migrations to the United States, they were excluded from our analyses.

The population of actual migrants from Canada to the United States in our sample comprises 21,202 individuals, including both Canadians and foreign-born residents of Canada. Of these, 4,396 were French Canadians; 16,328 were Anglo-Canadians; and 4,874 were foreign-born residents of Canada (mostly Europeans). These three subgroups have provided the structure for chapters 3–5. The representativity of our sample may be observed in chart A.1, showing the close correspondance between the yearly fluctuations we reconstituted from the *Index* and those based on official U.S. Bureau of Census data.

Our analysis has taken into account all major variables provided by the *Index*, thus resulting in a large number of cross-tabulations, tables, and charts. Because of editorial constraints and stylistic considerations, we included only those we considered essential to our narrative. Other data are either explained in the text or cited in the notes.

◆

Notes

Preface

1. Marcus L. Hansen and John B. Brebner, *The Mingling of the Canadian and American Peoples* (New Haven, 1940). Hansen passed away soon after the completion of his manuscript, whose publication was ensured by John Brebner.

2. A notable exception is Walter Nugent, *Crossings: The Great Transatlantic Migrations, 1870–1914* (Bloomington, 1992), where the author treats Canada's role as a receiver-sender society as part of a broader discussion, at a macrohistorical level, of the major transatlantic population movements.

3. Bruno Ramirez, *On the Move: French-Canadian and Italian Migrants in the North Atlantic Economy, 1860–1914* (Toronto, 1991).

Chapter 1. Societies in Motion

1. *Report of the Special Committee on Emigration,* Journals of the Legislative Assembly (Toronto, 1857), appendix N. 47. Hereafter *Report on Emigration, 1857.*

2. Yolande Lavoie, *L'émigration des Québécois aux États-Unis de 1840 à 1930* (Quebec, 1979), p. 45.

3. Leon E. Truesdell, *The Canadian Born in the United States* (New Haven, 1943), pp. 10, 16, 57; Yolande Lavoie, *L'émigration des Canadiens aux États-Unis avant 1930: Mesure du phénomène* (Montreal, 1972), p. 21.

4. Michael Cross, ed., *The Frontier Thesis and the Canadas: The Debate on the Impact of the Canadian Environment* (Toronto, 1970).

5. See, for instance, the reports submitted to the Special Committee on Emigration by T. Boutillier, of Saint Hyacinthe; A. Fraser, of Temiscouata; N. Nadeau, of Cape Saint Ignace; B. Guay, of Notre Dame de la Victoire. *Report on Emigration, 1857.*

6. Gerald M. Craig, *Upper Canada: The Formative Years, 1784–1841* (Toronto, 1963), pp. 1–19, 42–65; R. Cole Harris and John Warkentin, *Canada before Confederation* (New

194 *Notes to pages 3–6*

York, 1974), pp. 110–30; Fred Landon, *Western Ontario and the American Frontier* (Toronto, 1967); Marcus Lee Hansen and John B. Brebner, *The Mingling of the Canadian and American Peoples* (New Haven, 1940); D. Aidan McQuillan, "Les communautés canadiennes-françaises du Midwest américain au dix-neuvième siècle," in Dean R. Lauder and Eric Waddell, eds., *Du continent perdu à l'archipel retrouvé* (Quebec, 1983), pp. 97–115.

7. Ian Wallace, "The Canadian Shield: The Development of a Resource Frontier," in L. D. McCann, ed., *Heartland and Hinterland: A Geography of Canada* (Scarborough, Ont., 1981), pp. 372–409; Robert L. Jones, *History of Agriculture in Ontario, 1613–1880* (Toronto, 1946), pp. 289 ff.; Cole Harris and Warkentin, *Canada before Confederation*, p. 114.

8. Richard J. Hathaway, "From Ontario to the Great Lake State: Canadians in Michigan," *Michigan History* 67, 2 (1983): 42–45; Gregory S. Rose, "The Origins of Canadian Settlers in Southern Michigan, 1820–1850," *Ontario History* 79, 1 (1987): 31–52.

9. Quoted in Landon, *Western Ontario*, pp. 188–89.

10. Matthew Josephson, *Edison* (New York, 1959), pp. 2, 8–9.

11. R. S. Longley, "Emigration and the Crisis of 1837 in Upper Canada," *Canadian Historical Review* 17 (1936): 29–40.

12. Josephson, *Edison*, p. 2.

13. Charles F. Kovacik, "A Geographical Analysis of the Foreign Born in Huron, Sanilac, and St. Clair Counties of Michigan, with Particular Reference to Canadians: 1850–1880" (Ph.D. diss., Michigan State University, 1970), p. 70.

14. Richard C. Ford, "The French-Canadians in Michigan," *Michigan History* 27 (1943): 243–57; Benoît Brouillette, *La pénétration du continent américain par les Canadiens français, 1763–1846: traitants, explorateurs, missionnaires* (Montreal, 1939); Elzéar Paquin, *La colonie canadienne française de Chicago* (Chicago, 1893); Marc Potvin, "Le déclin d'une communauté franco-américaine: Fort Benton, Montana" (M.A. thesis, Université de Montréal, 1989), pp. 31–47.

15. Allan Greer, *Peasant, Lord, and Merchant: Rural Society in Three Quebec Parishes, 1740–1840* (Toronto, 1985), pp. 181–87, 226–28; Potvin, "Le déclin," pp. 24–31.

16. Charles B. Campbell, "Bourbonnais or the Early French Settlements in Kankakee County, Illinois," *Transactions of the Illinois State Historical Society* 11 (1906): 65–72; Hansen and Brebner, *The Mingling*, pp. 128–30.

17. McQuillan, "Les communautés canadiennes françaises," pp. 98–112.

18. Kovacik, "A Geographical Analysis," p. 70.

19. Alan A. Brookes, "The Exodus: Migration from the Maritime Provinces to Boston during the Second Half of the Nineteenth Century" (Ph.D. diss., University of New Brunswick, 1979), p. 81.

20. I. L. MacDougall, "Commercial Relations between Nova Scotia and the United States of America, 1830–1854" (M.A. thesis, Dalhousie University, 1961); William H. Bunting, *Portrait of a Port: Boston, 1852–1914* (Cambridge, Mass., 1971), pp. 88, 217–19; Alan A. Brookes, "Out-Migration from the Maritime Provinces, 1860–1900: Some Preliminary Considerations," *Acadiensis* 5, 2 (1976): 42–44; Cole Harris and Warkentin, *Canada before Confederation*, p. 188.

21. These debates are critically assessed in Louise Dechêne, "Observations sur l'agriculture du Bas-Canada au début du XIXe siècle," in Joseph Goy et Jean-Pierre Wallot, eds., *Évolution et éclatement du monde rural, France-Québec, XVIIe–XXe siècles* (Montreal, 1986), pp. 189–202.

22. Robert Armstrong, *Structure and Change: An Economic History of Québec* (Toronto,

1984), pp. 82–83; Cole Harris and Warkentin, *Canada before Confederation*, pp. 85–86.

23. *Lord Durham's Report*, edited and with an introduction by Gerald M. Craig (Ottawa, 1964), p. 136.

24. *Report of the Select Committee of the Legislative Assembly, Appointed to Inquire into the Causes and Importance of the Emigration, from Lower Canada to the United States* (Montreal, 1849).

25. Gérald Bernier et Robert Boily, *Le Québec en chiffres de 1850 à nos jours* (Montreal, 1986), p. 25.

26. Cole Harris and Warkentin, *Canada before Confederation*, p. 69.

27. Serge Courville, *Entre ville et campagne: l'essor du village dans les seigneuries du Bas-Canada* (Quebec , 1990), p. 37.

28. Fernand Ouellet, *Lower Canada, 1791–1840: Social Change and Nationalism* (Toronto, 1980), p. 143.

29. Armstrong, *Structure and Change*, p. 167; Normand Séguin, *La conquête du sol au 19ème siècle* (Montreal, 1977).

30. *Report on Emigration, 1857*, p. 6.

31. Ibid.

32. David Gagan, "Land, Population and Social Change: The 'Critical Years' in Rural Canada West," *Canadian Historical Review* 59 (1978): 296; John McCallum, *Unequal Beginnings: Agriculture and Economic Development in Quebec and Ontario until 1870* (Toronto, 1980), pp. 3–4.

33. McCallum, *Unequal Beginnings*, pp. 45–46.

34. Jones, *History of Agriculture*, esp. pp. 199–202.

35. McCallum, *Unequal Beginnings*, table S.7, p.129.

36. Jacob Spelt, *Urban Development in South-Central Ontario* (Ottawa, 1972); McCallum, *Unequal Beginnings*, table S.8, p. 130.

37. Helen I. Cowan, *British Emigration to British North America, the First Hundred Years* (Toronto, 1961); Norman Macdonald, *Canada: Immigration and Colonization, 1841–1903* (Toronto, 1966).

38. D. A. Muise, "Parties and Constituencies: Federal Elections in Nova Scotia, 1867–1896," *Annual Report of the Canadian Historical Association*, 1972, pp. 83–101.

39. Brookes, "The Exodus," p. 19.

40. Quoted in Ian McKay, "Class Struggle and Merchant Capital: Craftsmen and Labourers on the Halifax Waterfront, 1850–1900," in Chad Gaffield, ed., *Constructing Modern Canada* (Toronto, 1994), pp. 33–34.

41. Stanley A. Saunders, *Economic History of the Maritime Provinces* (Ottawa, 1939), p. 112. On the centrality of timber and forest-derived products for the New Brunswick economy, see also Graeme Wynn, *Timber Colony: A Historical Geography of Early Nineteenth Century New Brunswick* (Toronto, 1981); Cole Harris and Warkentin, *Canada before Confederation*, p. 198.

42. John E. Nelligan, "The Life of a Lumberman," part 1, *Wisconsin Magazine of History* 13 (1929): 19.

43. Ibid., p. 31.

44. Brookes, "The Exodus," pp. 32–36.

45. Quoted in ibid., p. 36.

46. Nelligan, "Life of a Lumberman," p. 21 ff.

47. Bunting, *Portrait of a Port*, pp. 88, 217–19; Brookes, "Out-Migration from the Maritime Provinces," pp. 42–44.

48. D. C. Masters, *The Reciprocity Treaty of 1854* (Toronto, 1969).

49. Armstrong, *Structure and Change,* p. 158; Robert E. Ankli, "The Reciprocity Treaty of 1854," *Canadian Journal of Economics,* 4,1 (1971).

50. Paul-André Linteau, René Durocher, and Jean-Claude Robert, *Histoire du Québec contemporain* (Montreal, 1979), pp. 119–24; Armstrong, *Structure and Change,* pp. 158–66.

51. Census of Canada, 1871, Manuscript Schedules, St. Cuthbert, reel C-10039.

52. McCullom, *Unequal Beginnings,* tables S.4 and S.5, p. 127.

53. Linteau, Durocher, and Robert, *Histoire du Québec contemporain,* p. 120.

54. René Hardy et Normand Séguin, *Forêt et société en Mauricie* (Montreal, 1984); Christian Pouyez et al., *Les Saguenayens: Introduction à l'histoire des populations du Saguenay* (Quebec , 1983).

55. Bernard Bernier, "The Penetration of Capitalism in Quebec Agriculture," *Canadian Review of Sociology and Anthropology* 13, 4 (1976): 422–34.

56. Bruno Ramirez, *On The Move: French-Canadian and Italian Migrants in the North Atlantic Economy, 1860–1914* (Toronto, 1991), pp. 27–28.

57. Yves Otis, "Famille et exploitations agricoles: Quatre paroisses de la rive sud de Montréal, 1852–1871" (M.A. thesis, Université du Québec à Montréal, 1985).

58. Courville, *Entre ville et campagne;* Serge Courville and Normand Séguin, *Le monde rural québécois au XIXe siècle* (Ottawa, 1989).

59. Paul-André Linteau, *Histoire de Montréal depuis la Confédération* (Montreal, 1992), pp. 17–38.

60. Quoted in McCallum, *Unequal Beginnings,* pp. 96–97.

61. France Gagnon, "Parenté et migration: Le cas des Canadiens français à Montréal entre 1845 et 1875," *Historical Papers of the Canadian Historical Association,* 1988, pp. 63–85; Jean-Claude Robert, "Urbanisation et population: Le cas de Montréal en 1861," *Revue d'histoire de l'Amérique française* 38 (March 1982): 523–35.

62. Séguin, *La conquête du sol;* John Willis, "Urbanization, Colonization and Underdevelopment in the Bas-Saint-Laurent: Fraserville and the Témiscouata in the Late Nineteenth Century," *Cahiers de géographie du Québec* 27, 73–73 (1984): 125–61; John I. Little, *Nationalism, Capitalism, and Colonization in Nineteenth-Century Quebec* (Montreal, 1989).

63. Documents de la Session du Québec, 1869, vol. 1, doc. 4. (In this book all translations from French and Italian are by the author.)

64. Ralph D. Vicero, *Immigration of French Canadians to New England, 1840–1900: A Geographical Analysis* (Ph.D. diss., University of Wisconsin, 1968), p. 276.

65. Vicero, "Immigration of French Canadians," p. 275.

66. Studies dealing with the rise of French-Canadian communities in industrial New England include Yves Roby, *Les Franco Américains de la Nouvelle-Angleterre: 1776–1930* (Quebec, 1990); François Weil, *Les Franco-Américains 1860–1980* (Tours, 1989); Yves Frenette, "La genèse d'une communauté canadienne-française en Nouvelle-Angleterre, Lewiston, Maine, 1800–1880" (Ph.D. diss., Université Laval, 1988); Édouard Hamon, *Les Canadiens français de la Nouvelle-Angleterre* (Quebec, 1891).

67. Ramirez, *On the Move,* pp. 120–25.

68. Frances Early, "French-Canadian Beginnings in an American Community: Lowell, Massachusetts, 1868–1886" (Ph.D. diss., Concordia University, 1979); Frenette, "La genèse d'une communauté."

69. Ramirez, *On the Move,* pp. 35–41.

70. Jean Lamarre, "La migration des Canadiens français vers le Michigan, 1840–1914: Leur contribution au développement socioéconomique de la région" (Ph.D. diss., Université de Montréal, 1995); Lamarre, "Migration Patterns and Socio-Economic Integra-

tion of the French Canadians in the Sagginaw Valley, Michigan 1840–1900," *Mid-America* 80, 3 (1988): 176–208.

71. E. R. Forbes and D. A. Muise, eds., *Atlantic Canada in Confederation* (Toronto, 1986); David Frank, ed., *Industrialization and Underdevelopment in the Maritimes, 1880–1930* (Toronto, 1985).

72. Brookes, "The Exodus," pp. 72–75.

73. For some perceptive assessments of the major historiographical issues, see Eric Sager, "Dependency, Underdevelopment and the Economic History of the Atlantic Provinces," *Acadiensis* 17, 1 (1987): 117–37; Phillip Buckner, "The Maritimes and Confederation: A Reassessment," *Canadian Historical Review* 71, 1 (1990).

74. T. William Acheson, "The N.P. and the Industrialization of the Maritimes, 1880–1910," Acadiensis 1, 2 (1972); D. Alexander, "Economic Growth in the Atlantic Region, 1880–1940," *Acadiensis* 8 (autumn 1978), pp. 47–76.

75. David Frank, "The Cape Breton Coal Industry and the Rise and Fall of the British Empire Steel Corporation," *Acadiensis* 7 (autumn 1977), 3–34.

76. Acheson, "The N.P. and the Industrialization of the Maritimes," p. 3.

77. Alexander, "Economic Growth in the Atlantic Region."

78. Patricia A. Thornton, "The Problem of Out-Migration from Atlantic Canada, 1871–1921: A New Look," *Acadiensis* 15, 1 (1985), pp. 3–34.

79. "Margaret Pottinger," in Margaret Conrad, Toni Laidlaw and Donna Smyth, eds., *No Place Like Home: Diaries and Letters of Nova Scotia Women, 1771–1938* (Halifax, 1988), p. 193.

80. "Margaret Pottinger," p. 189.

81. Brookes, "Out-Migration from the Maritime Provinces," pp. 42–44.

82. See the pioneering works on a Canadian-U.S. transborder area by Béatrice Craig, "Early French Migration to Northern Maine, 1785–1850," *Maine Historical Society Quarterly* 25 (1986): 230–47.

83. Beatsy Beattie, "'Going Up to Lynn': Single, Maritime-Born Women in Lynn, Massachusetts, 1879–1930," *Acadiensis* 22, 1 (1992): 67–68.

84. "Hannah Richardson," in Conrad, Laidlaw, and Smyth, *No Place Like Home*, pp. 153–54; see Beattie's insightful discussion of Richardson's diary in "Going Up to Lynn."

85. Beattie, "Going Up to Lynn," p. 69.

86. Frederick A. Bushee, *Ethnic Factors in the Population of Boston* (reprint; New York, 1970).

87. Bunting, *Portrait of a Port*, pp. 88, 217–19; Brookes "Out-Migration from the Maritime Provinces," pp. 42–44.

88. For important exceptions, see references in chapter 4.

89. The impact of these developments on depopulation in southeastern Ontario are discussed in Randolph Widdis, *With Scarcely a Ripple: Anglo-Canadian Migration into the United States and Western Canada, 1890–1929* (Montreal, 1998), chap. 5.

90. D. A. Lawr, "The Development of Ontario Farming, 1870–1914: Patterns of Growth and Change," *Ontario History* 64, 4 (1972): 239–51; J. A. Ruddick, "The Development of the Dairy Industry in Canada," in A. H. Innis, ed., *The Dairy Industry in Canada* (Toronto, 1937); Robert E. Ankli and Wendy Millar, "Ontario Agriculture in Transition: The Switch from Wheat to Cheese," *Journal of Economic History* 42 (March 1982).

91. Lawr, "Development of Ontario Farming," p. 241.

92. Ibid., pp. 240–41.

93. David Gagan, *Hopeful Travellers: Families, Land, and Social Change in Mid-Victorian Peel County, Canada West* (Toronto, 1981), pp. 126–42.

94. Gordon Darroch, "Class in Nineteenth-Century Central Ontario: A Reassessment of the Crisis and Demise of Small Producers during Early Industrialization," in Gregory Kealey, ed., *Class, Gender and Region: Essays in Canadian Historical Sociology* (St. John's, 1988), pp. 49–72.

95. Quoted in Lawr, "Development of Ontario Farming," p. 251.

96. Terry Crowley, "Rural Labour," in Paul Craven, ed., *Labouring Lives: Work and Workers in Nineteenth-Century Ontario* (Toronto, 1992), p. 57.

97. Widdis, *With Scarcely a Ripple*, p. 90.

98. David Smith, "Paying the Price: The Rural Origins of Canadian Migration in the Great Lakes Region, 1870s–1890s" (unpublished). I am grateful to the author for making this manuscript available.

99. McCallum, *Unequal Beginnings*, table S.8, p. 130.

100. Craig Heron, "Factory Workers," in Craven, *Labouring Lives*, p. 497.

101. Ibid., pp. 497–98.

102. Olivier Zunz, *The Changing Face of Inequality: Urbanization, Industrial Development, and Immigrants in Detroit, 1880–1920* (Chicago, 1982), p. 106.

103. Ibid., p. 221.

104. Ibid., pp. 133, 248, 246.

Chapter 2. The Rise of the Border

1. Leon E. Truesdell, *The Canadian Born in the United States* (New Haven, 1943), p. 10.

2. Truesdell, *The Canadian Born*, pp. 16, 57.

3. R. C. Brown and R. Cook, *Canada, 1896–1921: A Nation Transformed* (Toronto, 1974); Kenneth Norris and Douglas Owram, *History of the Canadian Economy* (Toronto, 1990); Paul-André Linteau, René Durocher, and Jean-Claude Robert, *Histoire du Québec contemporain* (Montreal, 1979), pp. 351–456.

4. T. W. Acheson, D. Frank, and J. Frost, *Industrialization and the Underdevelopment in the Maritimes, 1880–1930* (Toronto, 1985); H. V. Nelles, *The Politics of Development: Forest, Mines, and Hydro-Electric Power in Ontario, 1849–1941* (Toronto, 1974); J. M. S. Careless, *Frontier and Metropolis: Regions, Cities and Identities in Canada before 1914* (Toronto, 1989).

5. The best analysis of Canadian immigration policies in the context of changing socioeconomic conditions is Donald H. Avery, *Reluctant Host: Canada's Response to Immigrant Workers, 1896–1994* (Toronto, 1995). See also the imaginative approach to Canadian immigration history taken by Dirk Hoerder, *Creating Societies: Immigrant Lives in Canada* (Montreal, 1999).

6. Avery, *Reluctant Host*, p. 33. The major study of American immigration to Canada during the early twentieth century remains Harold M. Troper, *Only Farmers Need Apply: Official Canadian Government Encouragement of Immigration from the United States, 1896–1911* (Toronto, 1972).

7. Yolande Lavoie, *L'émigration des Québécois aux États-Unis*, p. 45.

8. John E. Nelligan, "The Life of a Lumberman," part 1, *Wisconsin Magazine of History* 13 (1929), pp. 3–65; "Mr. Jones' Life in La Crosse County," *American Life Histories: Manuscripts from the Federal Writers' Project, 1936–1940* (American Memory; http://lcweb2.loc.gov, then search by title). The Joneses were one of several Canadian rural families who read about the availability of good farming land in the La Crosse County prairies. In 1853 the whole family—parents and four boys—crossed the border

and settled in the village of Bangor, Wisconsin. U.S. National Archives, *Soundex Index to Canadian Border Entries* (hereafter cited as *Index*), RG M1461, reel 116.

9. Diplomatic and territorial histories of the Canada–U.S. boundary include Marian Botsford Fraser, *Walking the Line* (Vancouver, 1989); George H. Classen, *Thrust and Counterthrust: The Genesis of the Canada–United States Boundary* (Don Mills, Ontario, 1965); Bruce Hutchison, *The Struggle for the Border* (Toronto, 1955).

10. Lee Hansen and John B. Brebner, *The Mingling of the Canadian and American Peoples* (New Haven, 1940).

11. U. S. Bureau of Immigration, *Annual Report of the Commissioner-General of Immigration, 1896* (Washington, D.C., 1896), p. 14.

12. Dominion of Canada, *Report on the Alleged Exodus to Western United States at Port Huron*, by John Lowe. Annex to the Report of Minister of Agriculture, 1883 (Ottawa, 1884), pp. 1–5; hereafter cited as *Lowe Report*.

13. John Lowe, "Population, Immigration, and Pauperism in the Dominion of Canada," appendix to *Lowe Report*.

14. *Lowe Report*, p. 6.

15. Ibid., p. 7.

16. Thomas A. Klug, "The Detroit Labor Movement and the United States–Canada Border, 1885–1930," *Mid-America*, vol. 80, 3 (1998): 209–34, provides a penetrating analysis of the Detroit situation and of organized labor's campaign for an efficient border control system.

17. U. S. Congress, House, *Report of the Select Committee to Inquire into the Alleged Violation of the Laws Prohibiting the Importation of Contract Laborers, Paupers, Convicts, and Other Classes*, 50th Cong., 1889; Klug, "Detroit Labor Movement," pp. 224–25.

18. U. S. Senate, *Report of the Select Committee on Immigration and Naturalization*, 51st Cong., 1891, p. vii.

19. Calculated from data provided by Walter F. Willcox, ed., *International Migrations*, vol. 1, *Statistics* (New York, 1969), p. 387.

20. *Report of the Select Committee on Immigration and Naturalization*, p. vii.

21. The jurisdiction of the U.S. Immigration Bureau and the new immigration inspection procedures are described in detail in U. S. Industrial Commission, *Reports of the Industrial Commission on Immigration*, vol. 15 (Washington D.C., 1901), pp. 659–66.

22. The report was made by Charles Goff, a U.S. immigrant inspector assigned to Montreal; see Constance Potter, "St. Albans Passenger Arrival Records," *Prologue* (spring 1990), p. 90.

23. For a detailed discussion of the "Canadian Agreement" see Marian L. Smith, "INS at the US-Canadian Border, 1893–1993: An Overview of Issues and Topics," paper presented at the meeting of the Organization of American Historians, Toronto, 23 April 1999.

24. U.S. Bureau of Immigration, *Annual Report of the Commissioner-General of Immigration, 1896* (Washington, D.C., 1896), p. 13.

25. Ibid., p. 14.

26. U.S. Bureau of Immigration, *Annual Report, 1897*, p.6.

27. Ibid., p. 6.

28. U.S. Bureau of Immigration, *Annual Report, 1898*, pp. 37–38.

29. Ibid., p. 39.

30. U.S. Bureau of Immigration, *Annual Report, 1899*, pp. 31–32.

31. U.S. Bureau of Immigration, *Annual Report, 1900*, p. 41.

32. Smith, "INS at the US-Canadian Border," p. 4.

33. Klug, "Detroit Labor Movement," p. 231.

34. *Index*, RG M1461, reel 116.

35. Smith, "INS at the US-Canadian Border," p. 15; Potter, "St. Alban Passenger Arrival Records," p. 92.

36. *Index*, RG M1461; "Hatty L.," reel 310.

37. Ibid., "James S.," reel 420.

38. Ibid., "Rachel F.," reel 155.

39. Quoted in Avery, *Reluctant Host*, p. 95; Avery also discusses diplomatic exchanges between Canadian and U.S. authorities on the issue of quota restrictions.

40. Ovila Lafrenière file, Projet d'Histoire Orale, Collection Ramirez-Rouillard, Département d'Histoire, Université de Montréal.

41. This pattern is discussed at length in chapters 3 and 4.

42. Niles Carpenter, *Immigrants and Their Children*, 1920 (1927; reprint, New York, 1969), p. 264.

43. Calculated from Willcox, *International Migrations*, vol. 1, *Statistics*, table 3, pp. 391–93.

44. U. S. Bureau of Immigration, *Annual Report, 1924*, p. 4.

45. Massachusetts Department of Labor and Industry, *Twelfth Annual Report of the Bureau of Statistics of Labor* (Boston, 1881), pp. 469–70. Lengthier discussions of this incident include Yves Roby, *Les Franco-Américains de la Nouvelle-Angleterre: 1776–1930* (Quebec, 1990), pp. 185–88; Pierre Anctil, "Chinese of the Eastern States, 1881," *Recherches sociographiques* 22, 1 (1981): 125–31; Bruno Ramirez, *On the Move: French-Canadian and Italian Migrants in the North Atlantic Economy, 1860–1914* (Toronto, 1991), pp. 111–13.

46. Klug, "Detroit Labor Movement," pp. 219–25.

47. U. S. Immigration Bureau, *Annual Report, 1896*, p.14.

48. U. S. Industrial Commission, *Reports of the Industrial Commission on Immigration*, vol. 15 (Washington, D.C., 1901), pp. 16, 93.

49. Studies covering the presence of Canadians in U.S. cities and towns during the early twentieth century include Tamara K. Hareven and Randolph Langenbach, *Amoskeag: Life and Work in an American Factory City* (New York, 1978); Tamara K. Hareven, *Family Time and Industrial Time: The Relationship between the Family and Work in a New England Industrial Community* (Cambridge, Mass., 1982); Gary Gerstle, *Working-Class Americanism: The Politics of Labor in a Textile City, 1914–1960* (Cambridge, Mass., 1989); Yukari Takai, "Migration, Family, and Gender: A Longitudinal Analysis of French-Canadian Immigrants in Lowell, Massachusetts, 1900–1920" (Ph.D. diss., Université de Montréal, 1998); Randolph Widdis, *With Scarcely a Ripple: Anglo-Canadian Migration into the United States and Western Canada, 1880–1920* (Montreal, 1998); Beatsy Beattie, "'Going Up to Lynn': Single, Maritime-Born Women in Lynn, Massachusetts, 1879–1930," *Acadiensis* 22, 1 (1992).

50. Catherine Collomp, "Immigrants, Labor Markets, and the State, a Comparative Approach: France and the United States, 1880–1930," *Journal of American History* 86, 1 (1999): 60.

51. Samuel Gompers, "America Must Not Be Overwhelmed," *American Federationist* 31, 4 (1924): 314–16.

52. Avery, *Reluctant Host*, p. 95.

53. On the AFL's attitude toward Mexican immigration during the 1920s see Harvey Levenstein, "The AFL and Mexican Immigration in the 1920s: An Experiment in Labor Diplomacy," *Hispanic American Historical Review* 48, 2 (1968): 206–19.

54. Gompers, "America Must Not Be Overwhelmed," p. 313.

55. Oliver Hoyem, "Immigration and America's Safety," *American Federationist* 29, 11 (1922): 820–21.

56. James J. Davis, "An American Immigration Policy," *American Federationist* 31, 4 (1924): 290.

57. Ibid., p. 292.

58. Quoted in U. S. Bureau, *Annual Report, 1923*, p. 26.

59. Ibid., pp. 26–27.

60. U. S. Bureau of Immigration, *Annual Report, 1923*, p. 26.

61. Ibid., p. 27.

62. Jane Perry Clark, *Deportation of Aliens from the United States to Europe* (New York, 1931), p. 254.

63. R. M. Lower, "The Case against Immigration," *Queen's Quarterly* 37 (spring 1930), p. 573.

64. "Ils s'en vont," *La Gazette de Berthier*, 15 April 1892.

65. For the life and thought of these two leading French-Canadian nationalists, see Susan Mann Trofimenkoff, *The Dream of Nation: A Social and Intellectual History of Quebec* (Toronto, 1983).

66. Linteau, Durocher, and Robert, *Histoire du Québec contemporain*, p. 292. For a lengthier discussion of the relationship between colonization and emigration to the United States, see Ramirez, *On The Move*, pp. 76–86.

67. Eugénie Savoie file, Projet d'Histoire Orale.

68. Avery, *Reluctant Host*, especially chap. 1; see also, Valerie Knowles, *Strangers at Our Gates: Canadian Immigration and Immigration Policy, 1540–1990* (Toronto, 1992); Reg Whitaker, *Canada's Immigration Policy since Confederation* (Ottawa, 1989); Donald Avery and Bruno Ramirez, "European Immigrant Workers in Canada: Ethnicity, Militancy and State Repression," in Dirk Hoerder, Horst Roessler, and Inge Blank, eds., *Roots of the Transplanted*, vol. 2, *Plebeian Culture, Class and Politics in the Life of Labor Migrants* (New York, 1994), pp. 411–40.

69. Calculated from *Canadian Immigration and Population Study* (Ottawa, 1974), p. 8.

70. Hansen and Brebner, *The Mingling*, pp. 248, 250.

71. Avery, *Reluctant Host*, pp. 82–107; Georges-Marie Bilodeau, *Pour rester au Pays* (Quebec , 1926).

72. John A. Stevenson, "Is Canada an Immigration Sieve?" *MacLean's Magazine*, 15 February 1923, p. 20.

73. Ibid., p. 20.

74. Ibid.

75. Ibid., pp. 20–21.

76. See, among others, Duncan McArthur, "What is the Immigration Problem?" *Queen's Quarterly* 35 (1928), pp. 603–14; Agnes C. Laut, "Our Lost Immigrants," *MacLean's Magazine*, 21 January 1921, pp. 13, 54.

77. Georges Pelletier, "La duperie de l'immigration," *Le Devoir*, 3 March 1922.

78. Ibid.

79. "Immigration-émigration-migration," *Le Devoir*, 18 January 1923.

80. Oral history interviews in Bruno Ramirez, *Les premiers Italiens de Montréal: Naissance de la Petite Italie du Québec* (Montreal, 1984), pp. 122, 128.

81. "Contre la desertion," *L'Union des Cantons de l'Est*, 2 June 1923.

82. "L'Épiscopat denonce les desertions," *L'Union des Cantons de l'Est*, 21 June 1923, which reproduced the entire text of the letter.

83. Bruno Noury file, Projet d'Histoire Orale.

84. Jean Syndical, "Pourquoi ils partent," *Le Devoir*, 20 August 1923.

85. Lower, "Case against Immigration," p. 571.

86. Ibid., p. 569.

87. Ibid., p. 572.

88. *Index*, RG M1461, "Michele Delforno," reel 120.
89. Ibid., "Eli Mason," reel 260.
90. Ibid., "Almira Lusk," reel 235.

Chapter 3. Emigration from French Canada

1. *La Gazette de Berthier*, 7 August 1903, p. 3. Migration from Berthier County is analyzed in detail in Bruno Ramirez, *On the Move: French-Canadian and Italian Migrants in the North Atlantic Economy, 1860–1914* (Toronto, 1991), pp. 21–49.

2. Leroy O. Stone, *Urban Development in Canada* (Ottawa, 1967), p. 29. The return to Quebec of French Canadians and their U.S.-born children is discussed in Paul-André Linteau, "L'apport des migrants américains et franco-américains au Québec: un état de la question," *Revue d'Histoire de l'Amérique Française*, 53, 4 (2000): 561-602.

3. Paul-André Linteau, René Durocher, and Jean-Claude Robert, *Histoire du Québec contemporain* (Montreal, 1979), pp. 409–27; Christian Pouyez et al., *Les Saguenayens: Introduction à l'histoire des populations du Saguenay* (Quebec, 1983).

4. Yolande Lavoie, *L'émigration des Québécois aux États-Unis* (Quebec, 1979), p. 45.

5. Felix Albert, *Histoire d'un enfant pauvre* (Nashua, N.H., 1909), pp. 45–57. For an excellent discussion of Albert's autobiography, see Francis Early's introduction to the English translation *Immigrant Odyssey: A French-Canadian Habitant in New England*, ed. Francis H. Early (Orono, Maine, 1991).

6. Bruno Noury interview, Projet d'Histoire Orale, Collection Ramirez-Rouillard, Département d'Histoire, Université de Montréal.

7. Béatrice Mandeville interview, Projet d'Histoire Orale; U.S. National Archives, *Soundex Index to Canadian Border Entries* (hereafter cited as *Index*), RG M1461, "Marie Hetu," reel 249.

8. My thinking on migration fields has been influenced by James P. Allen, "Migration Fields of French Canadian Immigrants to Southern Maine," *Geographical Review* 62, 1 (1974): 32–66. For a skillful application of this notion see Yves Frenette, "La genèse d'une communauté canadienne française en Nouvelle-Angleterre, Lewiston, Maine, 1800–1880" (Ph.D. diss., Université Laval, 1988).

9. For a recent thought-provoking discussion of spatial scales in historical analysis, see Richard White, "The Nationalization of Nature," *Journal of American History* 86, 3 (1999): 976–86; See also a discussion of spatial scales and the narrating of the past in Bruno Ramirez, "Clio in Words and in Motion: Practices of Narrating the Past," *Journal of American History 86*, 3 (1999): 907–1001.

10. *Index*, RG M1461, "T. Benoit," reel 43.

11. U.S. Senate, *Reports of the Immigration Commission*, 41 vols. (Washington, D.C., 1911), esp. vols. 2 and 10. For a study of that presence based on the Immigration Commission data, see Bruno Ramirez, "French Canadian Immigrants in the New England Cotton Industry during the Progressive Era: A Socioeconomic Profile," *Labour/Le Travail*, no. 11 (1983): 125–42. Other studies on French Canadians in textile manufacturing with a focus on the twentieth century include Tamara K. Hareven and Randolph Langenbach, *Amoskeag: Life and Work in an American Factory City* (New York, 1978); Tamara K. Hareven, *Family Time and Industrial Time: The Relationship between the Family and Work in a New England Industrial Community* (Cambridge, Mass., 1982); Gary Gerstle, *Working-Class Americanism: The Politics of Labor in a Textile City, 1914–1960* (Cambridge, Mass., 1989); Yukari Takai, "Migration, Family, and Gender: A Longitudinal Analysis of French-Canadian Immigrants in Lowell, Massachusetts, 1900–1920" (Ph.D. diss., Université de Montréal, 1998).

12. Eugénie Savoie-Côté interview, Projet d'Histoire Orale.

13. Daniel Walkowitz, *Worker City, Company Town: Iron and Cotton Worker Protest in Troy and Cohoes, New York, 1855–1884* (Urbana, 1978), pp. 48–54.

14. Frenette, "Genèse d'une communauté," appendix 3, pp. 385–88.

15. Computed by the authors from the lists compiled by E.-Z. Massicotte in his "L'émigration aux États-Unis il y a quarante ans et plus," *Bulletin de recherches historiques* 33 (1933): 21–27, 86–88, 179–81, 228–31, 381–83, 427–29, 507–9, 560–62, 697, 711–12; 34 (1934): 121.

16. For a fuller discussion of these data as well as out-migration from Berthier County, see Ramirez, *On the Move*, chap. 1.

17. Lucien Dumontier interview, Projet d'Histoire Orale.

18. Ralph D. Vicero, "Immigration of French Canadians to New England, 1840–1900: A Geographical Analysis" (Ph.D. diss., University of Wisconsin, 1968); Frances Early, "French-Canadian Beginnings in an American Community: Lowell, Massachusetts, 1868–1886" (Ph.D. diss., Concordia University, 1979); Ramirez, *On the Move*, pp. 111–37; Yves Roby, "Québec in the United States: A Historiographical Survey," *Maine Historical Society Quarterly* 26, 3 (1987): 126–59.

19. *Index*, RG M1463, "Frederick Chaussé," reel 14.

20. Ibid., RG M1461, "Pauline Guthro," reel 64.

21. Ibid., RG M1463, "Oscar Brunelle," reel 54.

22. George Marion interview, Projet d'Histoire Orale.

23. *Index*, RG M1461, "Eugène Audette," reel 5; Philip T. Silvia, Jr. "The Spindle City: Labor, Politics, and Religion in Fall River, Massachusetts, 1870–1905" (Ph.D. diss., Fordham University, 1973), pp. 855, 860; L. J. Gagnon, ed., *Guide officiel des Franco-Américains 1916–1946* (Fall River, Mass., n.d.); Brigitte Violette, "Formation et croissance d'une classe moyenne: la communauté Franco-américaine de Fall River, Massachusetts, 1870–1920" (Ph.D. diss., Université de Montréal, 2000).

24. The data on French-Canadian migrants who previously resided in the United States break down as follows:

Age	15–29 (%)	30–44 (%)	45–59 (%)	60+ (%)
Males	40.7	65.8	74.6	76.3
Females	35.3	62.2	68.4	62.8

From *Index*, table 2.14. This and all subsequent tabulations in the notes have been compiled by Bruno Ramirez and Yves Otis from a sample drawn from the *Soundex Index to Canadian Border Entries*, RG M1461 and M1463. See the appendix for a discussion of the method employed.

25. *Index*, RG M1461, "Anthony Le Blanc," reel 232.

26. Ibid., "Laura Charbonneau," reel 95.

27. Ibid., "Joseph Albert Forcier," reel 153.

28. In *L'Étoile du Nord*, 24 August 1884, for instance, readers were informed that several mills had shut down in Fall River and in two Connecticut towns. One month later (20 September 1884) *l'Étoile* announced that one of its representatives was touring various New England centers "to seek new subscribers." And in its 2 May 1885 issue the paper gave the results of the municipal elections held in Spencer, Massachusetts, no doubt because it had resulted in the election of French Canadians to various public posts (one selectman, one superintendent of public charities, and two constables). Forty years later, one could read similar articles not only in *L'Étoile du Nord* but in a variety of French-Canadian newspapers. Examples may be found in *Le Canada français*

(Saint-Jean, Quebec), 2 August 1923; *L'Union des Cantons de l'Est* (Sherbrooke, Quebec), 22 July 1920, 9 March 1922, 18 May 1922.

29. As late as the 1920s, articles on Quebec and Canadian affairs appeared regularly in the leading Franco-American periodicals we have consulted, such as *La Tribune* of Woonsocket, *Le Jean Baptiste* of Pawtucket, *L'Étoile* of Lowell, *La Justice* of Holyoke, and *L'Opinion Publique* of Worcester.

30. *Index*, RG M1461, "Hervé Aubry," reel 16.

31. Studies analyzing the pattern of family migration among French Canadians moving to New England textile centers include Frenette, "Genèse d'une communauté"; Ramirez, *On the Move*, chap. 5; Takai, "Migration, Family, and Gender"; Sylvie Beaudreau and Yves Frenette, "Les stratégies familiales des francophones de la Nouvelle-Angleterre: Perspective diachronique," *Sociologie et société* 26, 1 (1994): 167–78.

32. *Index*, table 3.16.

33. Ibid., RG M1461, "Julia Arsenault," reel 16.

34. Ibid., "Elizabeth Saulnier," reel 349.

35. Ramirez, *On the Move*, pp. 120–25.

36. *Index*, RG M1461, "Rodrigue Trifili," reel 326.

37. Ibid., "Eugène Caron," reel 103.

38. The following figures indicate the consistently high proportion of unmarried women among French-Canadian migrants:

	1906–18 (%)	1919–24 (%)	1925–29 (%)
Unmarried men and women	23.8	27.7	33.3
Unmarried women only	14.4	20.1	25.6

From *Index*, table 3.18.

39. Alice Laliberté interview, Projet d'Histoire Orale.

40. *Index*, RG M1461, "Alice Magnan," reel 262; "Willy Charette," reel 99.

41. Linteau, Durocher, and Robert, *Histoire du Québec contemporain*, pp. 409–26.

42. Ibid., pp. 355–69.

43. Mrs. George Marion interview, Projet d'Histoire Orale.

44. Jacques Hamel interview, Projet d'Histoire Orale.

45. Anne Lagacé interview, Projet d'Histoire Orale.

46. *Index*, RG M1461, "Augustine Larocque," reel 248.

47. In order of importance, the following eleven cities were destinations for 33 percent of all migrating farmers: Detroit, Mich.; Biddeford, Maine; Manchester, N.H.; Lawrence, Mass.; Lowell, Mass.; Nashua, N.H.; Berlin, N.H.; Woonsocket, R.I.; Bristol, Conn.; Worcester, Mass.; Lewiston, Maine. From *Index*, table 3.21.

48. Horace Miner, *St. Denis: A French-Canadian Parish* (Chicago, 1939), pp. 151–52.

49. *Index*, table 3.22.

50. Ibid., RG M1463, "Joseph Remi Armand Bélanger," reel 8.

51. Charles Marion interview, Projet d'Histoire Orale.

52. Adrien Hamel interview, Projet d'Histoire Orale.

53. Gerald Nicosia, *Memory Babe: A Critical Biography of Jack Kerouac* (Berkeley, 1983), pp. 24–30.

54. Paul de la Riva, *Mine de rien: Les Canadiens Français et le travail minier à Sudbury, 1886–1930* (Sudbury, 1998); Gail Cuthbert Brandt, "The Development of French-Canadian Social Institutions in Sudbury, Ontario, 1883–1920," *Revue de l'Université Laurentienne, no.* 11 (1979): 5–22.

55. *Index*, table 3.25.

56. Gaétan Gervais, "L'Ontario français (1821–1910)," and Fernand Ouellet, "L'évolution de la présence francophone en Ontario: une perspective économique et sociale," both in Cornelius Jaenen, ed., *Les Franco-Ontariens* (Ottawa, 1993), pp. 49–124, 127–99; Morris Zaslow, *The Opening of the Canadian North, 1870–1914* (Toronto, 1971).

57. *Index*, table 3.31.

58. Ibid., RG M1461, "Leontine Guenette," reel 173.

59. Josephine Dumontier interview, Projet d'Histoire Orale.

60. *Index*, RG M1461, "Odette Guendon," reel 166; "Marie Hetu," reel 249.

61. Ibid., table 3.35.

62. Ibid., RG M1461, "Thèrese Roy," reel 332.

63. Ibid., "Louise Guerin," reel 189.

64. Elmire Boucher interview, Projet d'Histoire Orale. Excerpts from Elmire Boucher's oral history interview appear in Jacques Rouillard, *Ah Les États!* (Montreal, 1985), pp. 87–99.

65. Anne Lagacé interview, Eugénie Coté interview, Projet d'Histoire Orale.

66. *Index*, RG M1463, "France Guerin," reel 7; "Rose Dubois," reel 22.

67. Ibid., RG M1461, "Arthemise Pion," reel 306; "Alma Kerouac," reel 225; "Lorette Beaulieu," reel 33.

68. Ibid., RG M1463, "Jean Gosselin," reel 51.

Chapter 4. Emigration from English Canada

1. Yolande Lavoie, *L'émigration des Québécois aux États-Unis de 1840 à 1930* (Quebec, 1979), p. 45.

2. *Century* 28 (September 1884), quoted in Randolph Widdis, *With Scarcely a Ripple: Anglo-Canadian Migration into the United States and Western Canada, 1880–1920* (Montreal, 1998), pp. 213–14.

3. For out-migration from the Maritimes, see Alan A. Brookes "Out-Migration from the Maritime Provinces, 1860–1900: Some Preliminary Considerations," *Acadiensis* 5, 2 (1976): 26–55; Alan A. Brookes, "The Exodus: Migration from the Maritime Provinces to Boston during the Second Half of the Nineteenth Century" (Ph.D. dissertation, University of New Brunswick, 1979); Brookes, "The Golden Age and the Exodus: The Case of Canning, Kings County," *Acadiensis* 11, 1 (1981): 57–82; William G. Reeves, "Newfoundlanders in the 'Boston States': A Study in Early Twentieth-Century Community and Counterpoint," *Newfoundland Studies* 6, 1 (1990): 34–56; Patricia A. Thornton, "The Problem of Out-Migration from Atlantic Canada, 1871–1921: A New Look," *Acadiensis* 15, 1 (1985): 3–34. As a nonprofessional historian, Gary Burrill has rendered an invaluable service with his collection of oral histories, *Away: Maritimers in Massachusetts, Ontario, and Alberta* (Montreal, 1992). In addition to *With Scarcely A Ripple*, the pioneering work by Randy Widdis includes: "We Breathe the Same Air: Eastern Ontario Migration to Watertown, N.Y.," *New York History* 68 (1987): 261–80; "With Scarcely a Ripple: English Canadians in Northern New York State at the Beginning of the Twentieth Century," *Journal of Historical Geography* 13 (1987): 169–92; "Scale and Context: Approaches to the Study of Canadian Migration Patterns in the Nineteenth Century," *Social Science History* 12 (1988): 269–303. See also the recent special issue of *Mid-America*, no. 3 (fall 1998), edited by John J. Bukowczyk and David R. Smith, and containing essays on English-Canadian emigration by Donald Avery, Thomas Klug, and David Smith (cited in previous chapters).

4. U.S. National Archives, *Soundex Index to Canadian Border Entries* (hereafter cited as *Index*), RG M1461, "Eli Mason," reel 260; "Roderick Morrison, " reel 280; "Daisy Dean," reel 122; "Zoriana Neterpka," reel 296; "Archibald McLane," reel 258.

5. Tamara K. Hareven, "The Laborers of Manchester, New Hampshire, 1900–1940: The Role of Family and Ethnicity in Adjustment to Industrial Life," *Labor History* 16 (spring 1975): 249–65; Tamara K. Hareven, "Family Time and Industrial Time: Family and Work in a Planned Corporation Town, 1900–1924," *Journal of Urban History* 1 (May 1975): 365–89.

6. U.S. Senate, *Reports of the Immigration Commission*, 41 vols. (Washington, D.C., 1911).

7. *Reports of the Immigration Commission*, 11:481.

8. Ibid., 13:424.

9. For some insightful comments on the distinction between "old" and "new" immigration, see Charlotte Erickson, *Leaving England: Essays on British Emigration in the Nineteenth Century* (Ithaca, 1994), pp. 116–17.

10. The growing number of studies dealing with the ongoing arrival of "old" immigrants after the turn of the century include Klaus J. Bade, "German Emigration to the United States and Continental Immigration to Germany in the Late Nineteenth and Early Twentieth Centuries," in Dirk Hoerder, ed., *Labor Migration in the Atlantic Economies* (Westport, Conn., 1985), chap. 5; Jon Gjerde, "Chain Migration from the West Coast of Norway," and Dirk Hoerder, "International Labor Markets and Community Building by Migrant Workers in the Atlantic Economies," both in Rudolph Vecoli and Suzanne Sinke, eds., *A Century of European Migrations, 1830–1930* (Chicago, 1991), pp. 158–81; Erickson, *Leaving England*, chap. 3.

11. *Reports of the Immigration Commission*, vol. 20, pt. 1, pp. 76, 94–95.

12. Ibid., vol. 20, pt. 2, pp. 290, 314; 19:318.

13. Ibid., 9:290–91.

14. Ibid., 14:430.

15. Ibid., 19:95.

16. Ibid., 14:410.

17. Ibid., 19:168.

18. Ibid., vol. 20, pt. 2, pp. 322–23, 330.

19. Ibid., 19:95.

20. Ibid., 19: 318; vol. 20, pt. 2, p. 314.

21. Ibid., 19:95.

22. Ibid., 19:168.

23. Ibid., vol. 20, pt. 2, pp. 322–23, 330.

24. Ibid., 19:43; vol. 20, pt. 2, p. 57.

25. *Index*, RG M1461, "Frank Hearst," reel 200; "J. Nermiah," reel 290; "Joseph Gettings," reel 165.

26. *Index*, table 4.3.

27. Ibid.

28. For a more detailed regional study of out-migration from the Maritimes based on the *Index* data, see Yves Otis et Bruno Ramirez, "Nouvelles perspectives sur le mouvement d'émigration des Maritimes vers les États-Unis, 1906–1930," *Acadiensis* 28, 1 (1998): 27–46.

29. Oral history interview, in Burrill, *Away*, p. 45.

30. *Index*, table 4.3.

31. Widdis, *With Scarcely a Ripple*, esp. chap. 5.

32. *Index*, table 4.4.

33. Oral history interview, in Burrill, *Away*, p. 35; *Index*, RG M1461, "Angus Crowdis," reel 100.

34. *Index*, table 4.5.

35. Ibid., table 4.7.

36. Ibid.

37. Ibid.

38. Ibid., table 4.10.

39. Ibid., RG M1461, "Anna Gibson," reel 159; "Frank Cleversey," reel 79; "Olive Doyle," reel 119.

40. Ibid., table 4.12.

41. Ibid.

42. Ibid., table 4.13.

43. Ibid., table 4.23.

44. Ibid., RG M1461, "Herbert Drury," reel 132.

45. Ibid., RG M1461, "Roy Smith," reel 354.

46. Ibid., "John Alfred O'Regan," reel 295.

47. Contemporary critics of Canadian emigration who came close to formulating the notion of "brain drain" include John Nelson, "The Problem of Our Provinces—the Maritimes," *MacLean's Magazine*, 15 August 1923, pp. 16–17, 61; John A. Stevenson, "Is Canada an Immigration Sieve?" *MacLean's Magazine*, 15 February 1923.

48. *Index*, table 4.25.

49. *Index*, RG M1461, "Arthur Goulding," reel 170.

50. Ibid., "William Little," reel 241; "Harry Scales," reel 347.

51. Donald H. Avery, *Reluctant Host: Canada's Response to Immigrant Workers, 1896–1994* (Toronto, 1995), pp. 25–26; for some vivid accounts of the "harvest excursions" see Burrill, *Away*, pp. 17–41.

52. Oral history interviews, in Burrill, *Away*, pp. 22–25; 38–40. *Index*, RG M1461, "Owen Caldwell," reel 80; RG M1463, "Louis Bannister," reel 9.

53. *Index*, table 4.22.

54. *Index*, RG M1461, "William Calvin," reel 79; *New York Times*, 28 January 1962, p. 74; Gary M. Fink, ed., *Biographical Dictionary of American Labor* (Westport, Conn., 1984), p. 141.

55. Fink, *Biographical Dictionary*, p. 409.

56. *Index*, table 4.26.

57. Ibid.

58. Ibid., table 4.28.

59. Ibid., RG M1461, "John Sweeney," reel 349; "Harold Walker," reel 390.

60. Ibid., table 4.26.

61. For a skillful historical analysis of immigration in the Montreal region see Paul-André Linteau, "La monté du cosmopolitisme montréalais," *Questions de culture*, no. 2 (1982): 23–54, and by the same author, *Histoire de Montréal depuis la Confédération* (Montreal, 1992), esp. chap. 7 and 12. Studies of immigration and the ethnic segmentation of the labor markets in Montreal include Bruno Ramirez, "Brief Encounters: Italian Immigrant Workers and the Canadian Pacific Railway, 1900–1930," *Labour/Le Travail* 17 (spring 1986), pp. 9–28; Robert Nahuet, "Une expérience canadienne de Taylorisme: Le cas des usines Angus de Montréal" (master's thesis, Université du Québec à Montréal, 1984); Denise Helly, *Les Chinois de Montréal, 1877–1951* (Quebec, 1987).

62. *Index*, table 4.27.

63. Marian L. Smith, "INS at the US-Canadian Border, 1893–1993: An Overview of Issues and Topics," paper presented at the meeting of the Organization of American Historians, Toronto, 23 April 1999, p. 12.

64. *Index*, RG M1461, "W. Blampin," reel 38; RG M1463, "Cynthia Kelley," reel 17.

65. Ibid., table 4.30.

66. Ibid., table 4.14.

67. "George Beattie," in *Life Histories of Twenty Five Native and Foreign-Born Unemployed Laborers*," Research Document of the U.S. Commission on Industrial Relations, 1912–1915 (U.S. National Archives, microfilm edition), reel no. 6.

68. Olivier Zunz, *The Changing Face of Inequality: Urbanization, Industrial Development, and Immigrants in Detroit, 1880–1920* (Chicago, 1982), pp. 34–35, 106; Widdis, *With Scarcely a Ripple*, pp. 5–6; Beatsy Beattie, "'Going Up to Lynn': Single, Maritime-Born Women in Lynn, Massachusetts, 1879–1930," *Acadiensis* 22, 1 (1992): 82–83; yet, these few existing case studies contrast with the intense social relations and communal activities among Maritimers in the Boston area, as they emerge from Burrell, *Away*, pp. 7–109.

69. Donald Avery, "Canadian Workers and American Immigration Restriction: A Case Study of Winsor Commuters, 1924–1931," *Mid-America* 80, 3 (1998): 235–69; Smith, "INS at the US-Canadian Border," pp. 7–10.

70. *Reports of the Immigration Commission*, vol. 20, pt. 2, pp. 1035–36.

71. *Index*, RG M1461, "David Watkins," reel 385; "William Bailey," reel 33; "Sadie Karlofsky," reel 227.

72. Ibid., table 4.40.

73. Very little work has been done on the return migration of Canadians, exceptions include Widdis, *With Scarcely a Ripple*, chap. 7; and Paul-André Linteau, "L'apport des migrants américains et franco-américains au Québec: Un état de la question," *Revue d'Histoire de l'Amérique Française*, 53, 4 (2000): 561–602.

74. *Index*, RG M1461, "Edward Bulstrode," reel 35.

75. Ibid., table 4.41.

76. Ibid., table 4.42.

77. Ibid., RG M1461, "Mary McDonald," reel 266; "Stanley Murdock," reel 280.

78. Ibid., "J. M.," reel 262.

79. Ibid., table 4.45.

80. *Index*, RG M1463, "J. E.," reel 58.

81. Ibid., "R. E. M.," reel 80.

82. Ibid., RG M1461, "W. P.," reel 312.

83. Ibid., "C. H.," reel 188.

84. Ibid., "R. P.," reel 309.

85. Ibid., "H. L.," reel 231.

86. Ibid., "A. R.," reel 327.

87. Ibid., "A. R.," reel 322.

88. Ibid., "M. M.," reel 287.

89. Ibid., RG M1463, "B. R.," reel 73.

90. Ibid., RG M1461, "M. D.," reel 131.

91. Ibid., "C. D.," reel 130.

92. Ibid., "J. L.," reel 231.

93. Smith, "INS at the US-Canadian Border," p. 9.

94. *Index*, table 4.47.

95. *Index*, RG M1463, "Kathleen Boyd," reel 5; "Rose Blanche Charbonneau," reel 19.

96. Ibid., "Anna Howlett," reel 40; "Lydia Aubut," reel 1.

97. Ibid., "Vera Allen," reel 2; "Marie Jeanne Chamberland," reel 18.

98. Ibid., RG M1463, "D. B.," reel 21; "M. W.," reel 97; "Q. Q.," reel 76.

Chapter 5. The Remigration Movement from Canada

1. U.S. National Archives, *Soundex Index to Canadian Border Entries*, RG M1641, "Abraham Bellow," reel 31; hereafter cited as *Index*; Dennis K. McIntire, *International Authors and Writers Who's Who*, 16th ed. (Cambridge, 1999), p. 47; Saul Bellow, *Herzog* (New York, 1964).

2. Marcus L. Hansen and John B. Brebner, *The Mingling of the Canadian and American Peoples* (New Haven, 1940), pp. 101–3, 121; R. Cole Harris and John Warkentin, *Canada before Confederation* (New York, 1974), p. 181; Charlotte Erickson, *Leaving England: Essays on British Emigration in the Nineteenth Century* (Ithaca, 1994), pp. 137, 195.

3. M. C. Urquhart and K. A. H. Burley, eds., *Historical Statistics of Canada* (Toronto, 1965), ser. A 133–42, p. 19.

4. Works containing basic historiographical references to immigrants in Canada include Paul Robert Magocsi, ed., *Encyclopedia of Canada's Peoples* (Toronto, 1999); Jean R. Burnet with Howard Palmer, "Coming Canadians": An Introduction to a History of Canada's People (Toronto, 1988); Donald Avery and Bruno Ramirez, "Immigration and Ethnic Studies," in Alan F. J. Artibise, ed., *Interdisciplinary Approaches to Canadian Society* (Montreal, 1990), pp. 77–116.

5. *Index*, table 5.11.

6. Ibid., table 5.13.

7. Ibid., table 5.15.

8. Ibid., RG M1461, "Sara Rubinstein," reel 316.

9. Ibid., "John Baritokis," reel 55; "Saverio Varteo," reel 334.

10. Donald H. Avery, *Reluctant Host: Canada's Response to Immigrant Workers, 1896–1994* (Toronto, 1995), p. 23 ff.

11. *Index*, table 5.20.

12. Ibid., table 5.26.

13. Ibid., table 5.27.

14. Ibid., table 5.28.

15. Marilyn Barber, *Les domestiques immigrantes au Canada* (Ottawa, 1991), p. 8.

16. Ibid., pp. 11–16. On the significant proportion of domestics among Finnish immigrants, see Varpu Lindstrom-Best, *Les Finlandais au Canada* (Ottawa, 1985), pp. 6–11.

17. *Index*, table 5.30.

18. For works containing basic historiographical references on Italian immigrants in Canada, see Bruno Ramirez, *The Italians in Canada* (Ottawa, 1989), pp. 25–27; Franc Sturino, "Italians," in *Encyclopedia of Canada's People* (Toronto, 1999), pp. 787–832.

19. Ercole Sori, *L'emigrazione italiana dall'Unità alla seconda guerra mondiale* (Bologna, 1979), pp. 28–32; George E. Pozzetta and Bruno Ramirez, eds., *The Italian Diaspora: Migration across the Globe* (Toronto, 1992).

20. Luigi Favero e Graziano Tassello, "Cent'anni di emigrazione italiana (1876–1976)," in Gianfausto Rosoli, ed., *Un secolo di emigrazione italiana* (Rome, 1978), pp. 9–64. On early Italian settlements in Toronto and Montreal, see John Zucchi, *Italians in Toronto: Development of a National Identity, 1875–1935* (Kingston, 1988), pp. 34–67; Bruno Ramirez, *Les premiers Italiens de Montréal*, pp. 11–45.

21. L. S. Channel, *History of Compton County* (Belville, Ont., 1896), pp. 56–64; for a discussion of this strike relating it to the mobility of Italian migrants, see Bruno Ramirez, *On the Move: French Canadian and Italian Migrants in the North Atlantic Economy, 1860–1914* (Toronto, 1991), pp. 104–6.

22. For some life stories of Italian sojourners in North America, see "Passaggio di Antonio Andreoni nell' America del Nord," *Quaderni Culturali* 2, 1 (1982): 5–7; 2, 2

(1982): 28–31; "Nicola Manzo," in Ramirez, *Les premiers Italiens de Montréal*, pp. 91–95; John Potestio, "The Memoirs of Giovanni Veltri: A *Contadino* Turned Railway Builder," in John Potestio and Antonio Pucci, eds., *The Italian Immigrant Experience* (Thunder Bay, Ont., 1988), pp. 119–30; Archivio Centrale dello Stato, Rome, "Archivi parlamentari di inchiesta sulle condizioni dei contadini nelle provincie meridionali e nella Sicilia" (manuscripts reports and minutes), busta 4, fascicolo 3, "Fiorello P.," p. 100.

23. Karey Reilly, "Les Italiens de Copper Cliff, 1886–1912," *Revue du Nouvel-Ontario*, no. 17 (1995): 49–76; on Thunder Bay, Ontario, see Antonio Pucci, "Canadian Industrialization versus Italian *Contadini* in a Decade of Brutality, 1902–1912," in Robert Harney and Vincenza Scarpaci, eds., *Little Italies in North America* (Toronto, 1981), pp. 183–207; and Potestio, "Memoirs of Giovanni Veltri." See also Gabriele Scardellato, "Italian Immigrants in Powell River, British Columbia: A Case Study of Settlement before World War II," *Labour/Le Travail* 16 (fall 1985): 145–63; Scardellato, "Beyond the Frozen Wastes: Italian Sojourners and Settlers in British Columbia," in Roberto Perin and Frank Sturino, eds., *Arrangiarsi: The Italian Immigration Experience in Canada* (Toronto, 1989), pp. 135–61. Studies of urban ethnic services among Italians in Canada include Robert Harney, "Boarding and Belonging," *Urban History Review* 2 (October 1978): 8–37; Bruno Ramirez, "Montréal's Italians and the Socioeconomy of Settlement, 1900–1921," *Urban History Review* 10, 1 (June 1981): 39–48.

24. See *Royal Commission Appointed to Inquire into the Immigration of Italian Labourers to Montreal and the Alleged Fraudulent Practices of Employment Agencies* (Ottawa, 1905), and the skillful analysis by Robert Harney, "Montreal's King of Italian Labourers: A Case Study of Padronism," *Labour/Le Travail* 5 (1979): 57–84; Montreal's padronism is placed in a broader North American context in Gunther Peck, "Reinventing Free Labor: Immigrant Padrones and Contract Laborers in North America 1885–1925," *Journal of American History* 83 (December 1996): 848–71.

25. Dante Viola, "Ispezione dei campi di lavoro di La Tuque, Quebec," *Bollettino del Commissariato dell'Emigrazione* 13 (1910): 27.

26. Sylvie Taschereau, *Pays et patries: Mariages et lieux d'origine des Italiens de Montréal, 1906–1930* (Montreal, 1987); Zucchi, *Italians in Toronto*, p. 48 ff.; Frank Sturino, *Inside the Chain* (Toronto, 1993).

27. "Raffaele Tarasco," in Ramirez, *Les premiers Italiens de Montréal*, pp. 97–100.

28. "Nicola Manzo," in Ramirez, *Les premiers Italiens de Montréal*, pp. 91–95.

29. *Index*, table 5.5.

30. Ibid., RG M1461, "Enzo Mondolfo," reel 265; "Filippo Battista," reel 29.

31. Ibid., "Vincenza Trivalli," reel 371.

32. Ibid., "Rosina Tognetto," reel 364.

33. Ibid., "Hilda Baldini," reel 37.

34. Ibid., table 5.10.

35. Ibid., RG M1461, "Anna M.," reel 268.

36. Ibid., "Antonio Barbori," reel 47.

37. Ibid., "Liborio Rotolo," reel 327.

38. Robert Harney, "Men without Women: Italian Migrants in Canada, 1885–1930," *Canadian Ethnic Studies* 1, 1 (1979): 57–84; Ramirez, *On The Move*, chap. 4.

39. *Index*, table 5.20.

40. Reilly, "Les Italiens de Copper Cliff."

41. Bruno Ramirez, "Brief Encounters: Italian Immigrant Workers and the Canadian Pacific Railway, 1900–1930," *Labour/Le Travail* 17 (spring 1986).

42. "Costanzo D'Amico" and "Michele Marcogliese," in Ramirez, *Les premiers Italiens de Montréal*, pp. 115–20, 122.

43. Avery, *Reluctant Host*, p. 23.

44. Nicole Malpas, "Aux sources d'un réseau migratoire: Casacalenda-Montréal, 1861–1931" (thèse de doctorat, Université de Louvain, 1994).

45. *Index*, table 5.27.

46. Ibid., RG M1461, "Domenico Scolli," reel 345.

47. Ibid., "Giuseppe De Luchi," reel 124.

48. Ibid., "Luigi Ferri," reel 150.

49. Cole Harris and Warkentin, *Canada before Confederation*, pp. 118–19.

50. Erickson, *Leaving England*, esp. pp. 60–125; William A. Carrothers, *Emigration from the British Isles* (London, 1929); Rowland Berthoff, *British Immigrants in Industrial America, 1790–1950* (Cambridge, 1953).

51. Urquhart and Burley, *Historical Statistics of Canada*, ser. A 133–42, p. 19.

52. Carrothers, *Emigration from the British Isles*, p. 242.

53. Joy Parr, *Labouring Children* (London, 1980), p. 143.

54. Ibid., esp. p. 159 ff.; Valerie Knowles, *Strangers at Our Gates: Canadian Immigration and Immigration Policy, 1540–1990* (Toronto, 1992), pp. 68–70.

55. Marilyn Barber, "The Women Ontario Welcomed: Immigrant Domestics for Ontario Homes, 1870–1930," *Ontario History* 72 (September 1980): 155; Barber, *Les domestiques immigrantes au Canada*, pp. 7–16.

56. Parr, *Labouring Children*, pp. 143–59; Barbara Roberts, "'A Work of Empire': Canadian Reformers and British Female Immigration," in Linda Kealey, ed., *A Not Unreasonable Claim* (Toronto, 1989); Carl Berger, *The Sense of Power: Studies in the Ideas of Canadian Imperialism, 1867–1914* (Toronto, 1970).

57. Carrothers, *Emigration from the British Isles*, p. 242; Walter Nugent, *Crossings: The Great Transatlantic Migrations, 1870–1914* (Bloomington, 1992), p. 47.

58. Knowles, *Strangers at Our Gates*, p. 67;

59. A. Ross McCormack, "Networks among British Immigrants and Accommodation to Canadian Society: Winnipeg 1900–1914," *Histoire Sociale/Social History* 17, 34 (1984): 362, 363.

60. Lloyd Reynolds, *The British Immigrant: His Social and Economic Adjustment to Canada* (Toronto, 1935), p. 45; Nugent, *Crossings*, p. 46.

61. Mark Wyman, *Round-Trip to America: The Immigrants Return to Europe, 1880–1930* (Ithaca, 1993), pp. 10–11; Erickson, *Leaving England*, pp. 177, 247–48; Nugent, *Crossings*, pp. 44–48.

62. McCormack, "Networks among British Immigrants," pp. 366–68.

63. *Index*, RG M1461, "George Peaks," reel 297; "Douglas Ford," reel 153; "Ruby Arnold," reel 17.

64. Reynolds, *British Immigrant*, p. 45 ff.

65. These studies include Craig Heron, *Working in Steel: The Early Years in Canada, 1883–1935* (Toronto, 1988); Heron, "The Crisis of the Craftsman: Hamilton's Metal Workers in the Early Twentieth Century," *Labour/Le Travail* 6 (autumn 1980): 7–48; Ian McKay, *The Craft Transformed: An Essay on the Carpenters of Halifax, 1885–1985* (Halifax, 1985); Allen Seager, "Miners' Struggles in Western Canada: Class, Community, and the Labour Movement, 1890–1930," in Deian R. Hopkin and Gregory S. Kealey, eds., *Class, Community, and the Labour Movement: Wales and Canada, 1850–1930* (St. John's, 1989), pp. 162–98; Paul de la Riva, *Mine de rien: Les Canadiens Français et le travail minier à Sudbury, 1886–1930* (Sudbury, 1998); Donald Avery and Bruno Ramirez, "European Immigrant Workers in Canada: Ethnicity, Militancy and State Repression," in Dirk Hoerder, Horst Roessler, and Inge Blank, eds., *Roots of the Transplanted* (New York, 1994), 2:411–40.

66. Avery, *Reluctant Host*, pp. 25–26.

67. *Sixth Census of Canada, 1921*, vol. 4, pp. lxiv, lxvi.

68. On the impact of British immigrants on Canadian trade unionism and labor politics, see Avery and Ramirez, "European Immigrant Workers in Canada," p. 417 ff.; A. Ross McCormack, *Rebels, Reformers and Revolutionaries: The Western Canadian Radical Movement, 1899–1919* (Toronto, 1977).

69. Erickson, *Leaving England,* esp. chap. 3; Dudley Baines, *Migration in a Mature Economy: Emigration and Internal Migration in England and Wales, 1861–1900* (Cambridge, 1985).

70. *Index,* table 5B.6.

71. Ibid., RG M1461, "Ada Swain," reel 349; "John Kenny," reel 221.

72. Ibid., table 5B.14.

73. Ibid., RG M1461, "Robert Adams," reel 6.

74. Ibid., table 5B.10.

75. Ibid., table 5B.21.

76. Ibid., table 5B.24.

77. Ibid., RG M1461, "Edith Davis," reel 107.

78. Ibid., "Beatrice Pritchard," reel 312.

79. Ibid., table 5B.25.

80. Ibid., RG M1461, "Hilda Harris," reel 199; "Elizabeth Fincham," reel 149; "Louisa Roberts," reel 317.

81. Ibid., "Grace Hudson," reel 190; "Louisa Roberts," reel 317.

82. Ibid., table 5B.20.

83. Ibid., table 5B.26.

84. Ibid., RG M1461, "George Hope," reel 185.

85. Ibid., "Frederick Dawe," reel 105.

86. Ibid., "Thomas Mayor," reel 271.

87. "Trade circuits" in Canada and the United States are studied in Peter Bischof, "Tensions et solidarité : la formation des traditions chez les mouleurs de Montréal, Hamilton et Toronto, 1851 à 1893" (Ph.D. diss., Université de Montréal, 1992).

88. Erickson, *Leaving England,* p. 25.

89. *Index,* table 5B.27.

90. Ibid., table 5.11.

91. Ibid., RG M1461, "Filippo Battista," reel 29.

92. Nicoletta Serio, "L'emigrato va alla guerra: i soldati italiani nel corpo di spedizione canadese, 1914–1918," in Luigi Bruti Liberati, ed., *Il Canada e la guerra dei trent'anni: L'esperienza bellica di un popolo multietnico* (Milan, 1989), pp. 109–38.

93. *Index,* RG M1461, "Giovanni Politta," reel 305.

94. Ibid., RG M1463, "Luigi Finaro," reel 30.

Conclusion

1. Marcus L. Hansen and John B. Brebner, *The Mingling of the Canadian and American Peoples* (New Haven, 1940). Victor A. Konrad, "The Borderlands of the United States and Canada in the Context of North American Development," *International Journal of Canadian Studies/Revue internationale d'études canadiennes,* no. 4 (1991): 77–95; Stephen J. Hornsby, Victor A. Konrad, James J. Herlan, eds., *The Northeastern Borderlands: Four Centuries of Interaction* (Fredericton, N.B., 1989); Bruno Ramirez, "Labor Migrations and Borderlands: The Canadian-U.S. Case, 1900–1930" (paper presented at the IX Southern Labor Studies Conference, Austin, October 1995).

Index